The Mind Challenge

First published by Parragon in 2010
Parragon
Queen Street House
4 Queen Street
Bath BA1 1HE, UK

Cover design by Talking Design

ISBN 978-1-4075-9617-4

Printed in China

The Mind Challenge

PaRRagon

Bath • New York • Singapore • Hong Kong • Cologne • Delhi • Melbourne

Contents

Sudoku Puzzles

1	9	8
3	5	2
4	6	7

No 1

	7		3	1		9		8
5	8		4					
		3	9			4	5	
6	5		2			8		
4			5		9			7
		1			7		2	6
	9	2			3	6		
					2		7	1
3		6		8	4		9	

No 2

1	6					3		
	9	2		3		8		4
			9	7	5			
7	5	6	3					2
	8		5		9		6	
3					6	1	4	5
			4	9	8			
2		3		6		5	9	
		8					1	6

5	1	4
8	3	6
9	2	7

No 3

9	5					7		2
	1	4		7	8			
6	3			1		5		
	2		6					3
3		5	7		1	4		6
8					4		9	
		9		6			3	1
			8	2		6	5	
7		2					8	4

No 4

	7			3				5
6			8		9	7		
9		4	2		1	6		
		5	6				2	9
		8		1		4		
3	4				7	1		
		3	1		2	8		7
		7	5		4			2
4				8			6	

9

1	9	8
3	5	2
4	6	7

No 5

7						8	5	
1		2		8			4	6
			3	4	7			
		1			8	6	3	5
	7		6		4		8	
8	6	9	1			2		
			4	9	6			
2	4			1		3		7
	8	5						1

No 6

	1		5		3		7	
	7	2	9		8	3	1	
8				7				6
7			3	2	4			9
	4	5				7	2	
9			1	5	7			3
1				3				5
	6	8	4		5	9	3	
	5		7		2		6	

5	1	4
8	3	6
9	2	7

No 7

5	6	1		4				3
			1		3			8
			6	7	9			5
	5		7		1	8		
2	4						7	1
		9	8		4		5	
9			5	3	6			
4			9		2			
3				8		2	6	9

No 8

4	9	7		2			6	
					4		1	
			6	7			5	
5		2	1		7	9		4
9	8						7	3
6		4	3		8	1		5
	5			3	6			
	2		8					
	4			1		8	9	6

4	6	8
3	1	7
5	9	2

No 9

			1				5	
				4	2		9	
2	6	1		8			3	
3		6	8		7	5		9
4	7						1	6
9		8	4		1	3		2
	2			5		7	6	3
	9		2	7				
	8				3			

No 10

	6		7	3	2		9	
1	4		8				6	3
		7	6					5
		5	9					2
6	3						5	7
4					7	8		
2					9	4		
8	1				6		2	9
	7		2	5	4		1	

No 11

5			9			7	8	
		3	1				2	
9				2	8		3	4
	5			4		3		8
		4	8		9	1		
6		2		1			9	
3	6		2	7				5
	7				6	8		
	9	1			3			6

No 12

3		1				2	5	
5				9		7	6	
			4	3			9	8
	2		8			4		
8		7	9		3	6		5
		6			7		1	
7	5			1	4			
	6	9		7				2
	4	8				3		1

No 13

	3			5		7		8
6		5		3	2	1		
2	8	4	9					
			5	6			4	
3	1						7	6
	4			7	3			
					1	8	6	2
		7	4	2		9		3
9		1		8			5	

No 14

		2				6	8	3
4			5	2				
1	7		3				5	
		5	4	3		1		8
2			8		7			6
7		4		9	1	3		
	5				6		9	7
				1	3			4
6	4	9				2		

No 15

					7	3		
8	3		1	2			6	
		9			4		8	7
6	7				3		1	9
		5		1		6		
4	1		8				7	2
3	4		5			2		
	2			6	9		5	8
		8	2					

No 16

2		7		5			6	4
5						8	3	
			9	1	6			
8	7	9	3			5		
	3		6		9		2	
		4			5	1	9	3
			2	6	7			
	8	3						2
9	6			3		4		5

No 17

9			5			7		
	3		1			2		8
	1			7	2	9	6	
		3		6			2	9
6			2		1			5
7	4			5		1		
	9	4	7	8			3	
5		1			9		4	
		8			4			2

No 18

			9			4		
4	8			6	1		9	
		9	8				7	5
9	2		4				3	7
		6		3		8		
1	3				5		2	6
2	4				7	1		
	6		3	9			5	4
		5			2			

No 19

8	3				1		5	2
5				4				7
4		7	2			3		6
				6	8	9	4	
	8						1	
	9	5	3	7				
2		8			9	6		1
7				2				9
9	6		5				2	4

No 20

	1		3	8	6		7	
9					7	6		
8	7				5		4	2
3					1	9		
6	9						8	7
		5	6					4
1	3		7				2	5
		4	1					3
	2		4	9	3		6	

No 21

6					7	2		
4	7				1		3	8
	5		9	4	2		7	
		1	2					3
2	6						4	7
9					5	6		
	8		3	6	9		2	
5	9		7				8	1
		3	5					9

No 22

9				6	1			5
	7				8		3	
1	6	8				4	7	9
5			3				9	
		9	4		7	1		
	8				2			6
8	9	4				5	1	2
	2		5				4	
7			8	2				3

18

No 23

	3		9	8			1	
5	8	6				7	9	2
7			6					8
2			3				6	
		5	7		1	2		
	4				8			9
3					9			1
1	2	7				9	5	4
	6			4	5		2	

No 24

3	2					7		
	1	5		7		9		8
			1	4	6			
4	6	2	7					5
	9		6		1		2	
7					2	3	8	6
			8	1	9			
5		7		2		6	1	
		9					3	2

1	9	8
3	5	2
4	6	7

No 25

9		5			6	7		4
	4	3	2			6	1	
		1		5		9		
1	8			9	4			
	3						2	
			3	7			5	8
		9		6		8		
	7	8			1	5	6	
3		6	8			2		7

No 26

9	1		8				3	6
	3		7	6	4		2	
		7	3					5
		5	2					4
3	6						5	7
1					7	8		
4					2	1		
	7		4	5	1		9	
8	9				3		4	2

5	1	4
8	3	6
9	2	7

No 27

	9		8				3	
7			6	3				1
3	5	8				9	4	6
	4		7					8
		5	9		1	4		
2					3		6	
4	1	9				6	2	5
8				2	5			4
	7				6		1	

No 28

4			7					
	7			6	3	4	1	
	8	9	1					7
	5	8	4			7	2	
1				5				6
	2	6			9	3	5	
3					8	2	4	
	9	4	5	7			6	
					2			9

1	9	8
3	5	2
4	6	7

No 29

	2		3	8	5		1	
	1	4	9			6	5	
		5	6					3
8					6	5		
	7	9				2	8	
		3	2					4
2					9	8		
	3	1			4	7	9	
	9		5	7	2		6	

No 30

1			9		5			3
	2	7		4		5	1	
		5		2		9		
	5	6	8		2	3	4	
2			4		3			5
	3	9	5		7	8	2	
		4		3		6		
	7	2		8		1	3	
6			2		9			7

5	1	4
8	3	6
9	2	7

No 31

7			2				9	
		6		9	5	8	2	
		2	8				3	4
8		7		1			6	
4			3		7			1
	3			4		2		5
9	7				3	6		
	8	1	7	5		3		
	5				4			8

7	8	5
2	9	6
4	3	1

No 32

		9		7			4	2
3	1	2			5			
6	7		3	9			8	
		1	9	4				
9		8				4		6
				6	7	1		
	4			3	1		5	9
			8			6	2	3
5	8			2		7		

4	6	8
3	1	7
5	9	2

1	9	8
3	5	2
4	6	7

No 33

1			5			7	4	
		6	3	2			5	
9		3			8			6
			9	5		6	2	1
		4				8		
6	9	2		1	7			
3			4			1		2
	8			7	3	4		
	7	1			9			5

No 34

		2	3		5		8	
8				6		7		
	9	3	4		1		2	
	7				2	3		1
	5			4			9	
9		6	8				4	
	6		1		4	8	5	
		9		5				2
	8		9		7	1		

5	1	4
8	3	6
9	2	7

No 35

8		2			5			1
1	5			3	4	2		
					8	7	6	
6					7	8	1	
	4		9		2		7	
	1	9	8					3
	9	3	4					
		7	5	6			3	2
5			2			9		4

No 36

2		6					5	8
			9	6		3	4	
		5		4			1	7
1					7		2	
7		3	4		6	5		1
	8		3					9
4	1			7		8		
	5	7		2	9			
3	9					2		6

25

No 37

	7				8	1	4	
3	6	8	9					
		5		2	6			8
2		9		8			3	
	3		2		7		5	
	8			9		6		1
6			3	7		2		
					4	9	1	5
	9	4	1				6	

No 38

		8	5			3	2	
	5	4	1	7				
	7		8		9	1		
3			7	4				8
4		7				2		6
1				8	2			4
		9	2		6		5	
				3	8	4	7	
	3	2			7	9		

No 39

	5	8		1		6	9	
6		3				2		7
1			7		2			9
		7				8		
5			1		8			3
8		1				4		6
	2	5		9		1	3	

No 40

				6			2	5
		4			8	6		
							8	3
3		1	9					
7				3				6
					4	8		1
5	8							
		7	2			9		
6	3			7				

No 41

4				6			8	
		6			7		3	4
	9	5				2		
7		9			4			
			1			4		2
		3				5	2	
6	2		5			7		
	8			1				9

No 42

	7						2	
3		9		6		7		8
		8	7		9	5		
4				2				7
			3		1			
7				4				6
		5	4		7	3		
9		4		5		6		2
	3						1	

No 43

			9	2		6	4	
5			7					2
						1	7	
			8					7
		3		4		2		
1					5			
	7	4						
3					9			8
	6	2		3	4			

No 44

		5	3		8	1		
	6		9		4		2	
1				6				7
8		3				4		1
	2						3	
6		7				2		9
5				9				4
	1		5		3		6	
		2	1		6	8		

No 45

		1	3		8	6		
5	7						3	8
		9				1		
7				5				1
		4	7		9	5		
2				4				9
		2				7		
6	3						9	4
		8	6		3	2		

No 46

	1		4		7		3	
		6	1		8	4		
7				9				2
4	3						2	9
		2				8		
8	9						1	5
2				7				1
		1	3		2	5		
	5		9		6		7	

No 47

		4	3	8	7	1		
	6	3	4		1	2	5	
4		5	9		8	6		7
8								2
3		6	2		4	8		1
	4	8	1		9	7	2	
		2	8	7	3	4		

No 48

	4	2		9				
			1					6
		5		6	2		7	
					6			5
		9		4		3		
1			8					
	3		9	8		4		
8					7			
				3		9	2	

No 49

2	4						7	1
				7				
3	5			2	1	8		
			7			4		5
		4				7		
7		8			5			
		9	6	3			8	4
				1				
6	7						1	3

No 50

				5	3			7
2	6	5		1				3
			6					8
	3					8		
4	2						9	5
		1					6	
1					4			
6				8		4	3	2
7			3	9				

No 51

				1				6
			9		6	1	3	
			3		4	8	2	
		4	6		5	2	9	
7								3
	9	3	2		7	4		
	1	9	5		3			
	7	6	1		8			
4				6				

No 52

5		1	2		6	9		4
		4	7	1	9	5		
	6	9	4		5	3	7	
	5						9	
	1	3	9		2	8	4	
		6	1	9	7	4		
8		5	6		4	7		3

No 53

	2		6		7		3	
				8				
		8	3		2	4		
	8	2	7		1	5	4	
9				3				7
	4	5	2		8	1	6	
		1	8		9	6		
				7				
	9		4		6		5	

No 54

			6		3	7		4
			7			1		8
				8			3	
4		3	8		5	6		9
	1						4	
7		6	2		4	5		1
	4			6				
6		2			7			
1		9	3		2			

No 55

5		2		4		8		3
		1	3		8	5		
3								7
			8		4			
8								9
			5		7			
9								2
		4	2		9	1		
1		7		5		6		8

No 56

		6						
			7	9				
3	7		6	1			9	4
6				5		2		
2			8		9			3
		9		3				6
1	5			8	4		3	2
				7	5			
						8		

1	9	8
3	5	2
4	6	7

No 57

6		3		7		2		8
	1						4	
	5		1		2		9	
8				3				4
			5		7			
4				1				9
	8		6		3		7	
	4						3	
9		6		5		1		2

No 58

6			4		2			9
		4	9		3	7		
				1				
5		2	6		1	3		7
	4			8			1	
7		3	2		5	9		6
				2				
		5	1		9	8		
2			5		8			3

5	1	4
8	3	6
9	2	7

No 59

5			6		2			9
	9			8			2	
		8	4		7	5		
	5	9				4	1	
1								2
	4	2				6	3	
		6	3		8	9		
	2			4			8	
3			9		1			7

No 60

4			9		2			1
	7		3		6		2	
		6				5		
		3	4	9	1	2		
8								7
		1	2	7	8	3		
		4				9		
	6		8		9		3	
9			1		7			5

No 61

	4				7			
8			3	4		2		
				8		3		6
					9		1	
		3		2		8		
	5		4					
2		6		3				
		1		9	6			7
			5				9	

No 62

			8	5	9			
	7	9	4		3	5	6	
		3		7		4		
	6						7	
		4				3		
	1						2	
		6		8		1		
	9	2	6		4	7	8	
			1	2	7			

No 63

3			4		7			6
				1				
		4	6		9	2		
4		2	9		5	3		7
	1			8			6	
7		3	2		1	5		9
		7	5		8	9		
				9				
8			1		4			5

No 64

	4		7		1		3	
3								2
	1	6		4		5	9	
		7		1		9		
			2		3			
		1		5		7		
	6	3		9		8	7	
7								5
	8		6		7		4	

39

No 65

9		8		4		7		3
		5	6		8	2		
	9	2				3	5	
5	6						7	8
	8	3				4	1	
		1	9		2	8		
2		6		3		1		4

No 66

9	2			1			5	4
6		7				9		3
		2	6		7	1		
4								7
		3	4		1	5		
8		9				4		1
1	3			2			6	5

40

No 67

			7				6	
				4	8		2	
4	5	7		9			8	
9						7		
	3	5				1	4	
		8						6
	7			6		8	5	3
	2		8	1				
	9				3			

No 68

		9				5		
	3		2		5		8	
5			9		6			7
6		4	1		9	8		3
1		8	4		7	9		6
2			3		8			4
	4		5		1		6	
		7				2		

1	9	8
3	5	2
4	6	7

No 69

5								4
	3	2		7		9	6	
8			9		5			1
	4			5			1	
			7		8			
	6			2			4	
6			2		3			7
	1	3		8		5	9	
4								2

No 70

	4	7		9		8	6	
		5	1		7	2		
7		6				9		3
1	5						7	8
4		2				6		5
		3	4		2	7		
	2	1		6		3	9	

5	1	4
8	3	6
9	2	7

No 71

	6		8		3		1	
9			6		7			5
		3				6		
	4	5	1		2	3	8	
	8	2	3		4	5	9	
		1				7		
2			4		6			8
	7		5		9		2	

No 72

	2		3		8		7	
3			6		9			8
				7				
6	4		8		7		1	2
		9		3		5		
2	1		9		4		8	7
				9				
1			2		6			5
	6		7		5		4	

No 73

	4		2	8	3		9	
	1	5	4		9	7	3	
2	7		8		6		5	9
1								8
4	8		9		1		7	3
	2	1	6		4	9	8	
	9		3	2	8		1	

No 74

1			4		6			7
	9		8		3		5	
		4				2		
	2	5	3			4	9	7
	6	3	7		1	5	8	
		8				6		
	4		2		8		1	
9			6		7			5

44

No 75

5	4	3		6		1		
					5	8		
			9	1		3		
6							9	
	7	2				5	8	
	9							3
		9		7	3			
		6	2					
		1		8		9	4	2

No 76

	4		6		9		7	
6			7		1			9
				8				
4	9		8		2		6	5
		5		4		8		
2	8		1		5		9	3
				3				
5			2		7			1
	2		5		6		3	

No 77

		4		9		5		
7			8		4			2
	1		2		7		6	
	8	6				7	5	
1								8
	3	2				9	1	
	4		6		8		7	
2			5		9			1
		7		2		3		

No 78

9	4					5		
		6	5			2		7
7			8				3	
			3					8
	1						7	
2					1			
	5				9			3
8		2			3	9		
		9					4	6

No 79

4			2		9			7
		2				1		
	3		6		1		5	
	9	7	8		5	4	6	
	1	4	9		3	8	2	
	4		1		8		7	
		6				5		
9			5		2			3

No 80

				5		4	9	
					9		2	
3			7		2			
			3				6	7
	1			2			5	
6	2				8			
			2		4			8
	9		8					
	5	2		1				

No 81

	1						3	
					6	2		
	7		2	8			9	
				4			2	3
3	4		1		9		7	6
1	5			6				
	8			9	2		5	
		4	8					
	9						6	

No 82

		2		5		1		
	8						6	
6			3		7			2
	7	1	4		2	3	5	
			8		1			
	6	4	5		3	8	1	
9			7		4			1
	4						7	
		3		8		9		

No 83

9	6						4	5
	5	1		8		3	7	
4			7		8			3
	7						9	
1			6		9			8
	8	4		1		6	3	
5	2						8	7

No 84

2	8			9			1	7
7								3
	5		7		1		2	
			2		3			
1								6
			1		9			
	9		8		6		5	
6								8
5	3			2			4	1

No 85

		4	7			5	6	
				1				
	1		6		4		2	
	4	1	5		9	2	3	
8				6				5
	3	2	4		1	7	9	
	9		1		8		7	
				5				
		8	2		7	3		

No 86

4			3		1			7
		8	2		6	9		
	7			8			5	
3	1						7	6
		9				3		
5	8						2	9
	4			2			6	
		7	4		3	8		
9			7		8			1

No 87

	1			3	9		8	
			8					7
	6						3	
				6		5	1	
	2	6	5		3	4	7	
	9	4		7				
	4						5	
9					6			
	3		9	8			2	

No 88

4	2			7			9	3
1			5		3			6
7		8				3		2
	3	4				5	6	
2		6				9		1
3			9		1			8
8	7			2			1	5

51

No 89

3	2		9					
		1		3				
7	8		2		6			
9	3		1		2		4	7
		7				1		
1	6		4		5		3	8
			6		3		9	1
				5		6		
					9		7	5

No 90

5	6							7
		2		8			3	
8					1	2	4	
			9			7		2
6		1			2			
	7	8	5					1
	3			9		6		
4							7	5

No 91

2			1		4			9
	5		8		3		4	
		4				8		
	9	2	6		8	7	3	
	3	8	7		5	2	6	
		1				5		
	7		9		2		1	
3			4		6			7

No 92

7	8	9		1				5
			9					3
				8	5			4
		5					3	
6		7				2		8
	1					9		
4			5	2				
1					6			
9				3		5	6	7

No 93

		5	6			9	8	
	4		1		2		9	
2								7
1			5	6	8			9
		3				4		
8			9	4	3			1
5								6
	2		3		6		1	
		6	8		4	7		

No 94

				8				
7			1		5			6
	5		2		6		9	
9	2		3		1		6	7
		5		4		8		
3	1		8		7		2	9
	3		6		8		4	
1			4		3			2
				1				

No 95

4			1		6			9
	6						1	
		9		5		2		
	4	5	2		7	1	8	
			4		5			
	7	2	3		1	4	6	
		4		7		3		
	8						5	
3			6		2			8

No 96

	6						8	
	3	8	6		1	7	5	
			3	5	8			
	8	3	7		9	5	2	
		5				4		
	2	4	8		5	3	9	
			2	7	4			
	7	2	5		6	8	4	
	1						7	

No 97

6	9		1	2		4		
3	2						1	8
				3				
	7	9	8					
		8				9		
					7	6	8	
				8				
8	3						5	9
		6		5	3		2	7

No 98

4	5					3		
		9	3			7	2	
	2		1					8
	7				6			
6								2
			8				1	
3					5		8	
	1	7			8	5		
		5					9	4

No 99

	4	3						
1					8			2
	5	9		1				
			7			6		4
		1		5		9		
6		5			2			
				9		3	8	
7			4					9
						5	4	

No 100

	6	7		1	4			
					5			9
	3							
7		6	9					3
	1			7			8	
5					2	9		7
							7	
2			4					
			7	8		6	1	

No 101

	6		8		9		2	
		3		4		6		
2								7
4		8	1		6	3		9
			7		3			
3		7	4		8	1		2
9								1
		5		7		8		
	3		9		1		5	

No 102

7			5	8				
		9	3			4		5
		8				9		7
9					3			
2	8						9	4
			8					6
3		5				8		
4		2			8	6		
				5	7			1

No 103

7			1		2			9
		8				7		
	4		3		7		6	
		6	8	7	1	5		
3								2
		1	5	2	3	6		
	2		6		4		5	
		4				9		
8			7		5			1

No 104

						4		
			4	1		7	3	
5			8					
6					5		2	4
		7		4		1		
4	3		2					9
					6			2
	4	3		7	8			
		9						

7	8	5
2	9	6
4	3	1

4	6	8
3	1	7
5	9	2

No 105

		2	1		5	9		
4			9		3			7
	1						8	
	5		7	3	4		9	
6								2
	7		6	2	9		5	
	4						3	
3			2		7			8
		1	3		6	5		

No 106

9		2				6		8
1		7	6	2			4	
				9				
					3	8	1	
	8						7	
	7	3	8					
				8				
	1			5	9	2		3
8		9				5		7

No 107

			4		6	5		8
			5			3		1
				1			6	
8		6	1		2	4		9
	3						8	
5		4	7		8	2		3
	8			4				
4		7			5			
3		9	6		7			

No 108

8				3				7
		6	1		4	8		
	5						6	
7	4		9		8		3	1
			5		7			
9	6		3		1		7	5
	9						4	
		2	4		9	7		
1				5				2

No 109

							9	2
		4			9	3		
				3	5		8	7
				1	9			
6				8				3
		2	4					
3	7		8	6				
		6	5			1		
8	9							

No 110

		6				1		
9			6		1			2
	8			4			9	
	6	5	8		3	2	4	
			2		4			
	2	1	7		6	3	8	
	7			3			2	
5			1		8			7
		4				5		

No 111

7			2					3
				3		5	4	
						9	6	
9	8				1			
	4			5			3	
			7				5	8
	5	9						
	6	2		4				
4					9			1

No 112

		2	9		3	7		
	3	8		4		2	1	
9		3				4		5
8	5						7	6
7		4				1		2
	9	7		1		6	4	
		5	8		7	3		

No 113

		6	4		8	5		
1				5				9
	9		2		1		6	
3		4				9		6
	1						3	
7		2				1		4
	8		9		3		7	
5				4				1
		9	7		5	2		

No 114

								3
					8			
9				5	1			
	7	3					2	
	5			6			1	
	4					8	9	
			3	2				4
			7					
1								

No 115

5	8		1					6
				2		9	5	
	9	2	4					
4	5					2		
		6					1	4
					3	1	7	
	6	1		5				
9					7		6	8

No 116

8			9					
	1					6		
		7		1		3	4	
			5		1			2
		3		6		1		
7			3		8			
	6	4		3		2		
		2					9	
					7			5

No 117

					8			
							5	
	7			6	2			
1						8		7
6				3				2
4		5						9
			5	9			1	
	2							
			4					

No 118

	9				6			
6				4		7		5
		2						8
			2		9		6	
2				8				4
	1		3		4			
5						1		
4		8		2				7
			7				3	

No 119

	1	4	2				8	
		8	4					
9				6		3		
					8	4		7
	5						1	
1		6	9					
		1		5				8
					3	7		
	6				2	9	5	

No 120

2						9		
7		3		5				4
			4				1	
			5		6		8	
5				3				7
	9		1		7			
	6				8			
8				7		4		2
		5						3

1	9	8						
3	5	2						
4	6	7						

No 121

	5			8			2	3
8							7	
		1			9			
		5	1		2			
	2			7			8	
			8		4	6		
			5			4		
	6							9
7	3			2			6	

No 122

7						2		
	4				8			
		6		7		5		9
			7		3		1	
		5		2		7		
	6		4		5			
2		9		5		1		
			6				3	
		1						8

5	1	4
8	3	6
9	2	7

No 123

					4	5		
		6		9				2
	5				8	4	1	
3		4	5					
	1						7	
					2	9		1
	7	2	8				9	
5				7		1		
		3	6					

No 124

		9			6			
1				8		3		
	2	6			5		9	
			9			6		7
	4						2	
2		8			1			
	8		5			1	4	
		2		4				9
			3			7		

No 125

		4			7			
7				1				6
5	3				6	7		
			3				8	9
		6				1		
9	5				4			
		8	5				2	4
3				7				1
			2			3		

No 126

	1		7					
		2		6			5	
8	7		3					1
					1	4	7	
9								8
	6	8	2					
6					3		2	9
	8			9		1		
					5		4	

No 127

7			3		2			
						2	5	
		1				9		8
				5			3	
6			9		7			1
	5			3				
8		2				6		
	7	9						
			4		1			7

No 128

					4		7	3
7	9			3				
		8			5	9	2	
	5	4						8
3						4	9	
	8	2	1			7		
				9			8	5
5	1		6					

No 129

7								
			2					
			6	8				5
		5				4	9	
		3		1		7		
	6	2				8		
4				3	7			
					9			
								6

No 130

7		5	4		8		9	
			5	6			8	
3								6
			9			5	6	
9								7
	1	4			7			
1								5
	7			2	5			
	2		1		6	8		3

	7	8	5
	2	9	6
	4	3	1

No 131

	6	7	3					8
		4		1		9		
9			6					
	8	2	9					
4								5
					7	2	3	
					1			7
	5		4			1		
1					5	3	9	

No 132

2	6		7					
							7	
	9			2	4			
5				7		3		
8			2		9			7
		4		1				5
			1	8			6	
	8							
					6		9	3

73

4	6	8
3	1	7
5	9	2

1	9	8
3	5	2
4	6	7

No 133

		4				9		
	1			4	2			
	5		1		7	3		2
2	4				5			
		3				5		
			3				8	7
1		9	4		8		6	
			2	6			3	
		2				8		

No 134

					2	4		5
		1						
			7	1		2		
9				6			5	
1			8		4			6
	3			7				9
		4		8	3			
						6		
8		2	6					

5	1	4
8	3	6
9	2	7

74

No 135

8			5					1
	2				7	9		
6	1		8			7		
							4	3
		2				8		
9	5							
		8			9		3	7
		1	2				9	
7					5			6

No 136

		9			6			
	7	2					4	
	8			1				5
6				7				3
			6		9			
2				5				1
5				4			8	
	1					7	2	
			9			5		

75

1	9	8
3	5	2
4	6	7

No 137

		9						
			7	6		3		
					9	8		6
5				4			7	
9			3		6			2
	1			9				5
1		3	8					
		8		2	4			
						2		

No 138

	5	2		8			9	
			9					1
	4					3		
9			1		3			
	8			4			3	
			8		7			6
		6					5	
7					2			
	2			3		4	8	

5	1	4
8	3	6
9	2	7

No 139

					3	2		7
						8	5	
				7		4		
4	9		8				3	
5			2		1			6
	2				5		7	4
		8		9				
	6	5						
2		9	1					

No 140

	6	4		2		9		
	5				1			
					9		3	6
5	1		2				9	
8								3
	7				6		8	5
7	2		8					
			5				7	
		8		6		5	4	

No 141

		5	9					
2		8		1				6
			6			4	8	
	5	9			1	6		
	7						4	
		3	8			7	5	
	3	1			7			
7				8		2		5
					5	3		

No 142

	5				6			1
1		3	8			7		
	6				7			
5		6		3	1			
			2	7		6		4
			1				2	
		5			8	9		3
2			7				5	

No 143

	8		3					
			5				6	9
	9	4		2		5		
	7		9				1	8
1								6
8	3				2		5	
		1		9		8	4	
7	2				1			
					8		7	

No 144

	6			9			8	4
5		7	6					
			8					7
7					9	8		6
		6				1		
2		8	5					3
8					2			
					3	9		1
9	4			5			3	

No 145

9			4		7			
8	6	5						
		7		1	6			
		4		2	9			
	7						3	
			8	5		2		
			6	9		5		
						3	8	9
			3		5			1

No 146

	4		1		6			
2							3	8
						5		6
				5		1		
	9		8		4		2	
		5		1				
8		4						
6	3							9
			7		2		4	

No 147

1								
				3	8			9
			1				3	7
	6			2		8		
	1		3		9		4	
		5		1			6	
9	5				7			
7			2	4				
								4

No 148

			1				7	
		3			9	2		4
7			6				3	
3		8		4	1			
			7	6		8		5
	3				8			1
1		4	9			6		
	8				6			

1	9	8
3	5	2
4	6	7

No 149

6								9
		1	3		6		5	2
		7	9	1				
	4	6	7					
8								7
					8	3	9	
				3	9	5		
7	9		5		4	8		
2								3

No 150

		1		4				5
					8		2	
6							3	9
		4		1		3		
			8		2			
		7		9		8		
3	9							4
	1		2					
5				6		1		

5	1	4
8	3	6
9	2	7

Wordsearch Puzzles

No 1
A Warm Start

```
Y R Z B A E N I H S N U S P A
Y T F F A A Y O N I D K O T Y
R K I K Q X H W F H B Z I B T
N Q E C J Y E F N Z J I V B W
I Q Q R I F A O C P Q Y O Y A
D K J B O R I D F X N V N F R
I O V V A S T R G L G N R C M
P H L P S T E C E L U I H R T
E V U A B E V N E S O S A T H
T O P X Q K A A E L I W H G U
A C P H M N W O D R E D I E Z
I N S U L A T E E K U T E N D
D K N V A L A V U V K O Y I G
A K J Q O B E L E W N L L A V
R E V O C F H T D G I R B L H
```

BLANKETS	HEATWAVE
COAL	INSULATE
COVER	KEROSENE
DUVET	LUKEWARM
EIDERDOWN	PARAFFIN
ELECTRICITY	PASSION
FEVERISH	RADIATE
FIRESIDE	SUNNY
FLUSHED	SUNSHINE
GENIAL	TEPID
GLOWING	WARMTH

Soft Words

```
B O U E G E O K C R C D S L S
Q D P K C S Z T P L Z A M Q X
W E W Q I Z L D O W N Y O Y R
Q X B J S N W U Z Y M S O E J
D U R N D W D O F N J U T W Y
J G I E V S R F V I E O H O B
R Q I E C E U Q P Q C I V L N
Y Q Z Y T L L O Y S S R R L I
A D A T F U R V I P G U E E Z
W Z U E Y Y S L E D P X L M Y
G B I L Y C K R L T O U A A J
O I I T C E W L D R Y L X A M
B P S N N E P L I A B L E J Y
Z I E E T L T E N D E R D M W
M J A G B F X R G D B Z B F C
```

BUTTER	MERCIFUL
CLOUDS	MISTY
DOWNY	PLIABLE
DULCET	QUIET
FLEECY	RELAXED
FLUFFY	SILKEN
GENTLE	SMOOTH
KIND	TENDER
LUXURIOUS	VELVETY
MELLOW	WHISPER
MELODIOUS	YIELDING

U Words

```
J S U G Y K J E A J M E P T Z
C L N P W T S E I L G U H P I
R I O U S Z I A X Y W I W M D
E S N U S E F U L N E S S X E
C N K O K C T E Q L U F T U D
L E J W S R T T J I E C A F A
U T O P I A A L I O B R M A R
C U M N M S R I M N H U B N G
M D N I W P U T N D G U T M P
U L T E R I O R L I K R R U U
U L A S R E V I N U A Z C I M
U R C H I N V V L T Q N N N P
S D B F O L H E S Q O Z R A I
P H O A A U L P G Z L Y Y R R
P Y P I N E U R G E N C Y U E
```

UBIQUITY	UPGRADED
UGLIEST	UPSETTING
UKRAINIAN	UPSTART
UKULELE	UPWIND
ULCER	URANIUM
ULTERIOR	URBAN
ULTIMATELY	URCHIN
ULTRASONIC	URGENCY
UMBRELLA	USEFULNESS
UMPIRE	UTENSILS
UNIVERSAL	UTOPIA

No 4
Computers

```
U B B L E P A C S T E N W J R
Y N W N T R K K O H K V A F R
I K S J Y E W M F A A V Y R A
S E T Y B S T I S C A N N E R
F Y L L A W E R I F C X X C S
W B D M G O N O S T D R H A W
D O A O E R R U Y X R S E P O
Q A O N M B E G L E O C R A D
Y R L I D L T V A T M O A C N
T D N T U W N N R C M W I I
C C W O C X I I A E Q P T T W
J I O R H N C D S P D U F Y I
W K D L Z A Z S T Y Y T O K B
D B X F M N O U U H P E S A O
T F O S O R C I M J D R G P M
```

ANALYSIS	JAVA
BANDWIDTH	KEYBOARD
BROWSER	MACINTOSH
BYTES	MEGABYTE
CAPACITY	MICROSOFT
CD ROM	MONITOR
COMPUTER	NETSCAPE
DOWNLOAD	PROCESSOR
FIREWALL	SCANNER
HYPERTEXT	SOFTWARE
INTERNET	WINDOWS

Lord of the Rings

```
L T R V B I M P T Z S H E Z K
O K N Y W O E F S F T P R Z O
D Z M H T X R R E L R O N D N
S N I G G A B O B L I B L A Z
L R D M W F M D M N D P H F T
J T D C C A U O E I E O P T K
L B L A T R L B C G R I H I O
F L E B G A L A D R I E L J G
J L E W M M O G Z E O M E R A
A E A D N I G G A D I P O Y T
I E R D N R N I E G V G I V L
R Q T O N E N N R O G A R A Q
O O H G W A V S A L O G E L S
M E R R Y W G I F D I Z Q A R
C K A N N A M U R A S A M B Z
```

ARAGORN	GIMLI
ARWEN	GOLLUM
BILBO BAGGINS	LEGOLAS
BOROMIR	MERRY
ELROND	MIDDLE EARTH
EOMER	MORIA
EOWYN	RIVENDELL
FARAMIR	ROHAN
FRODO BAGGINS	SARUMAN
GALADRIEL	STRIDER
GANDALF	THEODEN

Sixties Pop

```
B U W B W V L O E B I V J G N
S I B E A C H B O Y S A P S I
R K C L J I M I H E N D R I X
F A N A T N A S U I I E O C I
D Q T I M T L L S A A E C V Z
Z S H U K D B J N R B P O B E
B U E N E Y O A L W E P L O A
P P W C D P R O X Z A U H B B
L R H O L O G E W R T R A D N
I E O I S U V G W T L P R Y A
T M N S T O M A K Y E L U L O
Y E O H M N W O R B S E M A J
B S R E K C O C E O J G L N C
C I H K J I S P O T R U O F Z
E T M O N K E E S D R Y B E P
```

ARLO GUTHRIE	JIMI HENDRIX
BEACH BOYS	JOAN BAEZ
BEATLES	JOE COCKER
BOB DYLAN	KINKS
BYRDS	MONKEES
DEEP PURPLE	MOODY BLUES
DIANA ROSS	PROCOL HARUM
FLEETWOOD MAC	SANTANA
FOUR TOPS	SUPREMES
JAMES BROWN	THE MOVE
JANIS JOPLIN	THE WHO

Star Trek

```
T A B N K N A R T T O T S D V
B R B M R S U L U D E N E R S
N U R S E C H A P E L A N P E
O H I H I Q S C O T T Y O Q N
G U D G T R E S A H P C B L T
N S G K N L D F G F K J E V E
I T E A O W A R P F A C T O R
L P R R R S I S M M N H Q K P
K Y L E F P E I E C A Z V E R
R O M U L A N S F S C U W H I
J E X H A A T I W W L O E C S
P K O D N K D N I N U U Y R E
E L B B I R T E U B V X P M Z
W O I R F S T A R S H I P M I
I R K Q F U S L M Q C X R Q I
```

BONES	NURSE CHAPEL
BRIDGE	PHASER
DEATH GRIP	RED ALERT
DR MCCOY	ROMULAN
ENTERPRISE	SCOTTY
FINAL FRONTIER	SPOCK
IMPULSE	STARSHIP
JAMES T KIRK	TRIBBLE
KLINGON	UHURA
MR CHEKOV	VULCAN
MR SULU	WARP FACTOR

No 8
Gone Fishin'

```
M F S W O L L A H S I F T A C
E I Y P C W Z W O D A P D U Z
R S A W R R I V E R B A N K L
R H E N M I G T X I S S E D Q
O E W D O K N V J F K D N V T
B R E A K I N G S T R A I N U
R M P N T L T Y T L F F L R O
A E M A V E N I G I A H E G R
H N K P O E R K T N D D R N T
I N S H O R E P Z E N E O I E
L O B S T E R I R U P M H T P
N H S I F G O D O O L M S S G
H E R R I N G L T A O W O A M
C P O Z R O F W S Q J F Z C L
W H C T A C V W A D E R S H V
```

BREAKING STRAIN

CASTING

CATCH

CATFISH

COMPETITION

CONGER EEL

DOGFISH

DRIFTLINE

FISHERMEN

FLOUNDER

HARBOR

HERRING

INSHORE

LOBSTER

RIVERBANK

SALMON

SHALLOWS

SHORELINE

SPRING TIDE

TROUT

WADERS

WATERPROOFS

No 9
Skiing Vacation

```
G N Z P U H C E L N Y J Q O X
T E O A X B W Z E R M A T T Q
P D D T R J K P H S L W Y N D
P L H V N G S R U N G H H K Y
J O A C E A E W B S R I I J S
E S H B G Q T N Z T U S N O J
N O L L N S R S T W G T L W Z
I V C B I V T A I I R L L T A
D A H R R V M J K D E E I W I
R D A A I R V Z O Q B R Y R R
K L M N E M A Y R H O F E N O
L G O D M R E L L M A U P D V
A I N I V R E C T M L N M I A
U A I S R E T S O L K N N T X
X Y X K P C T R Y W U Q U W X
```

ANDERMATT	LECH
ARGENTIERE	MAYRHOFEN
ASPEN	MEIRINGEN
AVORIAZ	OBERGURGL
BRAND	SOLDEN
CERVINIA	SOLL
CHAMONIX	ST ANTON
DAVOS	ST JOHANN
ELLMAU	ST MORITZ
KITZBUHEL	WHISTLER
KLOSTERS	ZERMATT

F Words

```
V S U O L U B A F T A P O Y T
Q D M X M D P E E K A L F N K
F G V K Z U S P B S R L T N T
O K R X F T F E R V E N T U Y
R E P P I L F L U F R A E F R
M U R V G X R O A T E G D I F
U A A R H E E U R B Z N S G A
L L Z O T L A P Y T U C L M D
A Y T S I E F P L L R U J E E
N U O T N E M A L I F E Y N D
B F U B G H R E V E T B S T I
U F U B Y E F A C T U A L S V
P Z C S D Z K R O V A L F U H
C J J E G U O N Q D Q X K E T
L H F T A F V D Y Z P N U S M
```

FABULOUS	FIGMENT
FACTUAL	FILAMENT
FADED	FLAKE
FEARFUL	FLAVOR
FEBRUARY	FLIPPER
FEDERAL	FORCEFUL
FEISTY	FORMULA
FERVENT	FORTRESS
FESTIVAL	FOSTER
FIDGET	FUNNY
FIGHTING	FUTILE

No 11
Woody Words

```
K D V F M F L G Y T D W M T N
H L Z H W H I T E O A K P W U
L M E R B A U B O G C S M W T
G S Z A T N A W N Z L B Y F O
R R Z B T U P T P S T E A K V
U M U S Z I N A A L D E R X F
R A E T L B E L R K H C V P E
K H B U B I N G A A Y H R E P
C O T E U B P O N W D U B L W
O G A P L C D M A B I E N I P
L A K R S E D N I H C L C E Y
M N D I R K P R S V I X L B L
E Y R R E H C A G U N P L O P
H D P V N H T P S X A F J N W
I L E I O X F R J M K W E Y U
```

ALDER	MAPLE
ASH	MERBAU
BEECH	PARANA
BIRCH	PINE
BUBINGA	RED OAK
CEDAR	SAPELE
CHERRY	TEAK
CHESTNUT	TULIPWOOD
EBONY	WALNUT
HEMLOCK	WHITE OAK
MAHOGANY	WILLOW

No 12
ARM Words

```
L T M A F S D X L Y W V Q H A
O E L U F M R A R M C H A I R
E P X A A Q R Y R O M R A X M
R A D A R M O R E D N F Y V I
X O R A A M Q A D A M R A Q G
O E E M R D R N Q N Q O L T E
L L E A A W O E A U A I L I R
W N L C S G A I S R R B I P Q
T Z B I G S N R M T M X M M E
E N O D D E G A M R A F R R N
M P W M M A L Y C O T R A A A
R B G R E I M D E R U O M R A
A F A Z T R F R G H R R S E D
M T Z E A R D I A V E C E N D
F R E R O M R A E L O H M R A
```

ARMADA	ARMET
ARMADILLO	ARMFUL
ARMAGEDDON	ARMHOLE
ARMAGNAC	ARMIGER
ARMALITE	ARMILLA
ARMAMENT	ARMORED
ARMATURE	ARMORER
ARMBAND	ARMORY
ARMCHAIR	ARMPIT
ARMED	ARMREST
ARMENIA	ARMY

No 13
Sailors of Note

```
U L T P A R R Y B V R U V H P
W M X M B J B C N M G N O F T
V O A Z N S E E O P B O C R E
F J R G E E L Q H U D S O N M
N G T R E H S I B O R F L T N
A W O D A L B D Z E U O U B F
N C B O W B L Q N A P G M T X
S O A K R Z D A E U A F B N T
E O C D R O M B N R M R U F D
N K P A X F A M R I N A S N T
X B V B S F G A N D O N L N C
M C L N F M F O L O S K M M K
G C Y I N W E O C I L L E J B
D V N S G N D R A K E I Z Q E
L T S R Q H Z K D J N N A N X
```

AMUNDSEN	FRANKLIN
BAFFIN	FROBISHER
BARROW	HOOD
BEAUFORT	HUDSON
BLIGH	JELLICOE
CABOT	MAGELLAN
COLUMBUS	NANSEN
COOK	NELSON
DRAKE	PARRY
FARRAGUT	SCORESBY
FOX	SINBAD

No 14
On Your Feet!

```
U I H O E H E P T R T R G J S
B B G K P K X X Q R F L O G S
E N H A L S N E A K E R S S I
S S P O L F P I L F Q E G R K
P N A L S O N Q V B W O N E S
A O S A Q E S O C K S S W P R
D T N K R S S H H G K G B P E
R G I S O A L O E A E O N I F
I N S E N N L J T S O L B L A
L I A L N D O E N T N C I S O
L L C U V A S W S H E P R H L
E L C M H L M K W E P L W O Y
S E O H S S I N N E T V I Q X
M W M Q A M L S R E D A W T R
K E C P U M P S M E I N M A S
```

BOOTS	SANDALS
CLOGS	SKATES
ESPADRILLES	SKIS
FLIP-FLOPS	SLIPPERS
FLIPPERS	SNEAKERS
GALOSHES	SOCKS
LOAFERS	STILETTOS
MOCCASINS	TENNIS SHOES
MULES	TRAINERS
PLIMSOLLS	WADERS
PUMPS	WELLINGTONS

No 15
Ballpark Words

```
N X C X L L W E V C G W S O A
O C D H I L V F R C L T A Q T
T M P F A O U E B T R I P L E
N J U O L N H G H I F E Z H K
W L S G T C G R K M B L E B S
J J L R T S O E R C V P A U D
T S A A A W T Y U M P I R E I
F P C N B U J R R P O U P A K
W I D D O E V H O M E R U N V
I T T S Q E S T U H E E L B B
O B Q L B Z L A E T S H T A J
G A J A F D S G B A Z C T L O
D L L M Q O H W N C M T A K V
D L E I F T U O K I E I W U T
S G N S F L I L P R S P X M V
```

BALK	PITCHER
BASEBALL	SHORTSTOP
BATTER	SINGLE
CATCHER	SPIT BALL
CHANGE UP	STEAL
CURVE BALL	STRIKE
FOUL	TEAM
GLOVE	THROW
GRAND SLAM	TRIPLE
HOME RUN	UMPIRE
OUTFIELD	WALK

Military Aircraft

```
N S H I S T R A T O J E T K Q
R C S U R V E X J D R A K E N
N I P E Q I S N B B C P X Z A
I M I H R N A M A L B S T Y C
G I T W D T K S L C R K L M L
F T F P R R E R E I Y O O U
D A I G H E H O I O L R B S V
Y R R O P T D R F I C A R Q J
V Y E U H S R U G R W Y E U P
T P S J S A O H A X E G D I H
M O S U H C T T O R M P N T U
Z R T O R N A D O R A G U O J
J Z F Z I A K U T S N M H S Y
N B V N T L M I R A G E T T W
B H G N A T S U M J L W T V Z
```

CORSAIR	MUSTANG
DRAKEN	SCIMITAR
HARRIER	SKYRAY
HELLCAT	SPITFIRE
HORNET	STRATOJET
HURRICANE	STUKA
LANCASTER	SUPER SABRE
LIGHTNING	SUPERFORTRESS
MARAUDER	THUNDERBOLT
MIRAGE	TORNADO
MOSQUITO	VULCAN

No 17
D Words

```
T E D A P P L E D A J O P S N
D N G D E S T I N Y D G G D M
A I X A C R S J A A R G E N X
N I F Y T P O K S P O L T O P
C T W F O N U T Y M I B A M N
E V L S E S A R C N O D R A Y
R B E W B R Y V Q O A I E I I
E D V C D R E U D L D S N D W
T A B L E F E N M A J J E E G
S F Y D P N S A T Y S O G A N
U F D E T G T O T G Z I E R I
D O E E S I U G S I D N D E N
D D E S A E R C E D D T Y S R
G I Y N A D E F E N D E R T A
S L X L W C D S M U R D L O D
```

<table>
<tr><td>DAFFODIL</td><td>DESTINY</td></tr>
<tr><td>DALMATIAN</td><td>DIAMONDS</td></tr>
<tr><td>DANCER</td><td>DIFFERENT</td></tr>
<tr><td>DAPPLED</td><td>DISADVANTAGE</td></tr>
<tr><td>DARNING</td><td>DISGUISE</td></tr>
<tr><td>DASTARDLY</td><td>DISJOINTED</td></tr>
<tr><td>DEAREST</td><td>DISPOSED</td></tr>
<tr><td>DECREASED</td><td>DOCTOR</td></tr>
<tr><td>DEFENDER</td><td>DODDERY</td></tr>
<tr><td>DEGENERATE</td><td>DOLDRUMS</td></tr>
<tr><td>DELINQUENT</td><td>DUSTER</td></tr>
</table>

Hobbies and Interests

```
E  G  N  I  D  I  R  J  E  P  P  C  H  V  H
G  M  N  U  R  Z  X  E  M  U  S  I  C  H  I
I  M  B  I  E  U  P  O  M  Z  L  T  V  V  K
S  W  S  R  K  A  L  G  Q  Z  B  B  G  L  I
Y  L  Y  K  O  L  N  W  V  L  E  M  N  G  N
D  Q  W  O  E  I  A  B  S  E  I  L  I  N  G
P  I  Y  F  G  T  D  W  K  S  B  Y  T  I  N
S  B  V  G  C  A  C  E  H  I  C  X  T  T  I
A  E  O  I  U  F  E  H  R  M  P  P  I  N  H
I  J  U  C  N  P  H  I  I  Y  I  A  N  I  S
L  N  B  Q  I  G  N  I  C  N  A  D  K  A  I
I  X  G  N  I  N  E  D  R  A  G  G  Z  P  F
N  P  G  P  O  T  T  E  R  Y  W  X  U  P  I
G  N  M  U  C  G  N  I  L  C  Y  C  E  F  C
F  U  W  G  N  I  D  A  E  R  L  Z  W  V  L
```

ABSEILING	KNITTING
ANTIQUES	MUSIC
BEEKEEPING	PAINTING
CYCLING	POTTERY
DANCING	PUZZLES
DIVING	READING
EMBROIDERY	RIDING
FISHING	SAILING
GARDENING	SKETCHING
HIKING	WALKING
JOGGING	YOGA

No 19
Sea Critters

```
U M H S I F E L T T U C A D Q
M U S S E L P Z U A Z P D B E
A S Q S T A R F I S H V O S R
L R U S K B A R C R L E P Q K
C O I U E L C N F L D R O Z V
Z Z D P C A E G E E J E L F V
F U S O N G H H D M E L A J I
V S E T J M S O W K O K H S I
J E A C C R I E R Q T N P U X
S A S O O E F R A S Z I E L J
A H N Z C T L Z E L E W C I I
G A A U K S L I M P E T Q T X
A R I Q L Y E W H Z D M P U Y
L E L H E O H B C D E N O A R
E D Z N A C S C A L L O P N G
```

CEPHALOPOD	SCALLOP
CLAM	SEA ANEMONE
COCKLE	SEA HARE
CRAB	SEAHORSE
CUTTLEFISH	SEA LEMON
LIMPET	SEA SNAIL
MUSSEL	SHELLFISH
NAUTILUS	SQUID
OCTOPUS	STARFISH
OYSTER	WHELK
RAZORSHELL	WINKLE

No 20
Moon Craters

```
N P M N D Y J J D P F V L Q P
E A H H O S W N G S X L U C G
S S S W I B K L M A R C O N I
D C G L O Q E Q P X G F F W D
N A H U M B O L D T U A A A R
U L P I E C L A V I U S R S E
M N U D A Z O E R F O W A I N
A N E Y X P L P B O I Z D S N
P V I F O O A O E N H P A P E
P E E E R G C R L R E C Y V J
I G F O T O O S E L N I Y Z C
R A K Y K S V O K L O I S T U
G V O O K C N A L P L P C P Q
A U Q M K K E I E J P I A U T
U K L E H C S R E H W D C S S
```

AGRIPPA	JENNER
AMUNDSEN	KOROLEV
APOLLO	LEBEDEV
CLAVIUS	MARCONI
COPERNICUS	NOBEL
DARWIN	PASCAL
EINSTEIN	PLANCK
FARADAY	SCHIAPARELLI
GAGARIN	TSIOLKOVSKY
HERSCHEL	TYCHO
HUMBOLDT	VEGA

No 21
House Pets

```
S D Z G L Q C D S T G V V E U
B R B O J P G E H I N F U S G
T B B A Y L Z O T F Y P P U P
H K U T L B P F O W T C I O G
Z H H D E I T M R S M N C M Q
I O Z U G R N Y R O E E N Y G
N R E C U E R B A A G S O V D
K S E K T K R E P X J I I O Z
Y E L T L H S I F D L O G A K
G N I T J A G S G A T T E P Z
H K Z J C M V F T A C R R U X
N A A R D S C M R U R O B U J
Z P R V C T I B B A R T I N U
H Y D U M E X M G K K I L G R
K M D N S R U Q K B L Q B Z C
```

BUDGERIGAR	HAMSTER
CAT	HORSE
DOG	KITTEN
DUCK	LIZARD
FERRET	MOUSE
FROG	PARROT
GERBIL	PUPPY
GOAT	PYTHON
GOLDFISH	RABBIT
GOOSE	RAT
GUINEA PIG	TORTOISE

No 22
Red

```
U U E B O O Y C J W H V Q L V
L Z Y Y D D L O B S T E R T D
M H S B D N O C H E R R Y E Q
P M O U N G Y O N R H M N L T
F V R R N V M A L A L I O R J
C A I O N E T E Z B R L O A E
E X C L A N I D R A C I R C L
C I A C E E N R Z N A O A S G
S I B G R T E I L N R N M C S
P R A Q U I L S Q I M A A A Y
E M E R W A M U I C I B T A Y
Y S K K P N J S A R N R L Z P
L E M E J C H R O M E I Q X C
Y W N L I N D I A N T C Z B I
L K H Y E H W F W U C K P D U
```

ALIZARINE	INDIAN
BLOOD	LOBSTER
BRICK	MAGENTA
CARDINAL	MAROON
CARMINE	ROSY
CERISE	RUBY
CHERRY	RUDDY
CHROME	SCARLET
CINNABAR	TURKEY
CONGO	VENETIAN
CRIMSON	VERMILION

No 23
Volcanoes

```
A S O I C A R G F V K W A M C
J V G N E R E B U S E M O T T
B I N I T A B A S N I U E R K
A R O B M A T I J J N J E V I
I L G P O P O C A T E P E T L
F E A L K E H R S F O S B O I
X Y R S L O U T F G U U U E M
E E I X S K H E N V I A R M A
A S Y Y A E R A I X T D A F N
Y T N S L S N U A A L U T I J
D R E E O E S P K Z N K U S A
Z U N N T L O A E A I O R H R
M S K A F T R X L A V N E E O
L Q C U O K L O F I K O B R F
E A H C M P A R I C U T I N H
```

ACATENANGO	LASSEN PEAK
BERUTARUBE	MAUNA LOA
COTOPAXI	MOUNT ST HELENS
DUKONO	NYIRAGONGO
EREBUS	PARICUTIN
FISHER	POPOCATEPETL
GRACIOSA	SABATINI
HEKLA	SAKURAJIMA
JEFFERSON	SURTSEY
KILIMANJARO	TAMBORA
KRAKATAU	VESUVIUS

Tropical Fish

```
O K R I B E N S I S V Q V Y B
W I M A R U O G U P P Y D G R
C N N F L Y I N G F O X M S A
O S C A R L P G S G H N A H B
S O T Y D L O U Q S M R F L R
X N S J E N C D I P T A A S E
G K W C H S I F R E H C R A G
O E O E I T L U T E K L R D I
S I R D K E U N Q M V O B K T
B U D R G G O O O E B L F F F
N G T N R E D L M S L V I O I
B Z A X N D L I A E D R V S M
V T I M E Y B R E T R W A G D
I I L J J P Q C A T F I S H S
U L S F U Y T A L P U F F E R
```

ANGELFISH	KRIBENSIS
ARCHER FISH	NEON TETRA
BLACK MOLLY	OSCAR
CATFISH	PLATY
DANIO	PLECO
DISCUS	PUFFER
FIREMOUTH	RAM
FLYING FOX	RASBORA
GOURAMI	SILVER DOLLAR
GUPPY	SWORDTAIL
HARLEQUIN	TIGER BARB

No 25
Pass the Pasta!

```
H K Q D P P Y G M M F S B J C
O V E U I X V R E D L A F A M
I E E L L H M B Q M I Q L E E
H N H I L L C X A K E H L N C
C K O B U A L M Z V U L I K I
R U B C S U F I T A E U L N N
O S Q H A J S R I N G T I I J
T I K Y R M E P A N B T T Z Q
T R H I J N U P I F O O M E G
E O G C N C M L V R Z Y J I R
L T U E C A N G I M A R G U I
L E K L C O N C H I G L I E H
E L A S A G N A F O I K I B V
I L O F F U T G H G U C S N W
W E N N E P C Y F U S I L L I
```

BAVETTE	LUMACONI
CAMPANELLE	MAFALDE
CONCHIGLIE	PENNE
FARFALLE	PILLUS
FUSILLI	ROTELLE
GEMELLI	ROTINI
GIGLI	SPIRALINI
GNOCCHI	TELLE
GRAMIGNA	TORCHIO
LASAGNA	TRENNE
LINGUINE	TUFFOLI

No 26
SUNny Words

```
L K Y T W G Y Q T Y T B I I D
V X Y A D N U S U N N I E S T
N E K N U S R Y S U N B U R N
A E S S C U U D Z A B K D Y E
N D E U B N A N E B L E P N E
L A S N W S N T V K K M I G R
S H U L Z T W N G I A H X E C
P S N I H R O A I E S B W Z S
A N S G K O D H B N U O N S N
S U P H R K N N U V L P R U U
U S O T X E U S O F N V Y I S
N K T Q M S S U N T A N N E D
S F K C E D N U S U N D O G S
E S I R N U S U N B L I N D W
T K I K B Q I Y S E V E M R L
```

SUN DECK	SUNKEN
SUN VISOR	SUNLIGHT
SUNBAKED	SUNNIEST
SUNBEAM	SUNRISE
SUNBLIND	SUNSCREEN
SUNBURN	SUNSET
SUNBURST	SUNSHADE
SUNDAY	SUNSHINE
SUNDOG	SUNSPOT
SUNDOWN	SUNSTROKE
SUNFLOWER	SUNTANNED

No 27
Phonetic Alphabet

```
G N M W Q T H O E Q O P U X F
G T H Y O H A C T U R Y N Q O
N T E G A S X R G D M T K Q H
P Q N F C I C C O K N H G O C
Y A G E G J I A Y M D U T I E
T S P O S N Z N R Z E E V R J
A M L A H L O J D O L O F E W
B F A Y N X E V Y I T U L U Z
E R O I Q J H E E O A C S I H
E R A X I E U I K M O R I U K
I A A V T F L L S N B J E V Z
U N I F O R M N I A A E R D Y
A H P L A R O Q H E Z Y R M C
K K Y H J C Q T W J T O A D X
O B C B U W X I F V A I O Q N
```

ALPHA	NOVEMBER
BRAVO	OSCAR
CHARLIE	PAPA
DELTA	ROMEO
ECHO	SIERRA
FOXTROT	TANGO
GOLF	UNIFORM
HOTEL	VICTOR
INDIA	WHISKEY
JULIET	YANKEE
KILO	ZULU

Islands

```
F R D Q J W M H W I Q M W J O
W A E N R J V V F I L V N R O
T W C V A Z A K N A L I R S I
G W I I C L A J A W D C K K E
C R C L S D D B N A X T A F A
Y H E D A R U N T H K O I Q C
P A L N G C O S U I N R D S I
R U A U A S O C C O E I O A N
U G N Q D D T Q K N F A K R I
S I D S A U A A E A D W F D M
M T I B M J F T T N P L E I O
K N R Y F R G R E E N L A N D
D A D I N I R T P G N K I I T
B X H T E B J R A B I Z N A Z
H T R D M Q L I Y U C I O V N
```

ANTIGUA	KODIAK
BARBADOS	MADAGASCAR
CORSICA	NANTUCKET
CUBA	NEWFOUNDLAND
CYPRUS	SARDINIA
DOMINICA	SRI LANKA
FIJI	STATEN
GREENLAND	TENERIFE
GRENADA	TRINIDAD
HAWAII	VICTORIA
ICELAND	ZANZIBAR

Getting Around

```
C E G U C L B S S F B K S N M
Z X N E U C R I B E H L I E W
O E O R T F A R C R I A V A V
D H O S T Z I T Y Y R E I E I
Z C L E E R L E A T C R W R T
E B L N R E W S T M S L Z O R
Y T A I E I A F U H A H E P A
K O B S O L Y S I B C R M L I
Y B R U M F M P L Y R A A A L
M O T O R B O A T H A O Y N E
H G A M G G F R E I G H T E R
I G E I R P M O D F F I W O I
G A J L D I N G H Y R N E V M
K N N C X A Z D F Y H F D L S
F G Z R C E F O R H P O O L S
```

AEROPLANE	HYDROFOIL
AIRCRAFT	LIMOUSINE
AIRSHIP	MOTORBOAT
BALLOON	MOTORBUS
BICYCLE	RAILWAY
CANOE	SLEIGH
CATAMARAN	SLOOP
CUTTER	TOBOGGAN
DINGHY	TRAILER
FREIGHTER	TRAIN
HORSE	YACHT

No 30
New York

```
T T O N G A U I N C H F L T D
B R O O K L Y N D O U L L I N
Y M A N H A T T A N A I W M A
K B O P M E L R A H N A F E L
R R A T U B V D E C L I B S S
A O Y T S N C I O L F Q R S I
P A K Y T T G L S T M U O Q N
T D S E V E N T H A V E N U E
C W N E N C R A C G V E X A T
E A F R E E V Y R Q H N U R A
P Y A N E E S N P G Y S S E T
S C T T N N W O T A N I H C S
O E E U H U D S O N R I V E R
R C E N T R A L P A R K N Q Q
P A R K A V E N U E W H A C U
```

BATTERY PARK	LINCOLN CENTER
BROADWAY	MACY'S
BRONX	MANHATTAN
BROOKLYN	PARK AVENUE
CARNEGIE HALL	PROSPECT PARK
CENTRAL PARK	QUEENS
CHINATOWN	SEVENTH AVENUE
FIFTH AVENUE	STATEN ISLAND
GRANT'S TOMB	TIMES SQUARE
HARLEM	UN HQ
HUDSON RIVER	WALL STREET

No 31
S Words

```
V S E M K E F V Y E S X E Z S
S K V F O Y S A I E F C T B E
O E A D L R W E I L N T U T S
S A L F E A E Z N E T F R H S
A A D F W T I R L I T G S E E
T N G O L N T I B M L I N C N
U W T A G E S E T M F E S I T
R S S N C M S Y U D O H D F F
D T T T R I H S R O O S S I O
A R E O H D T O N P H I A R S
Y U T F K E W Y P E R L N C E
N T S U N S H I N E S R I A A
V T O P L E N I T N E S T S N
X E N O H G R S T O R M Y Q C
X D N N T W B A Z R W S L A E
```

SACRIFICE

SAGACITY

SANITY

SATURDAY

SEANCE

SEDIMENTARY

SEIZING

SELFLESSNESS

SENTINEL

SHIRT

SHOPPING

SIDELINES

SILENCE

SILHOUETTED

SOFTNESS

SOMBRERO

STETSON

STORMY

STOWAWAY

STRUTTED

SUNSHINE

SWORDFISH

Anatomy

```
M H F A M Y B W E L C S U M M
D I T Y T I G N I A R B R Z R
H N M R A M R V E R T E B R A
G T A K C P G H U Y A V F D E
I E E L H B E A I N Q L C P R
H S R F G U T L R X F A D S O
T T T E X L M M V H P V H I F
F I S E D C A V F I P C U M F
W N D E Q L W N L Z S A B R N
N E O N I I U L E Z H I I E B
Q I O K P R A O W R B D C D L
Y G L K U R E I H A D R E I M
K T B M Y R W T P S R A P P F
P Q E J S U Q E R Q O C S E W
U F W I P S T O M A C H V E N
```

ADRENAL GLAND

ARTERIES

BICEPS

BLOODSTREAM

BRAIN

CAPILLARY

CARDIAC VALVE

DIAPHRAGM

EPIDERMIS

FEMUR

FOREARM

GUT

HEART

INTESTINE

KNEE

LARYNX

MUSCLE

PELVIS

SHOULDER

STOMACH

THIGH

VERTEBRA

No 33
US State Capitals

```
N L W I O J L T Q J O O H E K
C O R H U A I P M Y L O G N C
Y H T N N B N Q P T B I I O Q
J Q E S I L O P A N N A E S N
G A I Y O M G X H D J U L I N
U N A C E B N K I V E Q A D O
G S N I Q N N A U N Q N R A D
R I C H M O N D S Q E O V M K
L N S P S A C E A H F O A E Q
M G X K P J F U N T V N H G R
D Z C O X A G J R G S I D P A
T A L Z T U M A I B M U L O C
J I M N S J H H O N O L U L U
S V A T N A L T A H A F W U E
F S A N O T N E R T G P C J L
```

ANNAPOLIS

ATLANTA

AUGUSTA

BOSTON

CHEYENNE

COLUMBIA

DENVER

HARTFORD

HONOLULU

INDIANAPOLIS

JACKSON

JUNEAU

LANSING

LINCOLN

MADISON

NASHVILLE

OLYMPIA

PHOENIX

RALEIGH

RICHMOND

SANTA FE

TRENTON

Animals

```
F X G G D P V T R L F V M S D
G Z K H U O B I R A C X N U Z
W E S N I T O R S L E O Z M S
X W J O U A H R N O O C C A R
L M I P N K F R A B B I T T P
A M A L L R S J A G B M C O M
M W T X D E T B I V N P L P P
E X A N T E L O P E A A Z O B
W V B Q D M B J E A R L K P C
V D M X O T T E R B B A V P J
F O O T N A H P E L E K A I J
V E W H K I O A H S Z C J H Q
B T I G E R R I P G T A N H O
A M V E Y I S V O I D J I V I
G Z C E G J E H G W L W B Z U
```

ANTELOPE	LLAMA
BABOON	MEERKAT
CARIBOU	OTTER
DONKEY	POLAR BEAR
ELEPHANT	RABBIT
GOPHER	RACCOON
HIPPOPOTAMUS	SKUNK
HORSE	TIGER
IMPALA	WILDEBEEST
JACKAL	WOMBAT
KANGAROO	ZEBRA

Cold Words

```
N A D T A E W S Q T P W X I K
J C E D Y E K R U T A T V P M
K E A E A I Y E A T D C S A G
F Q O T C H I S E L L P Q M E
U V H R H A B R M Q V E Z R O
J E K A S O N C M A N K Z M T
R I N E T T D V J F W F C Y S
C A S H O E I E A I C R E A M
Z X R E D L U O H S E I W L H
V T R O F M O C N H S G F S D
Z W O B E B C C O S A I J I I
D L S Y T M K A I L I D N I L
B L H Y P O A A S T O R A G E
V P Q V I U P R U E R O S G G
S A Q T W F Z Q F S J G F I T
```

BLOODED	FRIGID
CANVASSING	FUSION
CASE	GELID
CASH	HEARTED
CATHODE	SHOULDER
CHISEL	SORE
COMFORT	STORAGE
CREAM	SWEAT
FEET	TURKEY
FISH	WATER
FRAME	WEATHER

No 36
Hallowe'en

```
Y T S E R I F N O B P J F X B
T S U L I D C W I Z A R D R Y
D A P H A L L O W E E N Y V J
L D E O F T R H S I L U O H G
L W R R O H N X D T G P L T N
A T N A T K P E Q L U L N A I
C H A O Y R Y T M M R M S L T
I A T C I E O A P E N Q E I N
T O U K K T V K E F L C H S U
S S R L K C I A C Z L E C M A
Y J A K D N A R R I X Y T A H
M E L E L R C L A G R L I N M
Q O V A O W O B B P L T W N X
Z I M S A T A N I C P D T Y G
L P H V W I T C H C R A F T B
```

APPARITION	HAUNTING
BLACK CAT	MYSTICAL
BONFIRES	PUMPKIN LAMP
CAULDRON	SATANIC
COSTUMES	SPOOKY
DEVIL	SUPERNATURAL
ELEMENTALS	TALISMAN
FLYING	TRICK OR TREAT
GHOULISH	WITCHCRAFT
GRAVEYARD	WITCHES
HALLOWE'EN	WIZARDRY

OLD...

```
V O L D M A I D O L D F A C E
L Y U V A T N L L O O Y O E I
O O E J H A D D D L L P L I H
F B L L H B W L E D D Z D T M
I V G D I I J Q S B T R S L L
M P L R F A A H T E I D O O J
G O D R A E B S N A M D L O E
Q N J B Z L L D E N E D D H G
P A R N D I L L L Z C F I C A
A M A U V L Y N O O Y F E S D
H O E O I T O O U W Z D R D L
C W D B S J B N E F I W D L O
D D D D P X T X S R S S I O S
L L L D L R O W D L O L D E R
O O O S Y Z Z E T F Z K N Q P
```

OLD AGE	OLD FELLOW
OLD BAILEY	OLD HAND
OLD BEAN	OLD MAID
OLD BILL	OLD MAN'S BEARD
OLD BIRD	OLD SCHOOL TIE
OLD CHAP	OLD SOLDIER
OLD COUNTRY	OLD STYLE
OLD DEAR	OLD TIME
OLDER	OLD WIFE
OLDEST	OLD WOMAN
OLD FACE	OLD WORLD

...and NEW

```
R N W W P L K A Y Q J N D E N
N S R H E V A W W E N E T T E
M Y Z O T C J E D M L W N A W
O N E W B L O O D G N F N G M
O V E S G W I Y N W N O E W O
R N L N R P E A Q N E U W E D
B E Y R E E F N E A W N C N E
W W T J D W J W C Z E D A N L
E M S T E E S W W Q L L S E B
N A W N E M V S E B G A T W V
W R E W A L B S H N J N L L I
L K N N C Z S G E E G D E O O
F E O Q Q N E W S V E N D O R
O T R O P W E N E L O T F K Y
R R S S E N W E N N J R P H U
```

NEW BLOOD

NEWBORN

NEW BROOM

NEWCASTLE

NEW DEAL

NEWEL

NEW ENGLAND

NEWFANGLED

NEWFOUNDLAND

NEWGATE

NEW JERSEY

NEW LOOK

NEWMARKET

NEW MODEL

NEWNESS

NEWPORT

NEWSLETTER

NEWSMAN

NEWS SHEET

NEW STYLE

NEWS VENDOR

NEW WAVE

No 39
Pirates!

```
L G M I U B U C C A N E E R W
U P M D O U B L O O N S D K B
A A L O I N A P S I H B I D T
H C T A P E Y E A G F Y S I D
L A R J N T U M T A R S D B I
E P A O A K H U E L D R A E C
E T W O W S S R L L A I O P A
K A P D I S U F N E E A R O R
C I K N A S N O B O H S B C H
M N A L A A N E B N E R I S X
L P T E E N U L S J R O F E H
S U R C A L L T L T U C L L Y
C T O C B U H T I Z G I J E Z
H P I E C E S O F E I G H T F
P A R R O T Q B K T F L N Z R
```

BLUEBEARD	FIGUREHEAD
BOTTLE OF RUM	GALLEON
BROADSIDE	HISPANIOLA
BUCCANEER	KEELHAUL
CANNON	OCEAN
CAPTAIN	PARROT
CORSAIRS	PIECES OF EIGHT
CROW'S-NEST	PLANK
CUTLASS	SPANISH MAIN
DOUBLOONS	TELESCOPE
EYEPATCH	TREASURE

No 40
H Words

```
K D L H M T E G D K U Q C M I
X B A W A G S W I H P Y S O M
F M H H E M L I N E F E H H X
L R B L H H S G N I G G U H L
E E C O H A W T H O R N H O H
S X U E Y G A M E A D R S N H
R S K V N G H X J R S E L E Y
E A E I I L A A U S L I H S D
H Q W L J E R E L K I L I T K
Y E E A P E C X C C U E T V P
H A I I K A H A T N Y T T Z E
D E D N U O H Y E N A O I F R
M U A Y A D D R A Z A H N H R
E H T X E G J O Y M T H G B K
T T I B A H J F W O U I C K Y
```

HABIT	HEMLINE
HACKLES	HERSELF
HAGGLE	HEWING
HAKE	HEYDAY
HALCYON	HITTING
HAMSTER	HOAX
HANKER	HONEST
HAPLESS	HOTELIER
HAWTHORN	HOUNDED
HAZARD	HUGGING
HEDONIST	HYENA

The Simpsons

```
C B N E D F L A N D E R S W A
W H P R B U Y N N E L H N V H
J U T N A M K C O R B T N E K
Q E M F H U D K H O M E R U A
W J A Y A A J E J R U A L C L
C K R U S T Y S V R G G H M S
D X T J M N T U H Y Y I E R Y
K M I B O B W O H S E D I S Z
Q B N S T S C H N F N M G B S
A E L Z R R U L W Y R C G O E
P E G R A M K I E B A P A U O
N Y O L B P G M U T B S M V M
I H P A I G B R Y D U H M I Q
W H G E U T N D S L I S A E C
Z P P M G S E Y M O U R G R E
```

BARNEY GUMBLE	MARGE
BART	MARTIN
CHIEF WIGGUM	MILHOUSE
CLETUS	MOE SZYSLAK
FAT TONY	MR BURNS
HOMER	MRS BOUVIER
KENT BROCKMAN	NED FLANDERS
KRUSTY	NELSON
LENNY	RALPH
LISA	SEYMOUR
MAGGIE	SIDESHOW BOB

No 42
US Universities

```
E B V X B P O U P N O W V C R
B A N H Q E P U W N A L H D C
Y E L L I V N O S K C A J O M
J L O E H G T E E T P W L O N
R P O G X E H F D M F U X W I
C M C A G A O P A I M U J H Q
X E D R K R N N O B C P T T E
U T O R E L R D I I I T U R L
K E M S A A A A R C N Y I O A
G N T K S V D N K I B T W N Y
T H T L I B R E D N A V A U E
D R O F D A R A L G W I L S P
I A X A V I E R H P D Q S M S
U R B A N A T M D N H O H Y A
F L O G J N C U I J C I B Z K
```

ADELPHI	OAKLAND
ALEXANDRIA	PICKERING
BENEDICTINE	RADFORD
CHAPMAN	TEMPLE
COLUMBIA	TUFTS
GEORGETOWN	URBANA
HARVARD	VANDERBILT
HIGH POINT	WAKE FOREST
INDIANA	WALSH
JACKSONVILLE	XAVIER
NORTHWOOD	YALE

No 43
Creepy Crawlies

```
F O O E L H C Y L F N E E R G
G F G H S I F R E V L I S B Y
X E I F C L V L A T A A E L F
V Y L F D A G E T N S X F O Q
B K E T D R O O E T E T J W L
J E Y S E F B R A W O F Y F L
I D H D K E Q G K B A T L L Y
X E I M U Q B G T C D Y F Y U
P P M L O E Y G L S O V R P J
S I B J E S W L N D U C E G A
T T M T W K Q R V U W C V U K
P N L H G P F U X N D S O B I
H E D E P I L L I M Q T H L Z
S C A R A B K C I T N A D E R
P Z G J T N O I P R O C S S Q
```

BLOWFLY	LOCUST
BLUEBOTTLE	MILLIPEDE
BOTFLY	MOSQUITO
CENTIPEDE	RED ANT
COCKROACH	SCARAB
CRANEFLY	SCORPION
DUNG BEETLE	SILVERFISH
FLEA	SPIDER
GADFLY	STAG BEETLE
GREENFLY	TICK
HOVERFLY	WEEVIL

No 44
Shapely Things

```
P N X N N N E R A U Q S R L F
S A O O G R H O M B U S R G P
N N R G R J S E P T A G O N E
O Q M A A C S C S K D K K K E
Q X E T L R O H T T R K S O H
X O L N W L T N E R I F Q C V
M L G E I C E E E X L U C T Y
S F N P T C E L T L A B U A S
I Z A R S O R G O D T G B G P
R B I E E K V N R G E I O O H
P Y R A M I D A M L R O I N E
H C T R C Q N T L X A A D V R
L R N K P G Z C L V L L M S O
C I R C L E J E L L I P S E I
C N G E V T T R A P E Z O I D
```

CIRCLE	PYRAMID
CONE	QUADRANGLE
CRESCENT	QUADRILATERAL
CUBOID	RECTANGLE
ELLIPSE	RHOMBUS
HEXAGON	SEPTAGON
OCTAGON	SPHEROID
OVAL	SQUARE
PARALLELOGRAM	TETRAGON
PENTAGON	TRAPEZOID
PRISM	TRIANGLE

No 45
Stop That Noise!

```
V C M J R C F U P F F R O K F
J R A Y S L R G W E Q U C D K
D H E A Q C W U G P P A G I G
V L L V U H D G N Q R C D T T
P E T I E I T N I C H U K K S
Q C S L L R Y I M I H B U X U
L H I B C R B T M T E L N A Z
Z A H H H U S E U G F N P Z G
W I W P C P C P R I N G I N G
B E V Z T E R M D A R F A H H
T Y T T I V E U Y C T B K I W
Y Y Q L W P A R M L W I C H S
V B O L Z E M T C H L W O H O
Z K W U L A E U Q S E A N N T
U L F W C J R T L P P V K B H
```

BANG	SCREAM
CHIME	SCREECH
CHIRRUP	SQUEAL
CRACK	SQUELCH
CRUNCH	THUD
DRUMMING	TRUMPETING
FIZZ	TWEET
HOWL	WAIL
KNOCK	WHINE
REVERBERATION	WHISTLE
RINGING	YELP

Rocks

```
P M E S N R A P S D L E F F J
W G T W W F J B K N T U F F M
J B A J T F X S S I E N G R L
W A L Q L R C Q M S O Y R S M
W G S I G H D O W U B E E A X
A A N P I O L I M E S T O N E
Y T T S E O G T T H I I L D T
Z E T R D R E E A C D H F S I
N Y M L A F R L A W I C T T Z
I I J N P C E R B E A A K O T
J X I Q L U H M F R N L J N R
H T F A C T O Y Z X A A Y E A
E P C U N P X G T H W M A V U
T T L A S A B N C E J W U E Q
T S X Y Q N O J T M K E Q U F
```

AGATE	LIMESTONE
ANTHRACITE	MALACHITE
BASALT	MARBLE
CALCRETE	OBSIDIAN
CHALK	QUARTZITE
DOLOMITE	SANDSTONE
FELDSPAR	SCHIST
FLINT	SHALE
GNEISS	SLATE
GRANITE	TRACHYTE
JASPER	TUFF

No 47
Airport Names

```
J G V P H S H E X U G C H W I
W O R H T A E H K R T P A G D
S C H I P H O L N C R S N S X
Y T D N C W F A L I M A E H M
F R K A F I V B N U H J D E A
P Q N R E K A C X C D A A R I
J P U O R T E M T I O R T E D
M R U E I G A N P T B A E M R
I R B R E R I N N I H B Y E A
R A U O T N U L I E N P B T U
A L R U E S A G Q L D O Y Y G
B G B W Y Q A L N G O Y R E A
E G A T W I C K I E P G V V L
L R N A R L A N D A B N A O C
K D K M D E R W X J X Q K N O
```

ARLANDA

BARAJAS

BEN GURION

BURBANK

CHANGI

CIAMPINO

DETROIT METRO

DULLES

GATWICK

HANEDA

HEATHROW

JOHN F KENNEDY

KASTRUP

LA GUARDIA

LINATE

LOGAN

MIRABEL

NEWARK

PRINCE GEORGE

QUEEN ALIA

SCHIPHOL

SHEREMETYEVO

Cartoon Folk

```
E J A Y U S U U B X Z P S H T
F E A W D K C U D Y F F A D S
D R A E B I G O Y V W E P P Y
R R J X I S M W D W N L W I L
O Y D U B P O R K Y P I G N V
O W S U P R Y N D G L X E O E
P I N K P A N T H E R J L C S
Y N E S U O M Y E K C I M C T
Y U I I O O A C F E V C E H E
E K U B W O O C X E W C R I R
L H O G R Y X P O Y J T F O X
A O L B O K F Y R E P M U H T
B I O T M S L O K P O B D L G
P R E N N U R D A O R F D O V
N J O O X O D H Y P O O N S H
```

BOO BOO	PINK PANTHER
BUGS BUNNY	PINOCCHIO
DAFFY DUCK	POPEYE
DROOPY	PORKY PIG
DUMBO	ROADRUNNER
ELMER FUDD	SNOOPY
FELIX	SYLVESTER
JERRY	THUMPER
MICKEY MOUSE	TWEETY PIE
MOWGLI	WILE E COYOTE
OLIVE OYL	YOGI BEAR

No 49
Green Things

```
T H W L Q G E F D H W B S T X
J U R V V U X O C L Y O G D E
G Z O B N F B A G C A J Q P Q
J U G R E E N G A G E R P C Y
N I E L P I L B G A F E E O P
B E P D P S B T L H R W D M L
E P N S E A S O T I U O A M E
A S Q V G H U L D O T L J J T
N A A E Y S R O E G B F H F T
S E F X Y Z T J E S D I T O U
L P S R E N H A O S S L I T C
D J L P I V E I M E S U S Z E
L S S M S W I S S C H A R D P
J R A L U I M L T C G C R B F
T W N L W Q A S O E H S Z G X
```

APPLE	JEALOUSY
BEANS	LEAVES
BOTTLE	LETTUCE
BRUSSELS SPROUT	MINT
CABBAGE	OLIVE
CAULIFLOWER	PEAS
EMERALD	PERIDOT
ENVY	SAGE
GRASS	SPINACH
GREENGAGE	SWISS CHARD
JADE	TURF

No 50
Olympic Sports

```
G N I M M I W S W D V U E A A
N A I R T S E U Q E L K W B G
I C J T D E C A T H L O N X X
T G A K K P N I L E V A J N J
F N R N N O L H T A T P E H Q
I I O S O L P W P S L P Z O Q
L V W H R E M M A H A E G C P
T I I O T V I G O T E N R K M
H D N T X A R N H N I T M E U
G S G P N U R L G L P A M Y J
I N T U E L E A T V T T E P G
E L I T W T L S M S Y H O Z N
W F R X I Z E W H T U L V I O
E F G C O R G N I T O O H S L
X N S H W B S A I L I N G T D
```

ATHLETICS   LONG JUMP

BOXING   MARATHON

CANOEING   PENTATHLON

DECATHLON   POLE VAULT

DIVING   ROWING

EQUESTRIAN   SAILING

GYMNASTICS   SHOOTING

HAMMER   SHOT PUT

HEPTATHLON   SWIMMING

HOCKEY   WEIGHTLIFTING

JAVELIN   WRESTLING

Saints Above

```
A T A X Q M A W H R Q A E J O
G T N E C N I V G R D F Y O N
I A E P N N M W E W B N C H N
D Y D J I I M T J T O H O N R
I F J F C Q E A C H R N G A Z
V S R H H P A I T I K U K Z U
A E A E O N G N S T D Z G A Y
D E F N L N A T D A H E Q I G
L T B I A Q O I S R O E N R I
F O N T S P B H T R E M W E N
J A I N H M S P G S B W W L B
F U I E N I R E H T A C P Y P
S M R L N K X S H H U B E R T
S P L A S A M O H T C F E O V
R E I V A X V J G M B C F S E
```

ANDREW	MATTHEW
ANTHONY	MICHAEL
BENEDICT	NAZAIRE
CATHERINE	NICHOLAS
CHRISTOPHER	PETER
DAVID	SEBASTIAN
GEORGE	THOMAS
HUBERT	VALENTINE
IGNATIUS	VINCENT
JOHN	WINIFRED
JOSEPH	XAVIER

No 52
STARTing Out

```
F E L T D E L T R A T S J O S
R I T K L O G S A Y H Y M I A
E S T A R T I N G B L O C K N
S T T S D T R A T S P U J I A
H A R A A G R N U C E I N C F
S R A E R N N A R L G O T K F
T T T S M T D I T U N G L S O
A I S U T V I S T S T B M T T
R N P P L A I N T R D R T A R
T G M R O H R A G A A A A R A
U P U O T P R T F L R T E T T
P O J R E T V Y E Z I T S H S
E S A N E W S T A R T N S N D
S T A R T I N G T I M E E E E
S T A R T O U T R A T S E R R
```

ASTARTE	STARTING BLOCK
FITS AND STARTS	STARTING DATE
FRESH START	STARTING LINE
HEAD START	STARTING POST
JUMP START	STARTING TIME
KICK START	STARTLED
NEW START	STAR TURN
NON-STARTER	START OFF
REDSTART	START OUT
RESTART	START UP
STAR THISTLE	UPSTART

No 53
Ice Cream Flavors

```
A N S Y Y R R E B P S A R M Q
L P O C A R A M E L W A A U X
L C R N Q C R S L I F N F G K
I R Z I I U R E L S G O F E M
N A I U C C M D B O R A I L B
A N H C T O C S R E T T U B H
V B X T N H T U S E U P W B C
E E E L E U F T P U Z L Q U A
E R P R N U F F J P H O B B E
F R R O D R E L P P A E N I P
F Y C G U D E T A L O C O H C
O O E I T T U R F I T T U T Q
C S T R A W B E R R Y E K P W
K S F D V B I L B E R R Y S K
X O M P J D Z Y G C C I P D K
```

APRICOT	FOREST FRUITS
BILBERRY	FUDGE
BLUEBERRY	LEMON
BUBBLEGUM	MANGO
BUTTERSCOTCH	PEACH
CAPPUCCINO	PINEAPPLE
CARAMEL	RASPBERRY
CHOCOLATE	STRAWBERRY
COCONUT	TUTTI FRUTTI
COFFEE	VANILLA
CRANBERRY	WILD CHERRY

No 54
Character Types

```
T X N U K G A O R F G S O Y S
A S S M F J E E B Z U J V I R
O M I S E R C N O O F F U B Q
Z B N D N N O P T I M I S T P
U R A Q A H D S G L C A S D T
C T E M I S I L R R E I G L V
Q R O M R T L P I J F M E H P
J R E F A A V M P I V A A O E
M W C M B E I F C I D C V N D
E H G D R N R A E E E I G D A
D O D G A A P D R I F T E R N
D O H L B A H M Y P A A N A T
L L U N A T I C F A T N I W Z
E J N C K T O V H T D A U O N
R B B Z Y R O X M S B F S C G
```

BARBARIAN	HIPPIE
BUFFOON	LEADER
CHARMER	LUNATIC
COWARD	MEDDLER
CRIMINAL	MISER
DAYDREAMER	ODDBALL
DOGMATIST	OPTIMIST
DRIFTER	PACIFIST
FANATIC	PEDANT
GENIUS	ROMANCER
GENTLEMAN	SADIST

No 55
L Words

```
E H M O H Y O S Q N K Y Q N N
L R J L I F T I N G Z B Q G Z
A O U C L Y C I L A E E L L J
R F C S C V T O L Q Y A U F B
E E W K I G W I T I N M D F C
B E T N E E N L V D B R C L H
I G E H R D L I I E A A Y X M
L R Z E G E E N R P G R I Z Z
I I D L A U G J O U I N Y L B
O P A D O H A E I C O D O X M
N K E W M C L L A Q J B Y L I
E R Q C K O I L O G I C A L H
S B O N Y L T G N I K O O L O
S D X A S V Y T F O L L G O K
I Q L G N I R O B A L T O G O
```

LABORING	LIFTING
LAKE	LIONESS
LANDING	LOCKED
LAUGHTER	LOFTY
LAZY	LOGICAL
LEADER	LONGEVITY
LEGALITY	LOOKING
LEISURE	LOWERED
LEOPARD	LOYAL
LIABILITY	LUMBERJACK
LIBERAL	LYRICAL

No 56
Major Mountains

```
M K Y U T O J T B F P S G L C
R A H Q S Y S T S B R R L N A
Z N T N E U R E G I E K A O T
J G N T R A E B M Z R L J S U
T C O B E I C H N Q B U S N Z
V H L Q V R C O B T N C M I N
X E L Q E I H R N G I H C V G
F N H Y R G O O F C X A M M D
T J O I E A M R R U A N E M X
K U T A D L A P Y N P G S A G
P N S P R U N O A N O T U K J
M G E Y F A O I E A T S W A C
I A N I S H R J K J O E L L L
K P Z H C D T A E C C Q F U I
F U P Z Q P Y S T E M A K E W
```

ACONCAGUA	JUNGFRAU
ARARAT	KAMET
BROAD PEAK	KANGCHENJUNGA
CHANGTSE	LHOTSE
CHO OYU	MAKALU
COTOPAXI	MATTERHORN
DHAULAGIRI	MCKINLEY
EIGER	MONT BLANC
ELBRUS	SINAI
EVEREST	TIRICH MIR
JANNU	VINSON

No 57
Walk in the Woods

```
K L T Z S D S R B F Y Q S B I
W O E X O E J E E P B T Z J Y
C O W A W E E N O M L I G I C
K T L I V R C N Z E A C L M T
C S R L T E A M R C C L A U M
I D B K I C S R B L K W D S Q
K A A Y R W I E E P B S O H K
W O D V H U G A I Y E B L R K
V T G C Q A R N M O R E B O C
P J E S I I E E I A R E V O G
E E R L N C W Z E P I T Q M G
B V O G O B L U E B E L L S W
O F K N E T T L E S S E I L Q
G R E K C E P D O O W I W F V
M S T R E A M A T K V O F P S
```

BADGER	LEAVES
BEECH	MUSHROOMS
BEETLE	NETTLES
BLACKBERRIES	OAK TREE
BLUEBELLS	OWL
CANOPY	PINE CONES
CLEARING	SQUIRREL
CROW	STREAM
DEER	TOADSTOOL
FENCE	WEEPING WILLOW
FOLIAGE	WOODPECKER

No 58
Smile at the Camera!

```
E U H H G T O T I A R T R O P
J S E C P A N N I N G B M T T
I R P L W A F Y L B R M O O Z
K J L A G R R D N I W E R H V
S O V X E N X G G N T K D P M
V C Q L R J A H O J W H Z E B
A O E A R E T E M T H G I L S
H L X N G N D R D V O L K E D
T X P D E N F N J I Z H E T V
C L O S E U P G I M W Q P N B
E L S C O L O R R F F W E I S
J H U A R E M A C L W M Y R P
B R R P A N O R A M A E B P A
U J E E U W I S N R V J I H U
S N R V U X H V F S G E T V F
```

BRIGHTNESS	PANORAMA
CAMERA	PHOTOGRAPH
CLOSE-UP	PORTRAIT
COLOR	PRINT
EXPOSURE	REWIND
FLASH	SCENE
FRAME	SUBJECT
LANDSCAPE	TELEPHOTO
LENS	VIEWFINDER
LIGHT METER	WIDE-ANGLE
PANNING	ZOOM

No 59
Superheroes to the Rescue!

```
S A F K Y O B R E P U S N C W
U R P L I V E D E R A D A A T
P N O U H J E O W H M P M P H
E S R H Z F W B M S T S O T E
R H I E T B A T M A N U W A P
M U N L T Y Q L I L N B R I H
A M A B V N T N C F A M E N A
N A M I T E A H B O Q A D M N
A N R D H M R L G O N R N A T
M T E E E J G S N I I I O R O
O O D R A V O I U E M N W V M
W R I C T M I S Q R E E D E E
T C P N O O R I U Y F R H L S
A H S I M S P E C T R E G T V
C X Q G W O R R A N E E R G A
```

BATMAN

CAPTAIN AMERICA

CAPTAIN MARVEL

CATWOMAN

DAREDEVIL

FALCON

FLASH

GREEN ARROW

GREEN LANTERN

HUMAN TORCH

INCREDIBLE HULK

ISIS

SILVER SURFER

SPECTRE

SPIDER MAN

SUB-MARINER

SUPERBOY

SUPERMAN

THE ATOM

THE MIGHTY THOR

THE PHANTOM

WONDER WOMAN

No 60
Shades of Blue

```
H A S T D A R K F F Q G S R T
E N S K Y H F B C Q R C N E N
W A Y T E C A M L O X O Z R Z
W C W U E N J Z Y T C B Q I C
H B R P H E I A U D Q A L H U
A T S R W R L R D R W L E P E
S S Y U F F Q W A R E T X P L
I H V S L U C X S M G F K A P
S M A S O J M E U B A N Z S R
G E N I R A M A R T L U A T U
O H S A B T D I K U L W Q E P
V E U N T H G I L I L Z S A C
S X B S K H N W N X O E Q L Y
Y A U G T O R E D W O P A Z I
P G K K R U J U O A Y T X N J
```

AQUAMARINE	POWDER
AZURE	PRUSSIAN
BRIGHT	PURPLE
CERULEAN	ROYAL
COBALT	SAPPHIRE
DARK	SKY
FRENCH	STEEL
LAZULINE	TEAL
LIGHT	TRUE
NAVY	TURQUOISE
PEACOCK	ULTRAMARINE

No 61
Waterfalls

```
T M C W X Y C H U R C H I L L
D S H O S H O N E R O V G J U
J V S S O F I T T E D B U N T
T I X S L L A F N I W T L M I
N O G E B W O H L C K Z L V G
Z I G U E O J Q I H R L F I O
M N A T A R W K E E I L O C R
A R I G H S O G V N M I S T D
Z H O B A C S I L B M G S O E
W R U R H R R U A A L G U R C
C N H W E S A A D C C N L I H
I K V I N P K D I H S I U A O
W K J N N N M Y R M K P E B I
N J U B I E A E B A P A R R M
N D R R M E C R O F H G I H J
```

ANGEL	KRIMML
BOW GLACIER	MINNEHAHA
BRIDAL VEIL	NIAGARA
CHURCHILL	REICHENBACH
DETTIFOSS	RHINE
DUNN'S RIVER	RINKA
EMPEROR	SHOSHONE
GAPING GILL	TWIN FALLS
GULLFOSS	UTIGORD
HIGH FORCE	VICTORIA
IGUASSU	WHITEWATER

END Words

```
E Q H T N K K A T V V N N W R
L G Y T I C A D N E M C P I U
B O M R E D N E F F O M N S S
A K A X A P I Y K D P N D D A
D R E A M D L J N X U I N A D
N E T N E D N E P E D E A O N
E N S F N D C E N M F P R J E
P D S E P S E D G E P E R T G
X E I E E E O D D E D N E M A
E R H R N R N E N N L N D H R
F E C U E D D D E E D N N L F
R D A D O N I L U E C Z E I O
R N N W E X H N N L N S V D N
O E B F X Q L C G T U U A R A
T G Z U I I Y U A J T M L S O
```

AGENDA	INNUENDO
AMENDED	LAVENDER
APPENDIX	LEGENDARY
ASCENDED	LENDER
CRESCENDO	MENDACITY
DEFENDS	OFFENDER
DEPENDENT	PENDULUM
EXPENDABLE	RENDER
FENDED	SENDING
FRIENDLY	TENDENCY
GENDER	TENDER

No 63
Native Americans

```
W U V L K A Y R E H G W O U Y
E M S Q Y C H O C T A W V T J
L D W C D S M O N O R U H Y W
P W T H I U H R M T A K U L F
V I S E M I N O L E P M X K R
A C R R E U B P S Q A E W W F
L Q F O M F A I J H H R B A S
I C E K Q W K E K O O N I H C
X C M E N U A C H K A N B O Z
I N R E N C O T A C M C E M H
X Y E O E W S I I L A G T U C
Y N T N W Q A H S H B P U X K
M E E O D Z O H J T C Z A Z P
T S W E A M M Y S T S I O U X
J V J P X N T O D N A Y W B X
```

APACHE	PAWNEE
ARAPAHO	SEMINOLE
BLACKFEET	SENECA
CHEROKEE	SHAWNEE
CHINOOK	SHOSHONE
CHOCTAW	SIOUX
CROW	TETON
HURON	UTE
IROQUOIS	WICHITA
MOHAWK	WYANDOT
MOHICAN	YUMA

Pizzas

```
C N R O C T E E W S N O I N O
H F W T O M A T O E S O X Q E
H X M U S H R O O M S V O A D
S Y G R O U N D B E E F N M E
P P E P P E R O N I W C A L E
F N E K C I H C J C H H G Y P
G B B N L Q H A D O D T E G P
B L A C K O L I V E S M R L A
C D C S A A C I K N F E O A N
A A O U P E E O K T K F V N C
P K N E D S M G J F Q A U U R
E S N P L S I L I H C L E T U
R O O G R E E N P E P P E R S
S R Q X X Z T S U R C N I H T
K E W S P I N E A P P L E Y N
```

ANCHOVIES	MUSHROOMS
BACON	ONIONS
BLACK OLIVES	OREGANO
CAPERS	PEPPERONI
CHICKEN	PINEAPPLE
CHILIS	SMOKED HAM
DEEP PAN CRUST	STUFFED CRUST
DICED PORK	SWEETCORN
GREEN PEPPERS	THIN CRUST
GROUND BEEF	TOMATOES
JALAPENOS	TUNA

No 65
Nobel Peace Prize Winners

```
F S D Y C O J S E R E P W E R
D L A W J U E C A Y J K M V J
Z X N D W T Y H V K I U Z O C
N A N N A Y D W R S H Q I D V
I G J Y L T M E S J Q A L H S
G B C B E H T I K F J O R J P
E I O J S R N T M L J A K O N
B Z R R A G A Z T K E U I U V
P I R C E H D E S A J R M H X
K C I R U P D R Z L L X K A N
R E G O R B A C H E V B N U I
Z C A P R M M E D D F B T X B
B I N F M K S T D N A R B O A
M L L A H S R A M A S F D I R
F K H P T E E N G M W T J Y U
```

ADDAMS	JOUHAUX
ANNAN	KISSINGER
BEGIN	MANDELA
BRANDT	MARSHALL
CARTER	PERES
CECIL	RABIN
CORRIGAN	ROTBLAT
DE KLERK	SADAT
GORBACHEV	SAKHAROV
HAMMARSKJOLD	SCHWEITZER
HUME	WALESA

No 66
Numbers

```
P M S M M N E E T E N I N D F
A N K O T R I L L I O N W S K
Q T Q Z X T G B K E F O R I K
D N A S U O H T Q N D W N X E
G S S O E Z T V I O N T D T K
R L X I D E E N W Y X Y E Y R
F M R F X Q E O W T Y T R O F
X I W I O T N D H F T X D N O
C L F F Y R Y N K I H I N E U
K L T T T T T S E F G S U E I
O I W Y E H N Y E V I L H T F
J O E T P E I E O V E Q T R P
K N L W K Q N R V N E L Y U L
E G V O T H I R T E E N E O M
W Y E H Y F K T Q Y S X L F J
```

EIGHTEEN	NINETEEN
EIGHTY	NINETY-TWO
ELEVEN	SEVENTY
FIFTEEN	SIXTY-ONE
FIFTY-ONE	SIXTY-SEVEN
FIFTY-TWO	SIXTY-TWO
FORTY-ONE	THIRTEEN
FORTY-TWO	THIRTY
FOURTEEN	THOUSAND
HUNDRED	TRILLION
MILLION	TWELVE

No 67
Rivers

```
M V A V N R A R J J I V Z A C
X G P N I G E R Q I N X E N A
E O T D U L I H E P C S N G G
L D C Q K B Z R L P E V I X P
U K E C U A N Y I I J T H I H
Q J K B M B E N N S V R R S K
C A X B U V K E T S T U W E F
Y O E R X N C L A I O A G M P
O Z L N O Z A M A S E G N A G
I U X O V W M D S S B L O H H
E D N A R G O I R I L O K T O
R B E E D A M E K M E V E C K
R O N H N A D R O J C H M W L
G C O N G O N O S D U H B L Z
E Z T G N A Y E K Y U R J J P
```

AMAZON	MISSOURI
COLORADO	NIGER
CONGO	NILE
DANUBE	RHINE
ELBE	RIO GRANDE
GANGES	SEINE
HUDSON	ST LAWRENCE
JORDAN	THAMES
MACKENZIE	VOLGA
MEKONG	YANGTZE
MISSISSIPPI	ZAMBEZI

No 68
Military Leaders

```
P K M P B M Q W K G V Q E S F
N W A L L E N S T E I N Z P J
S C R R Y K I T C H E N E R T
Q U L Z H E S S I R R A H Q E
V B B E H A L L E N B Y Y G A
H Y O U M U N D I N C L A N W
U C R W L M K N A M H R A I N
J V O E Y R O O I R I O N R Y
R W U L M W T R V B B G W L G
L H G L B O M N A P A Z G E O
K C H E O E G L A T O L L S R
A D S S F L D T E R H I O S D
H F Y L P I T M N L G O P E O
Y N O E L O P A N O O R A K N
X W W Y N R E K N A M R E H S
```

ALLENBY

BRADLEY

EISENHOWER

GARIBALDI

GORDON

GRANT

HANNIBAL

HARRIS

KESSELRING

KITCHENER

MARLBOROUGH

MONTGOMERY

NAPOLEON

PATTON

ROMMEL

SHERMAN

SLIM

WALLENSTEIN

WELLESLEY

WINGATE

WOLFE

ZHUKOV

No 69
Canadian Round Tour

```
C E D G R J G Z X A F I L A H
R E G I N A I T O C S A V O N
R E D N A G L O C Z K L J X M
F N K L O N D Y K E U L M X P
S G R G W T A A L A R I I C L
M L E Y A B N O S D U H M A S
L Y V P E O U O T N D C E L X
D U U S I I K D M T Q R F G T
H K O G S N U A S D T U P A O
Q O C E L C N M S N E H V R T
G N N E L I I I O U H C N Y T
O C A G T G N M W K H O Y N A
L I V O I R A T N O E V J B W
C E B E U Q A D A L B E R T A
I A B O T S U D Y R U B D U S
```

ALBERTA	MONTREAL
CALGARY	NOVA SCOTIA
CHURCHILL	ONTARIO
EDMONTON	OTTAWA
GANDER	QUEBEC
GOOSE BAY	REGINA
HALIFAX	ST JOHN'S
HUDSON BAY	SUDBURY
KLONDYKE	VANCOUVER
LAKE LOUISE	WINNIPEG
MANITOBA	YUKON

No 70
Fictional Sleuths

```
W R B Z I L L E C O R T E P Y
T M M C G I L L E L E W L X T
T J U H A R R Y O V O M L Y E
I O H N Q L T Z T L R I E C R
M N R O G P L T R N X S R N G
W A A I O A E A U W M S Y I I
G G N H O K M A H I N M Q U A
A E Y N C P E T W A O A U Q M
S R R O I S E R F B N R E R T
O A R L U X E L M X N P E V F
O C I O D T A O U C A L N R Q
Z H L S E G L B K C C E Y F D
P C F P R O C K F O R D L G H
R E Q I C J M F I G R E T O G
S E M L O H K C O L R E H S Z
```

CALLAHAN	MANNIX
CANNON	MCGILL
CHAN	MISS MARPLE
CLOUSEAU	PETER WIMSEY
COLOMBO	PETROCELLI
CROCKETT	PHILIP MARLOWE
ELLERY QUEEN	QUINCY
HARRY O	REGAN
HERCULE POIROT	ROCKFORD
MAGNUM	SHERLOCK HOLMES
MAIGRET	T J HOOKER

No 71
Hot Stuff

```
G S X D K H S M T N K X X T H
L R S T E A M D O R W A I T C
U M I A I O J I H R Y K U Q T
M A R D C I N D E R S S J M F
E T F R D O I N B Z M C D I K
H C C H I L I P E P P E R C L
S H X M E H E Y H P B E A R J
L E U A S V E R E P T U T O D
A S H N R R O C A O A C S W H
O A U S I T A T N D B E U A G
C S R F A N Q G S Y A B M V W
G G N I R P S T O H S R B E H
W O D U Z N E V O L C A N O V
B A F E Y X U C X S O B O T X
R W O O S J Q O M T D Z Z Q L
```

ASHES	MATCHES
BARBECUE	MICROWAVE
BONFIRE	MUSTARD
CHILLI PEPPER	ONION
CINDERS	OVEN
COALS	RADIATOR
FIRE TONGS	STEAM
FURNACE	STOVE
GRIDDLE	SUNSHINE
HEARTH	TABASCO
HOT SPRING	VOLCANO

Meat on the Menu

```
S P F H S A L U O G O D T O H
L A M B C H O P Y F K D N L M
T F L M T I Z V N Y T F M L C
N O C A B E W C N P R U L A O
D Y J N M D N D C A O R S B N
V V B M H I N D N R Q S D T E
X T E L T U C K E A E I N A K
F U E I M J F G S R S G G E C
S O F E H U R D O I L M F M I
X G S J R U V L F U R O A V H
F A T T B F E E B I L L I H C
Q R E M D X C V S V L P O N O
W R A T A L O P I H C L T I I
L H K R O P T L A S L A E V N
F E E B I L I H C G I G O T Y
```

BACON	HAM SANDWICH
BEEFSTEAK	HAMBURGER
CASSEROLE	HOT DOG
CHICKEN	LAMB CHOP
CHILI BEEF	MEATBALL
CHIPOLATA	RAGOUT
CUTLET	SALAMI
FILLET	SALT PORK
FRANKFURTER	SIRLOIN
GIGOT	TENDERLOIN
GOULASH	VEAL

No 73
Cards

```
Q Q C J P Q I X I G L A B W C
Y D K K D M Z Z Y M M U R T L
V W C V L J R T T E U Q I P U
L W I L D C A R D Q G X D Y E
V I R N M A L S D N A R G G R
T V T B N Y I E E D C E E E H
Q A D T G I U K R D E K K T C
C W R W L Q N F O L A O B A U
A D A A I E U G H O P P Z R E
N C C Z C X S C H D L W S T B
A T E D U C O L U A H A J S C
S B V H N N A T A U N R K T R
T N I N I X S B R M J D R I O
A E F P G G R C E N C P U U I
T R U M P S H U F F L E K S B
```

ACE HIGH	PINOCHLE
BACCARAT	PIQUET
BEZIQUE	RUMMY
BRIDGE	SHUFFLE
CANASTA	SPADES
DRAW POKER	STRATEGY
EUCHRE	STUD POKER
FIVE CARD TRICK	SUITS
GRAND SLAM	TRUMPS
KALOOKI	WILD CARD
LITTLE SLAM	WINNING HAND

No 74

Nuts and Seeds

```
L W A Y S D R F Z E Q U B M C
Y E A V T L E M Y R O K C I H
W Y K L U N P L C A S H E W G
R P E A N U T E V O W M H V T
E P G E B U Y T O T T A N N A
D S L K O N T T L I Z A R B N
N O C F C C T U N E N I P A N
A W Y E A H Y S L Z Q N L R C
I E C F R E E N R N I M U C X
R S T S D S U Y O V O T K P T
O I H C A T S I P N B C W Q B
C N T M M N P R D P A E X O I
N A E F O U O I S O O C I W V
S W B P M T L E E V L P E V I
B V W Y K L D Y P S P C N P R
```

ALMOND	DILL
ANISE	FENNEL
ANNATTO	HAZELNUT
BRAZIL	HICKORY
CARAWAY	PEANUT
CARDAMOM	PECAN
CASHEW	PINE NUT
CHESTNUT	PISTACHIO
COBNUT	POPPY
CORIANDER	SESAME
CUMIN	WALNUT

Red Things

```
E I F X P J Q A Q C R G N L A
G D Z U G V W O O D J C X R U
B D P M M X D T E P R A C J V
P E P P E R C A G C J A E V M
N D L B A H C K A U W A U H M
K A U C E N U M B K G O A G H
Y E L R S B I L B L E I N R Y
S H R E Q U O H A F E A A B K
O Y N S R O P K C I R B R N V
B X C C D R P R M U L L E T T
A P P E E W I I O T R Q F T H
G V D N E R L U L C G R L G I
Q L R T R Q O H Q D E C A F T
F S E O T T Z E L S S F G N B
T L P V E E H F V H A D L T T
```

ALGAE	DEER
BLOODED	EARTH
BRICK	FACED
CABBAGE	FLAG
CARD	GIANT
CARPET	GUARD
CHERRY	HEADED
CHINA	MULLET
CORPUSCLE	PEPPER
CRESCENT	SQUIRREL
CURRANT	WOOD

No 76
Shakespearean Characters

```
H C W R Z A J P U S T H H I J
Z Z M H C T E I L U J T A U W
V G W D A D N A R I M E M G L
O F F A T S L A F S Y B L L I
F R I A R L A W R E N C E F A
N D E Y Z I I A S C U A T I P
O U C P V U D R D T N M L S S
R P O A S M K I N G L E A R U
E U T R E O Z E W A H K S J T
B C H M T T R L X P B O C O U
O K E W N T S P O U P I A M R
E M L G O O D B T Y B A L T B
M U L S E B W T I T A N I A T
O W O R L E F N S L W P S O C
R U N R R X S H D D S P U L T
```

ARIEL	MIRANDA
BOTTOM	OBERON
BRUTUS	OCTAVIA
CALIBAN	OPHELIA
FALSTAFF	OTHELLO
FRIAR LAWRENCE	PROSPERO
HAMLET	PUCK
JULIET	ROMEO
KING LEAR	ROSENCRANTZ
LEONTES	TITANIA
MACBETH	TYBALT

No 77
Butterflies and Moths

```
Z B K S Z A T K F J E N B A V
K O W W S R Q E X C O M M A E
G Y P A D S R O L L O P A T A
R W D L G P A E A G V H T O M
E J R L M S O R Y O N B I X V
Y H Y O V P I X G S U I M P X
D T A W A M J E S T Y L R O M
A F D T D T L I T E O A E G U
G J R A L S L E S L G N H R O
G A D I B A R L O U K I K A U
E E Z L S F S A H V K D U Y S
R L U Y L A P B G I D R H L M
M E R Y D U D K L R T A U I B
D H F J P I T F F U B C P N O
C B W U R E P E E K E T A G U
```

APOLLO	GRAYLING
ATLAS BLUE	GREY DAGGER
BUFF TIP	HERMIT
BUTTERFLY	KNOT GRASS
CARDINAL	MOTH
CHRYSALIS	PUPA
CLEOPATRA	RED ADMIRAL
COMMA	RINGLET
DRYAD	RIVULET
GATEKEEPER	SWALLOWTAIL
GHOST	VOGEL'S BLUE

Crossword Puzzles

No 1

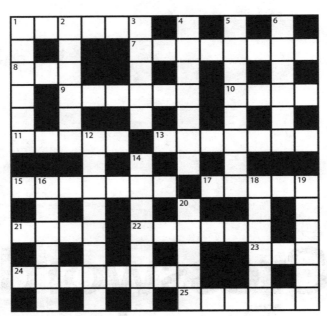

Across

1 Traveling show (6)

7 Relating to office work (8)

8 Unbroken series of events (3)

9 Hidden (6)

10 Adept (4)

11 Minor goddess of nature (5)

13 Swerve (7)

15 Incomplete (7)

17 Happen again (5)

21 Walk through water (4)

22 Time of year (6)

23 Very small circular shape (3)

24 Characteristic of a particular area (8)

25 Dealer, seller (6)

Down

1 Cardboard drink-container (6)

2 Redemption money (6)

3 Frighten away (5)

4 Not one nor the other (7)

5 Put the last touches to (8)

6 Money case (6)

12 Inciting pity (8)

14 Going by (7)

16 Rhododendron-like shrub (6)

18 Outspoken (6)

19 Curate (6)

20 Defect (5)

No 2

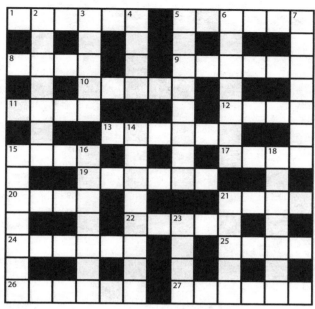

Across

1 Became less intense (6)
5 Imaginary place considered perfect (6)
8 Grassy garden area (4)
9 Retaliate (6)
10 Bundle, of straw eg (5)
11 Container for a bird (4)
12 Offshore area (4)
13 Persecute (6)
15 Mixer drink (4)
17 Expression of love (4)
19 Ebb (6)
20 Gives assistance (4)
21 Gloomy (4)
22 Ointment (5)
24 Gemstone (6)
25 At high volume (4)
26 Hair curler (6)
27 Organ of a flower (6)

Down

2 Swaggering show of courage (7)
3 Unrelaxed, taut (5)
4 Chop (4)
5 Fearless (8)
6 Tapering stone pillar (7)
7 Continuing forever or indefinitely (7)
14 Family member from the remote past (8)
15 Unsteady uneven gait (7)
16 Military structure where ammunition is stored (7)
18 Natural height of a person (7)
21 Triangular area where a river divides (5)
23 Transparent optical device (4)

No 3

Across

1 Foot-covering (4)
3 Characteristic of a woman (8)
9 Compound with a minty taste (7)
10 Type of firearm (5)
11 Mountain range in eastern California (6,6)
14 Consume (3)
16 Cow's milk gland (5)
17 Prevarication (3)
18 Till which calculates a bill in a shop (4,8)
21 Musical entertainment (5)
22 Bodily disorder or disease (7)
23 Vigilant (4-4)
24 Information reported in the papers (4)

Down

1 Academic term (8)
2 Unit of weight (5)
4 Snake-like fish (3)
5 Impossible to undo, permanent (12)
6 Unbeliever, pagan (7)
7 Level (4)
8 Public road from one place to another (12)
12 Prod (5)
13 Loose material, dust (8)
15 Circus swing (7)
19 Topic (5)
20 Ms Chanel, fashion designer (4)
22 Beer (3)

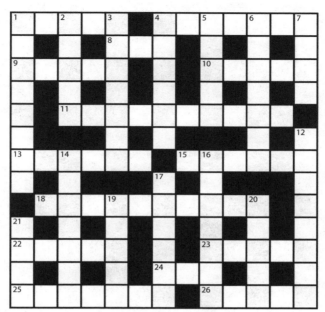

Across

1 Section of an orchestra (5)

4 Jemmy (7)

8 Consciousness of one's own identity (3)

9 Spicy tomato sauce (5)

10 Ordered series (5)

11 Armored seagoing vessel, used in war (10)

13 Number represented by the Roman XI (6)

15 Coiffure (6)

18 Moderately rich (10)

22 Similar (5)

23 Multitude (5)

24 So-named before marriage (3)

25 Perceived (7)

26 Relating to the kidneys (5)

Down

1 Infatuated (8)

2 Perform without preparation (2-3)

3 City in Washington (7)

4 Edible mollusc (6)

5 Watering-hole (5)

6 Metal container in which coal or charcoal is burned (7)

7 Submerged ridge of rock or coral (4)

12 Make a prediction about (8)

14 Item of jewelry (7)

16 One more (7)

17 After (6)

19 Smell (5)

20 Enchantress (5)

21 Raised platform (4)

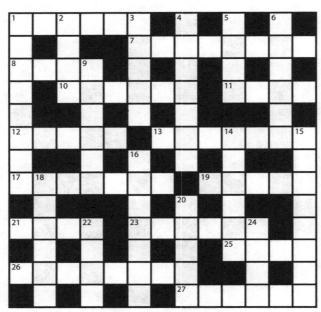

Across

1 Edible decapod (6)
7 Roomy (8)
8 Bloc (4)
10 Colorful flowering plant (6)
11 Give forth (4)
12 Monastery (5)
13 Unit of sound (7)
17 Design device (7)
19 Phoney (5)
21 Head honcho (4)
23 Very sad (6)
25 Manage, make do (4)
26 Systematic investigation to establish facts (8)
27 Tension (6)

Down

1 George Lucas film of 1977 (4,4)
2 Sudden attack (4)
3 Religious song (5)
4 Corpse (7)
5 Presidential assistant (4)
6 Unproductive of success (6)
9 Cotton fabric with a shiny finish (6)
14 Humorously sarcastic (6)
15 Lacking zest or vivacity (8)
16 Water tank (7)
18 Small hand tool with a flat metal blade (6)
20 Routes (5)
22 Appear to be (4)
24 Doves' home (4)

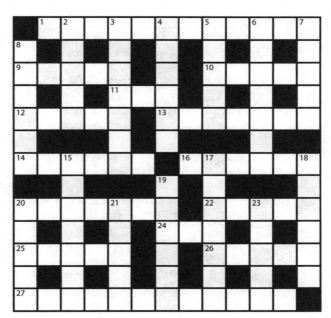

Across

1 Receptacles for business documents (7,5)

9 Pasture (5)

10 Direct descendant (5)

11 Definite article (3)

12 Fatuous, mindless (5)

13 *Origin Of* ___, work by Charles Darwin (7)

14 Gather or bring together (6)

16 Appraise (6)

20 Laugh quietly or with restraint (7)

22 Items of footwear (5)

24 Groove (3)

25 Superior (5)

26 Humble (5)

27 The entertainment industry (4,8)

Down

2 Royal headdress (5)

3 Morally strict (7)

4 Truthful (6)

5 Social position or status (5)

6 Self-annihilation (7)

7 Air cavity in the skull (5)

8 Self-centeredness (6)

15 Sign of the zodiac (7)

17 Keep (7)

18 Title given to a nun (6)

19 Similar things placed in order (6)

20 Playing card suit (5)

21 Pulse (5)

23 Form (5)

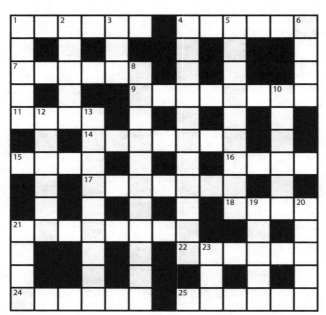

Across

1 Small informal restaurant (6)

4 Meal eaten outside (6)

7 Precious metal, symbol Ag (6)

9 Deliberately stayed clear of (8)

11 Desist (4)

14 The New World (7)

15 Stand to support a coffin (4)

16 Make a pretence (4)

17 Popeye's favorite vegetable! (7)

18 Holler (4)

21 Occurring every second year (8)

22 Preserve a dead body (6)

24 Cove (6)

25 Set in from the margin (6)

Down

1 Footing (5)

2 Simultaneous discharge of firearms (5)

3 Fish eggs (3)

4 Usable for a specific purpose (11)

5 Disliking being photographed (6-3)

6 Stiff paper (4)

8 Happening again and again, tediously (11)

10 Involve as a necessary accompaniment (6)

12 Capital city of Taiwan (6)

13 Rectory (9)

19 Wipe off (5)

20 Confine (5)

21 Ale (4)

23 Adult male person (3)

No 8

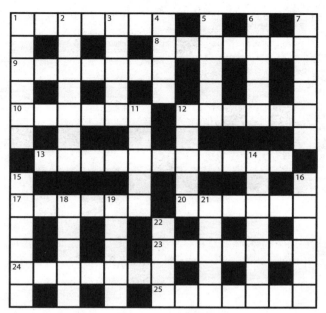

Across

1 Variety of mandarin orange (7)
8 Proportionately (3,4)
9 Send away (7)
10 Deported (6)
12 Strict (6)
13 Compositor (11)
17 Confront, solicit (6)
20 Part of the eye (6)
23 Deserving by one's own merits (7)
24 On edge (7)
25 Physician who performs operations (7)

Down

1 Abrupt (6)
2 Give evidence (7)
3 Join (5)
4 Domed recess (4)
5 Powerful effect or influence (5)
6 Emblem (5)
7 Sponsor, investor (6)
11 Finger or toe (5)
12 Step (5)
14 Building (7)
15 Yellow fruit (6)
16 Border (6)
18 Map (5)
19 Shop where hairdressers work (5)
21 Inadvertent incorrectness (5)
22 Not as great in amount (4)

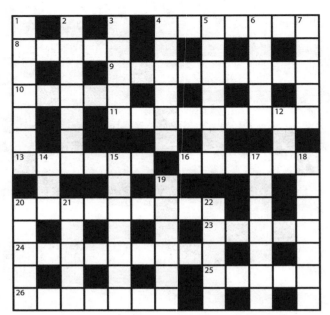

Across

4 Satisfy (thirst, for example) (7)
8 Tedium (5)
9 Setting down in permanent form (9)
10 French goodbye (5)
11 Able to feel or perceive (9)
13 Crumple (6)
16 Rich and fashionable people who travel widely for pleasure (3,3)
20 Of climate, free from extremes (9)
23 Golf course by the sea (5)
24 Social policy of racial segregation (9)
25 Lofty nest of a bird of prey (5)
26 Decay with an offensive smell (7)

Down

1 Relating to pottery (7)
2 Give the right to (7)
3 Software program capable of causing great harm to a computer (5)
4 Upward slope (6)
5 Fawning in attitude (7)
6 Excuse (5)
7 Legionary emblem (5)
12 Contend (3)
14 Regret (3)
15 Enfold (7)
17 Remove moisture by use of centrifugal forces (4-3)
18 Ballroom dance (3,4)
19 Bread shop (6)
20 Trudge (5)
21 Signified (5)
22 American ___, poisonous shrub (5)

No 10

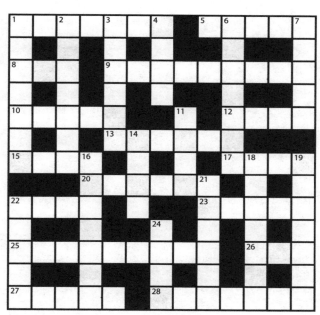

Across

1 Low wall along the edge of a roof (7)
5 Group containing one or more species (5)
8 Decompose (3)
9 Place of bliss (7-2)
10 Bring dishonor upon (5)
12 Contributed (4)
13 Lay waste to (6)
15 Sediment in wine (4)
17 Small narrow pointed missile that is thrown (4)
20 Pester (6)
22 Dandy (4)
23 Mountaineering spike (5)
25 Compass point at 135 degrees (5-4)
26 Witness (3)
27 Military trainee (5)
28 Lax (7)

Down

1 Umbrella which provides a source of shade (7)
2 Go back over (7)
3 Placard (6)
4 Nipple (4)
6 Infuriated (7)
7 Remove body hair (5)
11 Sea fish (4)
14 Unit of area (4840 square yards) (4)
16 Travel back and forth between two points (7)
18 Performer (7)
19 Line touching a curve (7)
21 Exactly right (4,2)
22 Staple (5)
24 Release after a security has been paid (4)

No 11

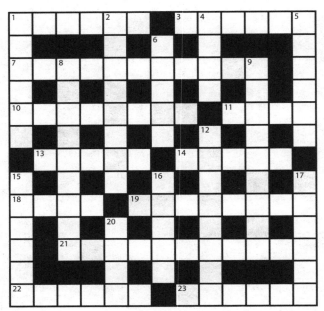

Across

1 Theatrical dance routine (6)
3 Rough area on the skin (6)
7 Notwithstanding (11)
10 Pennant (8)
11 Skin problem (4)
13 Spring-loaded door fastener (5)
14 Ring-shaped bread roll (5)
18 In the center of (4)
19 Producing offspring (8)
21 Transducer used to detect and measure light (8,3)
22 Dish for holding a cup (6)
23 Population count (6)

Down

1 Cast out (6)
2 Way in (8)
4 'So be it' (4)
5 Part added to a play that continues and extends it (6)
6 Disease with associated high temperature (5)
8 Message that tells the particulars of an act or occurrence (9)
9 Reticent (9)
12 Imaginary standard by which things are measured (8)
15 Annoy continually (6)
16 Thin, meat soup (5)
17 Emergence (6)
20 Had existence (4)

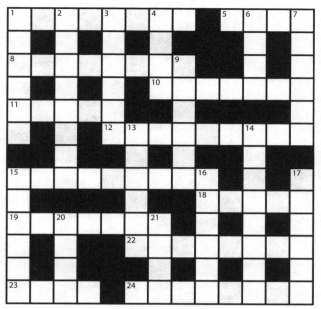

Across

1 Typewriter tab which changes the case of letters (5,3)
5 Grooved tooth of a venomous snake (4)
8 Minor celestial body composed of rock and metal (8)
10 Denial (7)
11 Army unit of two or more divisions (5)
12 Intense sorrow caused by loss of a loved one (9)
15 Takes unawares (9)
18 Flexible joint (5)
19 Stick fruit (7)
22 With the least delay (8)
23 Strap with a crosspiece on the upper of a shoe (1-3)
24 Going backwards (8)

Down

1 Rarely found (6)
2 Inside (8)
3 Stir about violently (6)
4 Independent ruler (4)
6 Sums up (4)
7 Framework of metal bars used as a partition (6)
9 Edict (6)
13 One who leaves a country to settle in another (6)
14 Wife of an earl (8)
15 Rigorous (6)
16 Hold back to a later time (6)
17 Plant grown for its edible seeds that are cooked like peas (6)
20 Waste product useful as a fertilizer (4)
21 Foundation (4)

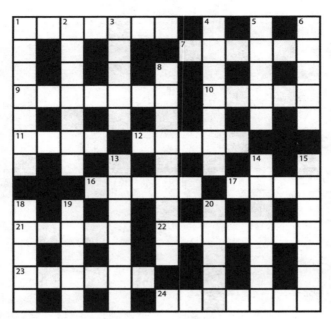

Across

1 Creation of the highest excellence (7)
7 World's largest desert (6)
9 Compress (7)
10 Thin pancake (5)
11 Stench (4)
12 Very thin candle (5)
16 Capital of Oregon (5)
17 Fête (4)
21 Close-fitting trousers of heavy denim (5)
22 Old horse-drawn vehicle (7)
23 Intelligent (6)
24 Listening (7)

Down

1 Husband or wife of a reigning monarch (7)
2 Egg white (7)
3 Spirally threaded cylindrical rod (5)
4 More decorative (7)
5 Showing impatient expectancy (5)
6 Biblical tower intended to reach to heaven (5)
8 Degeneration (9)
13 Herb with aromatic finely-cut leaves (7)
14 Pasta 'cushions' (7)
15 Going different ways (7)
18 Expel (5)
19 Cake-maker (5)
20 Animal life in a particular region (5)

No 14

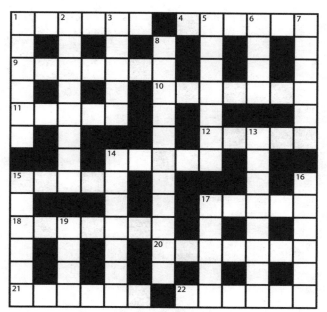

Across

1 Surface on which pictures can be projected (6)

4 Decimal measurement system (6)

9 Language native to Kabul, for example (7)

10 Highest in excellence (7)

11 Follow as a result (5)

12 Display stand for a painting (5)

14 Small army unit (5)

15 Dish out (5)

17 Lines on which music is written (5)

18 Consider in detail (7)

20 Conjecture (7)

21 Thinly distributed (6)

22 Father or mother (6)

Down

1 Uses jointly (6)

2 Record book (8)

3 Rub out (5)

5 Slipped away (7)

6 People who belong to the same genetic stock (4)

7 Breakfast food (6)

8 Lack of politeness (11)

13 Earmarked, reserved (3,5)

14 Lacking in playfulness (7)

15 Gardening scissors (6)

16 Desert in order to join the opposition (6)

17 Country, capital Damascus (5)

19 Operatic solo (4)

Across

1 Jelly based on fish or meat stock (5)

4 Extreme mental distress (7)

8 Bung (7)

9 Person afflicted with Hansen's disease (5)

10 Relating to them (5)

11 Contestant in a sports event (7)

12 Impose a penalty (6)

13 Type of monkey, macaque (6)

16 Emanating from stars (7)

18 Devoutly religious (5)

20 Scene of action (5)

21 Cookery (7)

22 Of the greatest possible degree (7)

23 Send (payment) (5)

Down

1 Valuable quality (5)

2 Authoritative declaration (13)

3 Evergreen conifer (7)

4 In a foreign country (6)

5 Narrow gorge with a stream running through it (5)

6 Style of painting associated with the late 19th century (13)

7 Restraining straps (7)

12 Corridor (7)

14 More euphoric (7)

15 Prophet, person who divines the future (6)

17 Depart (5)

19 Cleaned with a broom (5)

No 16

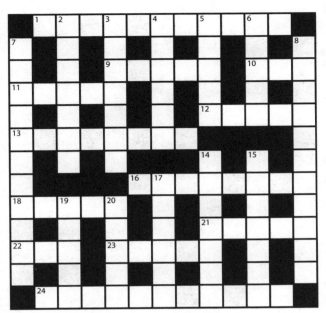

Across

1 Desire for wealth and possessions (11)

9 Less than the correct amount (5)

10 Expert (3)

11 Undergo a chemical change (5)

12 Strainer (5)

13 Clouding of the lens of the eye (8)

16 Oil used as fuel in lamps (8)

18 Holds fast (5)

21 Exhausted (5)

22 Cereal crop (3)

23 Cleanse the entire body (5)

24 Ill-fated (4-7)

Down

2 Moderately slow tempo in music (7)

3 Oriental (7)

4 Sloping print (6)

5 Asian water lily (5)

6 Partial darkness (5)

7 Farming (11)

8 Showing good judgment (5-6)

14 Woman who invites guests to a social event (7)

15 Admonish (7)

17 News chief (6)

19 Representative (5)

20 Somber (5)

No 17

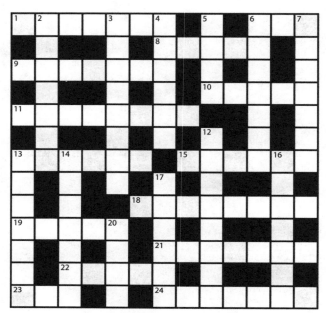

Across

1 Ardently serious (7)
6 Public transport vehicle (3)
8 Smell (5)
9 Strategy (7)
10 Intolerant person (5)
11 Primitive wind instrument (8)
13 Metal paper fastener (6)
15 Point where two lines meet or intersect (6)
18 Deceived, given away (8)
19 Time of life between the ages of 13 and 19 (5)
21 Breastbone (7)
22 Stone writing tablet (5)
23 Before long, poetically (3)
24 Flax derivative used as oil (7)

Down

2 Insistent (7)
3 Entitled (8)
4 Bunch of cords fastened at one end (6)
5 Explosive device (4)
6 Haggle (7)
7 Slide unobtrusively (7)
12 Number, the Roman XIV (8)
13 Sink a ship (7)
14 Contrary (7)
16 Put to death (7)
17 Object used as a container for liquids (6)
20 Mark of a wound (4)

No 18

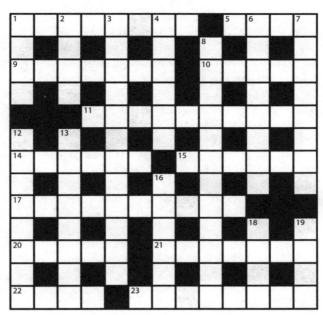

Across

1 Music tape container (8)
5 Live-action film about a piglet (4)
9 Nuclear plant (7)
10 Register (5)
11 Mourner carrying a coffin at a funeral (10)
14 Escaped, as through a hole or crack (6)
15 Pancake batter baked in an iron implement (6)
17 In a crosswise direction (10)
20 Beforehand (5)
21 Pear-shaped fruit with green skin ripening to black (7)
22 Long detailed story (4)
23 Showing profound respect (8)

Down

1 Cereal crop (4)
2 Chair (4)
3 Seemingly outside normal receptive channels (12)
4 Sudden intense sensation or emotion (6)
6 Plane (8)
7 Makes bigger (8)
8 Shop which sells a wide range of goods (7,5)
12 Duck-billed creature (8)
13 Marching in a procession (8)
16 Censure severely or angrily (6)
18 Arrived (4)
19 Young male horse (4)

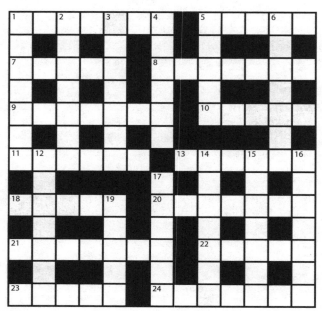

Across

1 Greek currency unit prior to the euro (7)

5 Shoot from a concealed position (5)

7 Sign of the zodiac (5)

8 Blood-red (7)

9 Enthusiastic recognition (7)

10 Brand name (5)

11 Flamboyantly elaborate, showy (6)

13 Hydrophobia (6)

18 Assistants (5)

20 Patron (7)

21 Meet head-on (7)

22 Freezing, glacial (5)

23 Digression (5)

24 Lockjaw (7)

Down

1 Precious gem (7)

2 Stir up (7)

3 Arctic sled dogs (7)

4 Missing (6)

5 Cloak, often knitted (5)

6 Come before (7)

12 Calamitous (7)

14 In the middle of (7)

15 Pancreatic hormone (7)

16 Long steps (7)

17 Characteristic to be considered (6)

19 Apartment consisting of a series of connected rooms (5)

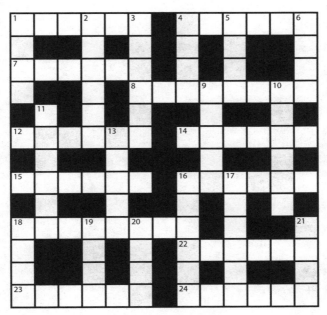

Across

1 Stroke tenderly (6)
4 Examination of substance from the living body (6)
7 Pincer (6)
8 Divulge, make known (8)
12 Act against an attack (6)
14 Severe shortage of food (6)
15 Woven shopping bag (6)
16 Supply or impregnate with oxygen (6)
18 Spinal bone (8)
22 Large-grained or rough to the touch (6)
23 Conflict (6)
24 Very tired (6)

Down

1 Division of a dollar (4)
2 Group of countries with one ruler (6)
3 Morally degraded (6)
4 Lowest adult male singing voice (4)
5 Egg-shaped (4)
6 Christmastide (4)
9 Stop (5)
10 Rationality (6)
11 Tranquilize (6)
13 Female relative (5)
16 Counting frame (6)
17 Refund of some fraction of the amount paid (6)
18 Word that denotes an action (4)
19 Written words (4)
20 Motorcycle (4)
21 Declare to be untrue (4)

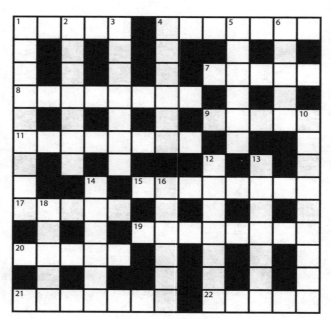

Across

1 Worthless material (5)

4 Kitchen utensil used for spreading (7)

7 Having existence (5)

8 Restricted computer network (8)

9 Ecstasy (5)

11 Locked in by frozen water (8)

15 Unaffected by the passing years (8)

17 Junk (5)

19 Country, capital Islamabad (8)

20 Gambol (5)

21 Lower someone's spirits (7)

22 Gesture involving the shoulders (5)

Down

1 Extremely pleasing to taste (9)

2 Acorn plant (3,4)

3 Legislator (7)

4 Organ of the body between the stomach and the diaphragm (6)

5 Threefold (6)

6 Connections (5)

10 Adding flavor to (9)

12 Tiresome (7)

13 Atmospheric condition (7)

14 Occupation for which one is trained (6)

16 Pictures (6)

18 Go after with the intent to catch (5)

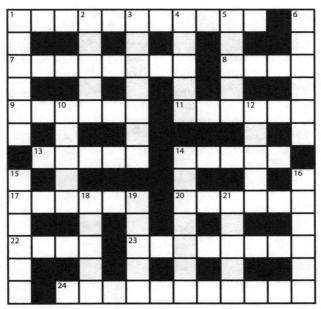

Across

1 Sun with the celestial bodies that revolve around it (5,6)

7 Set free (8)

8 Ripped (4)

9 Process for obtaining an objective (6)

11 Discord (6)

13 Landed estate of a lord (5)

14 Effrontery (5)

17 Serve (6)

20 Steal cattle (6)

22 Female operatic star (4)

23 Major Chinese city (8)

24 Having the power to enter or pierce (11)

Down

1 Scatter water (6)

2 Fend off (5)

3 Speech disorder (7)

4 Stalks of a plant (5)

5 Organic compound (5)

6 Hazard on a golf course (6)

10 Elegant water-birds (5)

12 Torpid (5)

14 Swift pirate ship (7)

15 Brigand (6)

16 Making stitches (6)

18 Fatuous (5)

19 Sense of good style (5)

21 The faculty of vision (5)

Across

1 Utterance made by exhaling audibly (4)
3 Bedtime drink (8)
9 Conundrums (7)
10 Rental (5)
11 North African country (5)
12 Commercial stoppage (7)
13 Stenographer (6)
15 Pursues relentlessly (6)
17 Flat area in a series of slopes (7)
18 Goes in advance of others (5)
20 Oily fruit (5)
21 Native of Haifa, for example (7)
22 Cased in a protective covering (8)
23 Male deer (4)

Down

1 Clandestine (13)
2 Suffering from vertigo (5)
4 Arch of the foot (6)
5 Sons of one's step-parent by a former marriage (4-8)
6 Strong feelings of embarrassment (7)
7 Making a positive impression on someone beforehand (13)
8 First half of the Christian Bible (3,9)
14 Relating to swine (7)
16 Compose, formulate (6)
19 Proficient (5)

No 24

Across

1 Heathens, infidels (6)
8 Stick of black carbon material used for drawing (8)
9 Team spirit (6)
10 Unnecessary (8)
11 Japanese woman trained to entertain men (6)
12 Competitor who finishes second (6-2)
16 Ribbon-like intestinal parasite (8)
18 Quantity much larger than is needed (6)
21 Diplomatic etiquette (8)
23 Strikingly strange (6)
24 Without mercy (8)
25 One who rides breaking waves (6)

Down

2 Love intensely (5)
3 Accumulate (5)
4 Synopsis of a play (8)
5 Gateau (4)
6 Surgeon's knife (7)
7 Capital of the Bahamas (6)
11 Person's manner of walking, pace (4)
13 Anonymous (8)
14 In addition (4)
15 Sure (7)
17 Cowardly (6)
19 Group of singers (5)
20 Cut into pieces (5)
22 Ship's company (4)

No 25

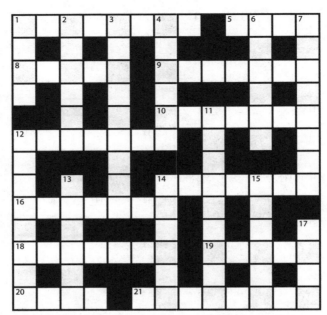

Across

1 Male horse (8)

5 Naked (4)

8 South American cud-chewing animal (5)

9 Save from ruin or destruction (7)

10 Bondage (7)

12 Have (7)

14 Dapple (7)

16 Passage (7)

18 Man who serves as a sailor (7)

19 Nearer to the center (5)

20 Neither good nor bad (2-2)

21 Computing term: large unit of information (8)

Down

1 Grain-storage tower (4)

2 Astonishes (6)

3 Periods of 366 days (4,5)

4 Be preoccupied with something (6)

6 Rouse (6)

7 All people (8)

11 South American country (9)

12 Hobbies (8)

13 Former name of the Indian city of Chennai (6)

14 Go without food (6)

15 Renal organ (6)

17 North American lake (4)

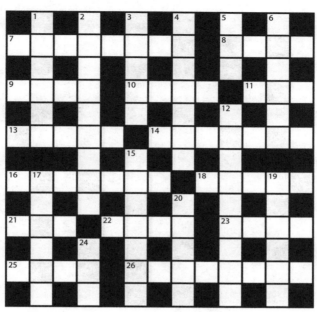

Across

7 Prince or king in India (8)

8 Not at home (4)

9 One thousand grams (4)

10 Location (4)

11 Feline mammal (3)

13 Engraving in relief (5)

14 Brickwork (7)

16 Entrance (7)

18 Foot lever (5)

21 Irritate (3)

22 Pay received for employment (4)

23 Component (4)

25 Sum charged for riding in a bus (4)

26 Monocle (8)

Down

1 Verdigris (6)

2 Device that measures atmospheric pressure (9)

3 Fictitious (5)

4 Relating to reality (7)

5 Short-lived fashion (3)

6 Eastern marketplace (6)

12 Native North American tribal emblem (5,4)

15 Series of acts at a nightclub (7)

17 Radio antenna (6)

19 Again but in a new or different way (6)

20 Precious stone (5)

24 Sleeping place (3)

No 27

Across

1 Uncouth (5)

7 Music of the 1930s (7)

8 Sharp knock (3)

9 Too soon (9)

11 Sharp part of a knife (5)

12 Country which is not a monarchy (8)

16 Exhibiting childlike credulity (4-4)

20 Residence (5)

21 Expert manner of speaking (9)

23 Noah's boat (3)

24 Feel of a surface (7)

25 Nickname of Corporal O'Reilly in *M*A*S*H* (5)

Down

1 Arctic deer with large antlers (7)

2 Earnest or urgent request (6)

3 Light evening meal (6)

4 Factual (4)

5 Statuesque (7)

6 At no time (5)

10 Light violet color (5)

13 Vote into office (5)

14 Teach (7)

15 Large wave which hits the shore (7)

17 Peril (6)

18 Person who shows fear (6)

19 Bed on board a ship (5)

22 Thought (4)

No 28

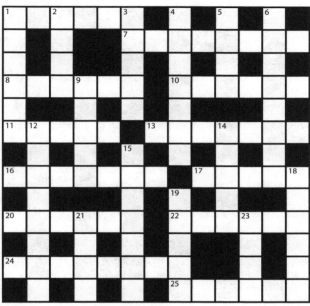

Across

1 Small stamp or seal on a ring (6)
7 Soft drink made with plant extracts (4,4)
8 Against (6)
10 Put to the test (3,3)
11 French composer of works such as *Boléro* (5)
13 Caused by earth vibration (7)
16 Implemented (7)
17 Cap made of soft cloth (5)
20 Pause uncertainly (6)
22 Emotion of great sadness (6)
24 Postpone the punishment of a convicted criminal (8)
25 Necessary for relief (6)

Down

1 Tremble with cold (6)
2 Cogwheel (4)
3 Twist of hair (5)
4 Sell illicit products such as drugs or alcohol (7)
5 Follow orders (4)
6 Act as a substitute (8)
9 Take without permission (5)
12 Came into view (8)
14 Lance (5)
15 Question after military operation (7)
18 In the direction of (6)
19 Trembling poplar (5)
21 Slab of grass (4)
23 Highway (4)

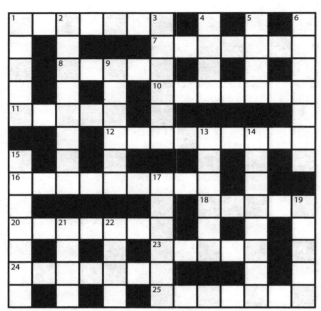

Across

1 Wife of a duke (7)
7 Greed (7)
8 Relating to the nose (5)
10 Not accurate (7)
11 Prospect (5)
12 Identification of the nature or cause of a phenomenon (9)
16 Of worldwide scope (9)
18 South Pacific island group (5)
20 Kitchen appliance (7)
23 Invalidate (5)
24 Volume, issue (7)
25 Family line (7)

Down

1 Woman's garment (5)
2 Small pieces of colored paper thrown at weddings (8)
3 Digestive fluid (6)
4 Renown (4)
5 Former unit of money in Italy (4)
6 Odontologist (7)
9 Vehicle for travelling on snow (6)
13 British naval hero (6)
14 Act intended to arouse action (8)
15 Gesture of respectful greeting, for women (7)
17 Filament (6)
19 Lay out in a line (5)
21 Caustic (4)
22 Work hard (4)

No 30

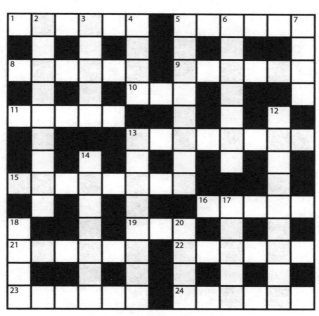

Across

1 Quagmire (6)
5 Chess piece (6)
8 Mission (6)
9 Begins (6)
10 (They) exist (3)
11 Make merry (5)
13 British currency (8)
15 Expresses great happiness (8)
16 Paid out money (5)
19 Hard-shelled seed (3)
21 Bureau, place of work (6)
22 Lessen the strength of (6)
23 Muscle that flexes the forearm (6)
24 Small chin beard trimmed to a point (6)

Down

2 Us (9)
3 Old saying or proverb (5)
4 Drink often mixed with alcohol (4)
5 Unwarranted, without foundation (8)
6 Restrain with fetters (7)
7 Basic unit of money in Uruguay (4)
12 Disingenuous (9)
13 Nausea (8)
14 Blend together (7)
17 Shopping mall (5)
18 Grave (4)
20 Small branch (4)

No 31

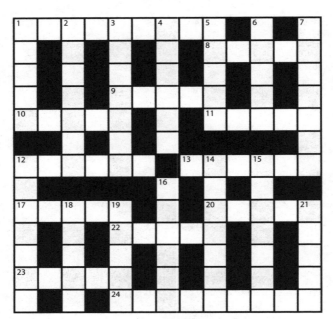

Across

1 Expectation, prospect (9)

8 *Key ___*, 1948 film (5)

9 Sudden forceful flow (5)

10 Musical which includes the song *It's the Hard Knock Life* (5)

11 Piece of poetry (5)

12 Pleasure obtained by inflicting harm on others (6)

13 Insect which rests with forelimbs raised as if in prayer (6)

17 Disgust (5)

20 Hawaiian greeting (5)

22 Expect (5)

23 Pandemonium (5)

24 Power to withstand hardship or stress (9)

Down

1 Plant life (5)

2 Freed from impurities (7)

3 Greek hero who slew the Minotaur (7)

4 Origin (6)

5 Senior (5)

6 Meat juices (5)

7 Own up to (7)

12 Work done that benefits another (7)

14 Lacking professional skill (7)

15 Broken by being stepped upon heavily (7)

16 Even-tempered (6)

18 Colorful part of a flower (5)

19 Fall out of date (5)

21 Forename of Mr Agassi, tennis champion (5)

No 32

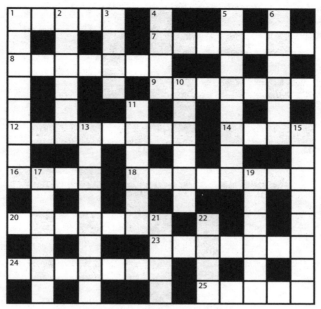

Across

1 Enchant (5)

7 Workplace where clothes are washed and ironed (7)

8 Word formed from the initial letters of a multi-word name (7)

9 Unspecified person (7)

12 Individuality (8)

14 Graven image (4)

16 Soap froth (4)

18 Treeless area in a forest (8)

20 Sweetheart (7)

23 With legs stretched far apart (7)

24 Malady (7)

25 Noise made by a sheep (5)

Down

1 Roman emperor who followed Caligula (8)

2 Scour a surface (6)

3 Hair on a lion's neck (4)

4 Charitable gifts (4)

5 Previous (8)

6 Unbroken mustang (6)

10 Gas found in air (6)

11 Airtight sealed metal container (3,3)

13 Young bird not yet fledged (8)

15 Connective tissue (8)

17 Ineffectual (6)

19 Antiseptic used to treat wounds (6)

21 Short intake of breath (4)

22 Poke or thrust abruptly (4)

No 33

Across

1 Ripe (6)
4 Substance that turns blue in alkaline solutions (6)
7 Skittles (8)
8 Spinning toys (4)
9 Natives of Kuwait or Qatar, for example (5)
10 Anticipate (7)
12 Meat pin (6)
13 Evoke (6)
15 Rejoinder (7)
18 Irrational passion (5)
20 Incline (4)
21 Nocturnal African mammal which feeds on termites (8)
22 Involuntary expulsion of air from the nose (6)
23 Wool of a sheep (6)

Down

1 Miraculous food (5)
2 Tax imposed on ships (7)
3 Take back ownership (9)
4 Long noosed rope used to catch animals (5)
5 Planetary satellites (5)
6 Infer from incomplete evidence (7)
11 Someone worthy of imitation (4,5)
12 Excess of revenue over expenditure (7)
14 Curving inward (7)
16 Location, whereabouts (5)
17 Tantalize (5)
19 Joint just above the foot (5)

No 34

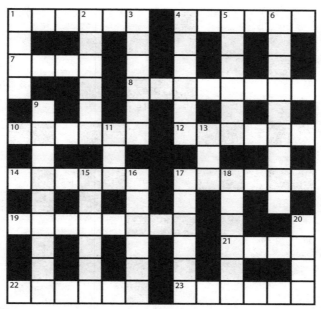

Across
1 Object thrown in athletic competitions (6)
4 Military action in which besieged troops burst forth from their position (6)
7 Disparaging remark (4)
8 Collect discarded material (8)
10 Close-fitting foundation garment (6)
12 Detective who follows a trail (6)
14 Refrains from taking (6)
17 Boil slowly (6)
19 Hard, dark wood used in furniture making (8)
21 Alone, unaccompanied (4)
22 Poetically, the drink of the gods (6)
23 Figurine (6)

Down
1 Twilight (4)
2 Slices (a joint of meat, for example) (6)
3 Time of day immediately preceding dusk (6)
4 Smudges, blurs (6)
5 Be in awe of (6)
6 Obtained illegally or by improper means (3-6)
9 Capable of being borne (9)
11 Biblical first woman (3)
13 Polynesian garland (3)
15 Color seen at one end of the spectrum (6)
16 Someone who skims across ice (6)
17 Needle (6)
18 Unwholesome atmosphere (6)
20 Fruit of a pine (4)

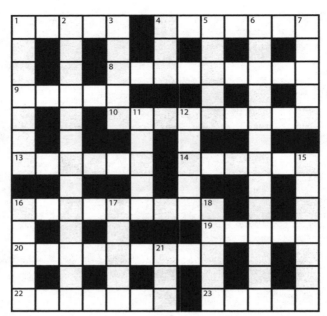

Across

1 Water vapor (5)
4 Cumulative amount involved in a game (7)
8 Place where sinners suffer eternal punishment (9)
9 Bore a hole (5)
10 Joyously unrestrained (9)
13 Confirm (6)
14 Feeling concern or interest (6)
16 Late news inserted into a newspaper (4,5)
19 Relieves (5)
20 Movement (9)
22 Beams made of wood (7)
23 Spooky (5)

Down

1 Involuntary vibration (7)
2 Extravagant behavior intended to attract attention (13)
3 Leaf which adorns the Canadian flag (5)
4 Cylindrical vessel (3)
5 Iciness (5)
6 Head of state (5,8)
7 Article of faith (5)
11 Purchaser (5)
12 Scottish lakes (5)
15 Cartilage (7)
16 Clever (5)
17 Quiet (5)
18 General conscious awareness (5)
21 Of a thing (3)

No 36

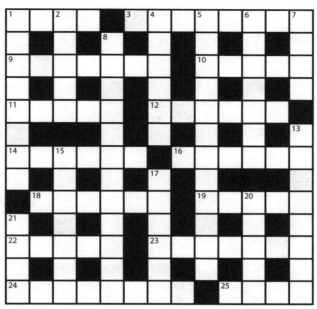

Across

1 Ardor (4)

3 Applied heat to (6,2)

9 Public medical examiner (7)

10 Fibre used for making rope (5)

11 Spiral, coil (5)

12 Brightly shining (6)

14 Coin worth one twentieth of a dollar (6)

16 Go back on a promise (6)

18 Relating to the sea (6)

19 Trick (5)

22 Aromatic, edible bulb (5)

23 Aseptic (7)

24 Exact correspondence of form on opposite sides of a dividing line or plane (8)

25 Belonging to that woman (4)

Down

1 Small vegetable marrow (8)

2 Pertaining to hearing (5)

4 Take into custody (6)

5 Construe in the wrong way (12)

6 Abominate (7)

7 Lacking color (4)

8 Lack of firsthand knowledge and understanding (12)

13 Generally incompetent and ineffectual (8)

15 Brain case (7)

17 Natural spring which gives out steam (6)

20 Endure (5)

21 Fling up (4)

No 37

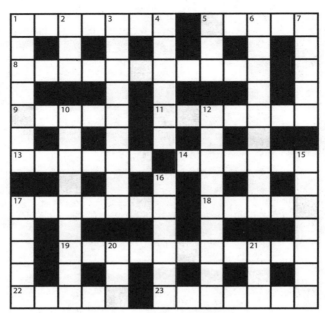

Across

1 Well-founded (7)
5 ___ del Sol, popular Spanish resort (5)
8 Patriotic love of one's country (11)
9 Profane or obscene expressions (5)
11 Make more attractive (7)
13 Eight-legged creature (6)
14 Mars, ruins (6)
17 Present for acceptance or rejection (7)
18 Picture placed within the bounds of a larger one (5)
19 Within or by means of a vein (11)
22 Saturated (5)
23 Socks, stockings and tights collectively (7)

Down

1 Flimsy (7)
2 Mesh (3)
3 Place to keep novels (9)
4 Jubilant (6)
5 Breath or spirit in Chinese philosophy (3)
6 Analysis or study of meaning (9)
7 Burning (5)
10 Making fit for a specific purpose (9)
12 Pleasure (9)
15 Fill a need (7)
16 Bring up (a topic for discussion) (6)
17 Trousers (5)
20 Plaything (3)
21 Metal-bearing mineral (3)

No 38

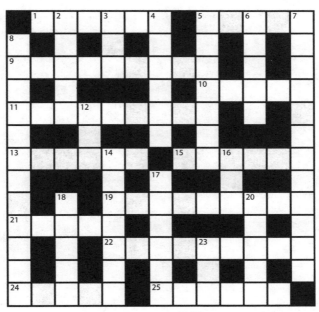

Across

1 Scavenging animal (6)

5 Quench (5)

9 This minute (5,4)

10 Mark placed over a vowel to indicate a short sound (5)

11 Bit by bit (9)

13 Grave (6)

15 Pauper (6)

19 Very difficult and demanding much energy (9)

21 Settle on a perch (5)

22 Power of mental concentration (9)

24 Vogue (5)

25 Woven floor covering (6)

Down

2 Slant (5)

3 Case for containing a set of articles (3)

4 Attorney (6)

5 Color similar to that of the atmosphere in daytime (3,4)

6 Small tropical fish (5)

7 Marked by imagination and a readiness to undertake new projects (12)

8 Ridiculous (12)

12 Prompt (3)

14 Error (7)

16 Wildebeest (3)

17 Judgmental reviewer (6)

18 Marriage settlement (5)

20 Sound off (5)

23 And not (3)

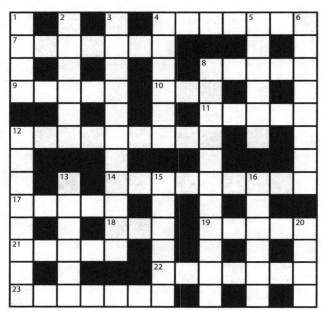

Across

- **4** Picks out (7)
- **7** Former (3-4)
- **8** Shore (5)
- **9** Vehicle's stopping device (5)
- **10** Pitch (3)
- **11** Remedy (5)
- **12** City in central Bolivia (5,4)
- **14** Underwater warship (9)
- **17** Colorful rice (5)
- **18** Field suitable for grazing by livestock (3)
- **19** Land surrounded by water (5)
- **21** Give qualities or abilities to (5)
- **22** Commissioned military officer (7)
- **23** Fashionable (7)

Down

- **1** Toothed implement used to disentangle hair (4)
- **2** Take back (6)
- **3** Container for preserving historical records to be discovered in the future (4,7)
- **4** Area (6)
- **5** Place of worship (6)
- **6** Agenda (8)
- **8** Capital of the Republic of the Congo (11)
- **12** Inhibit (8)
- **13** In a willing manner (6)
- **15** Cook (vegetables) briefly (6)
- **16** Away from the coast (6)
- **20** Mineral, hydrated magnesium silicate (4)

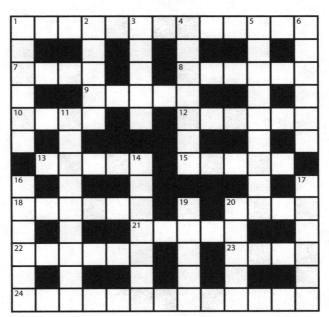

Across

1 Landlocked European country (5,8)
7 Secure (4)
8 Moderate (6)
9 Looks for (5)
10 Hard fruits (4)
12 Obstruct, hinder (6)
13 Very thin (5)
15 Rich man (5)
18 Trite or obvious remark (6)
20 Bazaar (4)
21 Ocean-going vessel (5)
22 Carpenter's tool (6)
23 Afflicts (4)
24 Thrown into a state of intense fear or desperation (5-8)

Down

1 Gambling place (6)
2 Green salad vegetable (5)
3 Develop fully (5)
4 Ardor (7)
5 Gracefully slender (9)
6 Annul (6)
11 Custom (9)
14 Latticework used to support climbing plants (7)
16 Polar feature (3-3)
17 Rational motive for a belief (6)
19 Fury (5)
20 Former French unit of currency (5)

No 41

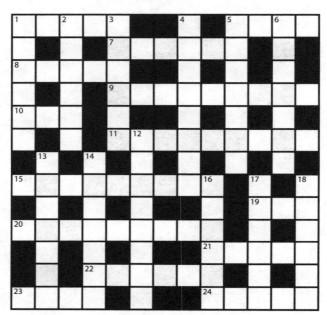

Across

1 Highest peak in the Alps, Mont ___ (5)

5 Nosegay (4)

7 Disease of the skin (6)

8 Make parallel (5)

9 Man-made (9)

10 Listening organ (3)

11 Quick reply to a question or remark (9)

15 Boundary (9)

19 Large monkey (3)

20 Diversion requiring physical exertion and competition (9)

21 Imbecile (5)

22 Unstable situation of extreme danger (6)

23 Great achievement (4)

24 Striped cat (5)

Down

1 Cup without a handle (6)

2 Collection of beehives (6)

3 Forbid the public distribution of (6)

4 Grape sugar (8)

5 Elaborate spectacle (7)

6 Wither, especially due to loss of moisture (7)

12 Operated by generated power (8)

13 Point at which to retire for the night (7)

14 Local idiom (7)

16 Express opposition (6)

17 Housing or outer covering (6)

18 One who owes money (6)

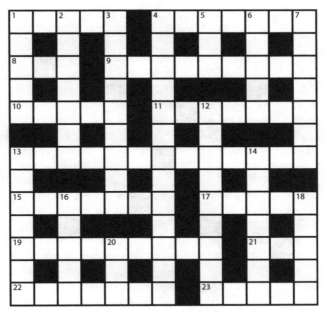

Across

1 Burn with steam (5)

4 Edible marine mollusk with a fan-shaped shell (7)

8 Melody (3)

9 Actor who played the lead in *Rocky Balboa* (2006), ___ Stallone (9)

10 First in rank or degree (5)

11 Acutely insightful (7)

13 Vision correctors (7,6)

15 Adrift (7)

17 Paragon (5)

19 Gossip spread by spoken communication (9)

21 Greek deity, a cross between a man and a goat (3)

22 Inhaled audibly through the nose (7)

23 Linger (5)

Down

1 Fill quickly beyond capacity (5)

2 Accuse of a wrong (7)

3 Marked by loss of hope (9)

4 Excessively complacent (4-9)

5 Plural of the word 'am' (3)

6 Supple (5)

7 Buccaneers (7)

12 United States head of state (9)

13 Fees (7)

14 Train carriage with berths for overnight passengers (7)

16 Florida resort (5)

18 Gangly (5)

20 Imp (3)

Across

1 Goes beyond (7)
5 Doctor in the armed forces (5)
8 Feeding only on plants (11)
9 American raccoon (5)
11 Gather together (7)
13 South American cud-chewing animals (6)
14 Tiny Japanese tree (6)
17 Belonging to the present time (7)
18 Large antelope (5)
19 Pipe which carries fluid around the body (5,6)
22 Brother of one's mother (5)
23 Transgression (7)

Down

1 Moral (7)
2 Motor vehicle (3)
3 Do away with (9)
4 Singe (6)
5 Sound made by a cow (3)
6 Indigestion (9)
7 Part of the body between the neck and the diaphragm (5)
10 Active in the absence of free oxygen (9)
12 Having pages that can be easily removed or rearranged (9)
15 Pamper (7)
16 Place for the teaching or practice of an art (6)
17 Soft fur, nutria (5)
20 Be obliged to repay (3)
21 Boy child (3)

No 44

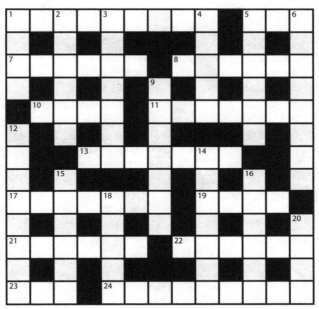

Across

1 Unspecified item (9)

5 Small drink (3)

7 Sunshade (6)

8 Horse's pace between a trot and a gallop (6)

10 Palm fruit (4)

11 Hang freely (7)

13 Inanely foolish (7)

17 Tread roughly (7)

19 Restaurant cook (4)

21 Country which shares a border with Egypt (6)

22 Want strongly (6)

23 Melancholy (3)

24 Take the place of (9)

Down

1 Marine mammal (4)

2 Madman (6)

3 Offers or presents for acceptance (7)

4 Drinking vessel (5)

5 Compositor (6)

6 Place of complete bliss (8)

9 Into pieces (7)

12 On a higher floor (8)

14 Atomic (7)

15 Kept out (6)

16 Next to (6)

18 Machine used for printing (5)

20 In this place (4)

Across

1 Egyptian god of the underworld (6)

5 Underground railway (6)

8 Flexible containers (4)

9 Mariner (8)

10 Griping tummy ache (5)

11 Complain (7)

14 Game played with racquets (6)

15 Reply (6)

17 Tool used to cut metal (7)

19 Coat with fat during cooking (5)

21 Giving delight and satisfaction (8)

23 Unit of length (4)

24 Twine (6)

25 Flow over or cover completely (6)

Down

2 Serialized TV program (4,5)

3 Native of Moscow, for example (7)

4 Waistband (4)

5 Set of steps (8)

6 Show off (5)

7 Plural of the word 'am' (3)

12 Doubtful or incredulous (9)

13 Breaking free (8)

16 Using frugally or carefully (7)

18 Military fabric (5)

20 Man-eating giant (4)

22 Ignited (3)

No 46

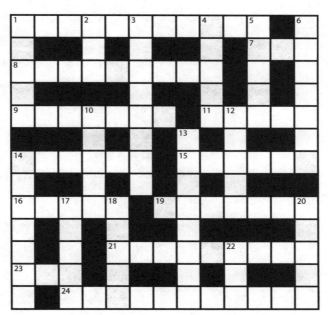

Across

1. Intelligence officer who undertakes work for a government (6,5)
7. Reproductive cells (3)
8. Island group including the Cook Islands (9)
9. Salad vegetable (7)
11. Deal with commercially (5)
14. Mentally or physically infirm with age (6)
15. Get around, circumvent (6)
16. Small wheel on a spur (5)
19. Space next to a sleeping place (7)
21. Discipline in personal and social activities (9)
23. Metal container (3)
24. TV program presenting the facts about a person or event (11)

Down

1. Floral leaf (5)
2. Shaft of light (3)
3. Wooden board or platter (8)
4. Precise (5)
5. Kingdom in the South Pacific (5)
6. Pitiable (7)
10. Clan (5)
12. Thick cords (5)
13. One who is not present (8)
14. Outer covering (7)
17. Coiled about (5)
18. Words of a song (5)
20. Way in (5)
22. Little insect (3)

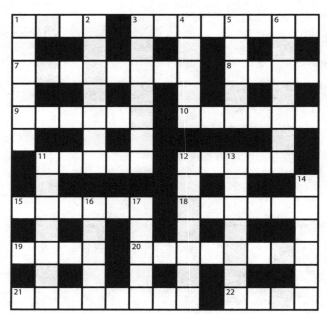

Across

1 Dish often served as a first course (4)

3 Baptize (8)

7 Light brown raw cane sugar (8)

8 Deposit of valuable ore (4)

9 Join the military (6)

10 Tried out (6)

11 Castrated bull (5)

12 X mark (5)

15 Came to rest (6)

18 Latin American country (6)

19 Peru's capital city (4)

20 In a quiet and tranquil manner (8)

21 Disturb the composure of (8)

22 Zealous (4)

Down

1 Make unhappy (6)

2 Command, control (7)

3 Division of a book (7)

4 Cook with dry heat (5)

5 Exchanges for money (5)

6 Perpetual (7)

11 Designated social position (7)

12 Garden vegetable (7)

13 Musical toy (7)

14 Toyed (6)

16 Cover with cloth (5)

17 Terminus (5)

No 48

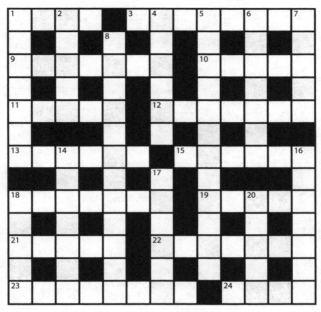

Across

1 Taper (4)
3 Unmarried man (8)
9 Petty (7)
10 Hidden, placed on watch, or in ambush (5)
11 Set securely or deeply (5)
12 Refuse to accept (7)
13 Tray for serving food or drinks (6)
15 Zero (6)
18 Staying power (7)
19 Lit by twilight (5)
21 Telling fibs (5)
22 South American river (7)
23 Psychological suffering (8)
24 Expired (4)

Down

1 Spectator (7)
2 Ascend (5)
4 Make a disguised reference to (6)
5 Abnormal anxiety about imaginary ailments (12)
6 Hanging around (7)
7 Line of travel (5)
8 Central digit of the hand (6,6)
14 Introductory sections of stories (4-3)
16 Gland located near the base of the neck (7)
17 Celebrated (6)
18 Dish of lettuce, tomatoes, cucumber, etc (5)
20 Push roughly (5)

No 49

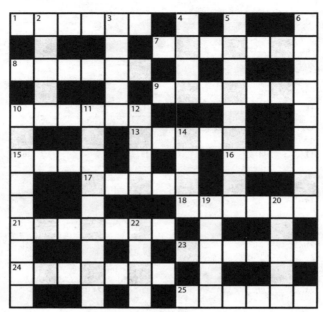

Across

1. Grimy (6)
7. Eyeglass (7)
8. On a ship (6)
9. Speculative undertaking (7)
10. Afternoon nap (6)
13. Country, capital Beijing (5)
15. Caramel brown (4)
16. King of beasts (4)
17. Particular items (5)
18. Married partner (6)
21. Gain the good will of (7)
23. Type of brandy (6)
24. Seeds used to flavor a traditional seedcake (7)
25. Water heater (6)

Down

2. Spiritual leader (5)
3. Explode (5)
4. Cipher (4)
5. Lowest female singing voice (9)
6. Profound emotion inspired by a deity (9)
10. Matter (9)
11. Play down or obscure (4-5)
12. Town and port in north-west Israel (4)
14. "Beware the ___ of March", advice given to Julius Caesar (4)
19. Picture recorded by a camera (5)
20. Use jointly or in common (5)
22. Block (4)

No 50

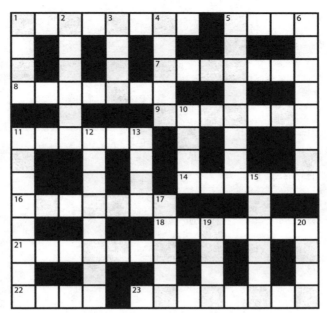

Across

1 Cultivated rural area (8)

5 Steep rugged rock or cliff (4)

7 Not devious (7)

8 Canvas shoe with a pliable rubber sole (7)

9 Quite a few (7)

11 Designate (6)

14 Fortress (6)

16 Beaming (7)

18 Enchant (7)

21 Meeting for an exchange of ideas (7)

22 Wheel shaft (4)

23 Hemisphere that includes North and South America (3,5)

Down

1 Commotion (4)

2 Wards off (6)

3 Destiny (4)

4 Comes close (5)

5 Educational institutions (8)

6 Type of fuel (8)

10 Long narrative poem (4)

11 The food of the gods (8)

12 Able to recognize or draw fine distinctions (8)

13 Midday (4)

15 Overwhelming fear (6)

17 Laconic (5)

19 Unfreeze (4)

20 Come to earth (4)

No 51

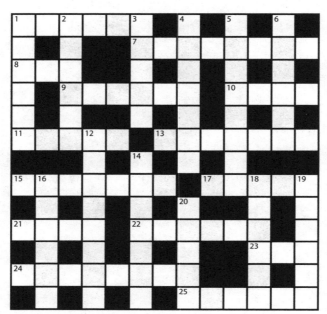

Across

1 Ought (6)

7 Sane (8)

8 Painting, sculpture, etc (3)

9 Choose (6)

10 Placed in position (4)

11 Drainage channel (5)

13 Period of 100 years (7)

15 Tool used to hold or twist a nut (7)

17 Stories (5)

21 Bends the body as a sign of reverence (4)

22 Paramour (6)

23 Grain of cereal grass (3)

24 Practice (8)

25 Rocky and steep (6)

Down

1 Looked at with fixed eyes (6)

2 Start, commencement (6)

3 Appliance that removes moisture (5)

4 Speak haltingly (7)

5 Cosmetic preparation (8)

6 Salted roe of a sturgeon (6)

12 Metallic cylinder used for storage (8)

14 In a murderous frenzy (7)

16 Marked by suitability (6)

18 Large gathering of people (6)

19 Traveled across the ice (6)

20 Serpent (5)

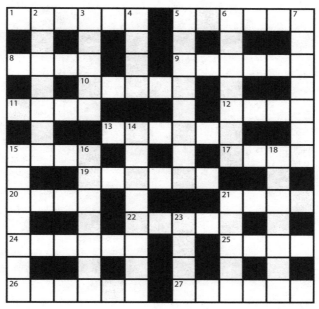

Across

1 To the opposite side (6)
5 Skin on the neck (6)
8 Partly opened flowers (4)
9 Drill used to shape or enlarge holes (6)
10 Large bird of prey (5)
11 Selection of foods (4)
12 Not in action (4)
13 Mastermind (6)
15 Harvest (4)
17 Young girl's title (4)
19 Slumbering (6)
20 Objectives (4)
21 Kill intentionally (4)
22 Civil or military authority in Turkey (5)
24 Science of morals (6)
25 Speed of progress (4)
26 Not if (6)
27 Pie covering (6)

Down

2 Person who carries a message (7)
3 Offensive against an enemy (5)
4 Musical composition with words (4)
5 Certain to be successful (4-4)
6 State of being actual (7)
7 Pair of pincers used in medical treatment (7)
14 Dots in a text showing suppression of words (8)
15 French castle (7)
16 Recreation (7)
18 Disperse (7)
21 Garments worn primarily by Hindu women (5)
23 Clip at (4)

No 53

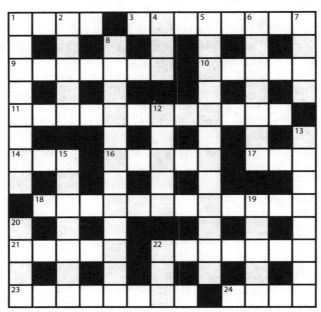

Across

1 Crust-like surface of a healing wound (4)

3 Attractive and tempting (8)

9 ___ *Glory*; romantic drama based on a Lavyrle Spencer novel (7)

10 Rice and raw fish wrapped in seaweed (5)

11 Use of water in the treatment of disease (12)

14 Negation of a word (3)

16 Musical study (5)

17 Scheduled to arrive (3)

18 Unable to become assimilated into the body (12)

21 Foreigner, stranger (5)

22 One of the 50 states (7)

23 Took one's time (8)

24 Give up (4)

Down

1 Long and complex sonata (8)

2 Harsh or corrosive in tone (5)

4 Over-worked horse (3)

5 Rebellion (12)

6 Flavorless (7)

7 Derive a benefit from (4)

8 Unwillingness to comply (12)

12 Typical dwelling-place (5)

13 One set to speak on behalf of a group (8)

15 Stress (7)

19 Green fabric used to cover gaming tables (5)

20 Precipitation in the form of ice pellets (4)

22 Fixed charge for a professional service (3)

No 54

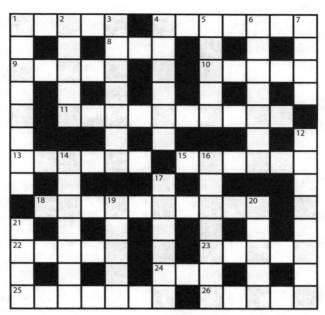

Across

1 Ancient unit of length (5)
4 Abusive attack on a person's character (7)
8 Section of a play (3)
9 Of the countryside (5)
10 Malicious burning of property (5)
11 Having wicked thoughts or intentions (4-6)
13 Firstborn (6)
15 Drag the bottom of a lake (6)
18 Retiring, not arrogant (10)
22 Something that happens at a given place and time (5)
23 Link up, connect (3,2)
24 Stretch (3)
25 Demolish (7)
26 Series of mountains (5)

Down

1 Unworried (8)
2 Canal boat (5)
3 Movies with synchronized speech and singing (7)
4 Mark of infamy (6)
5 Anew (5)
6 Go down (7)
7 Basic unit of money in South Africa (4)
12 Resistance (8)
14 Beasts of burden (7)
16 Engage in boisterous, drunken merry-making (7)
17 Wheel with a groove in which a rope can run (6)
19 Forest god (5)
20 Gather, as of natural products (5)
21 Part of a necklace (4)

No 55

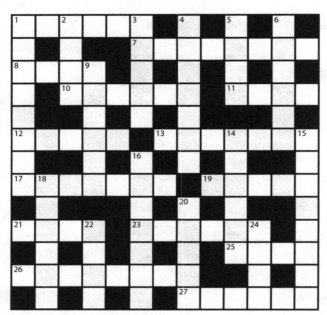

Across

1 Frozen dessert made with fruit juice (6)
7 Commendation (8)
8 Jumble (4)
10 Hurry (6)
11 Framework (4)
12 Acclaim (5)
13 Persevere, endure (7)
17 Police force member (7)
19 Committee having supervisory powers (5)
21 Word denoting a person or thing (4)
23 English landscape painter (1775-1851) (6)
25 Actor's portrayal (4)
26 Circular bands of metal used for holding lock-opening tools (3-5)
27 Pincers (6)

Down

1 Mexican headgear (8)
2 Sudden forceful flow (4)
3 Mouth-watering (5)
4 Sporting dog (7)
5 Instrument struck to announce a meal (4)
6 Dental decay (6)
9 Highly seasoned fatty sausage (6)
14 Bathroom fixture (6)
15 Trait of being neat and orderly (8)
16 Mounting that holds a gem in place (7)
18 Title taken by Hitler as leader of Germany (6)
20 Pleasantly cold and invigorating (5)
22 Variety (4)
24 Went on horseback (4)

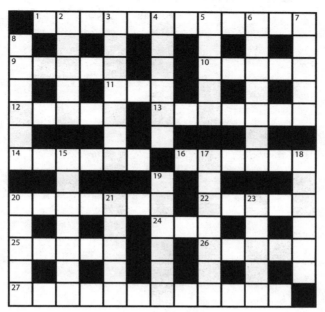

Across

1 Bacterial infection of the lungs (12)
9 Put to shame (5)
10 Tomb (5)
11 Common type of tree (3)
12 Judge tentatively (5)
13 Small fish (7)
14 Corrupt morally (6)
16 Domestic pet (6)
20 Fighter in an army (7)
22 Ruffle (5)
24 Entirely (3)
25 In line with a length or direction (5)
26 Extremely angry (5)
27 Exemption from some rule or obligation (12)

Down

2 Accepted practice (5)
3 Ancient Greek city, site of the Temple of Artemis (7)
4 Cumbersome (6)
5 Type of beer (5)
6 Fowl that frequents coastal waters (7)
7 Native of Stockholm, for example (5)
8 Having a sharply uneven outline (6)
15 Irritable as if suffering from indigestion (7)
17 Cause pain or suffering (7)
18 Area for food preparation on a ship (6)
19 Noisy quarrel (6)
20 Rise to one's feet (5)
21 Fireplace (5)
23 Adult insect (5)

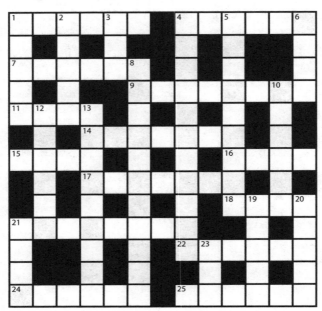

Across

1 Relating to the universe (6)

4 Containing salt (6)

7 Pitch dangerously to one side (6)

9 Unrestrained expression of emotion (8)

11 Highest level attainable (4)

14 Vote back into office (2-5)

15 Sword lily (4)

16 Building block (4)

17 Fought or struggled in a confused way (7)

18 Compass point (4)

21 Forceful and definite in expression or action (8)

22 Three times (6)

24 Glowing fragments of wood left from a fire (6)

25 Decapitate (6)

Down

1 Hot chocolate (5)

2 Scarper (5)

3 Water in a solid state (3)

4 Lack of attention to one's own person (4-7)

5 Listlessness (9)

6 Make money (4)

8 Poor enough to need help from others (11)

10 Planetary paths (6)

12 Radioactive transuranic metallic element (6)

13 Former, onetime (9)

19 Get up (5)

20 Pace (5)

21 Otherwise (4)

23 Weeding tool (3)

No 58

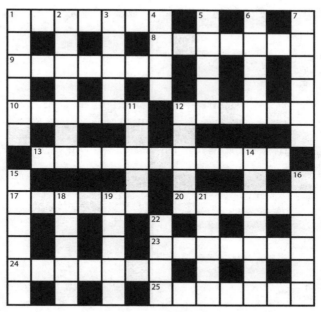

Across

1 Small pouches in a garment (7)
8 Issue forth (7)
9 Breed of hunting dog (7)
10 Looks at fixedly (6)
12 Headgear for a horse (6)
13 Woman who is considered to be dangerously seductive (5,6)
17 Ridiculous (6)
20 Snooze (6)
23 Overhead transport (7)
24 Fast train that makes a limited number of stops (7)
25 Earnest (7)

Down

1 Compound often used in agriculture and industry (6)
2 Savage and excessive butchery (7)
3 Deport from a country (5)
4 Withered (4)
5 Civic leader (5)
6 Destined (5)
7 Render unable to hear (6)
11 Velocity (5)
12 Facial hair (5)
14 Farthest ebb of the sea (3,4)
15 Hairdresser (6)
16 Hard-cased arthropod (6)
18 Sweeping blow (5)
19 Insurgent (5)
21 Repeat performance (5)
22 Overtake (4)

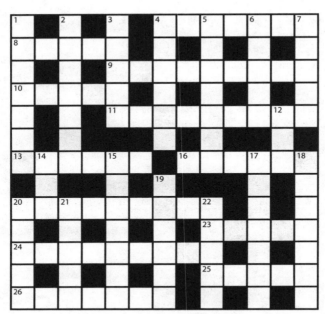

Across

4 Piece of embroidery demonstrating skill with various stitches (7)

8 Latin-American dance (5)

9 Ammunition casing containing an explosive charge and a bullet (9)

10 Thick stew made of rice and chicken (5)

11 Blasphemous behavior (9)

13 Conventional (6)

16 Elaborate party (often outdoors) (6)

20 Skillful in movements of the hands (9)

23 Approximately (especially of a date) (5)

24 Country in Europe (3,6)

25 Rile (5)

26 Castle cellar (7)

Down

1 Idealistic social reformer (7)

2 Front tooth (7)

3 Point of concentration (5)

4 Coniferous tree (6)

5 Cocktail of vermouth and gin (7)

6 Deep serving spoon (5)

7 Fasten by passing rope through a hole (5)

12 Fetched (3)

14 Single number (3)

15 Type of cellulose film (7)

17 Underwater breathing device (7)

18 Embarrassed (7)

19 External medicament (6)

20 Drugged (5)

21 Inert gas (5)

22 Range (5)

No 60

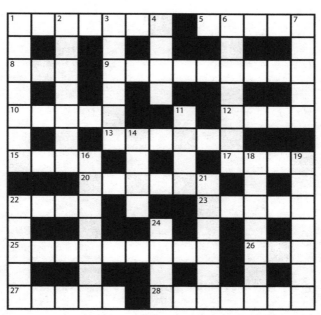

Across

1 Hair cleanser (7)
5 Thespian (5)
8 Boat's paddle (3)
9 Fatherhood (9)
10 Strong flame that burns brightly (5)
12 Graphic symbol (4)
13 Belonging to those people (6)
15 Wood file (4)
17 Russian emperor (4)
20 Exceedingly sudden (6)
22 Sleeping places (4)
23 Use to one's advantage (5)
25 Helper (9)
26 Time period (3)
27 Termagant (5)
28 Ethical or moral principle that inhibits action (7)

Down

1 Drool (7)
2 State of being behind in payments (7)
3 Marionette (6)
4 Sworn vow (4)
6 Belong, be a part of (7)
7 Synthetic fabric (5)
11 Flaccid (4)
14 Male red deer (4)
16 Peacefully resistant in response to injustice (7)
18 Agitate, excite (5,2)
19 Discharge (7)
21 Shred (6)
22 Alloy of copper and zinc (5)
24 Prohibits (4)

No 61

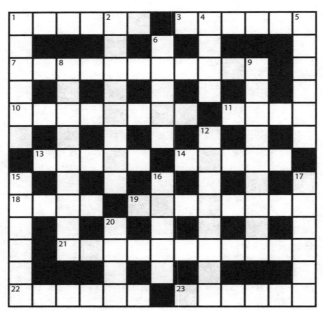

Across

1 Summer shoe (6)

3 Bone of the forearm (6)

7 Booking (11)

10 One who administers a test (8)

11 Fit of shivering (4)

13 Item of bed linen (5)

14 Everyone except the clergy (5)

18 High male voice (4)

19 Triumphant (8)

21 Well-informed (11)

22 Calm, with no emotional agitation (6)

23 Scottish dish (6)

Down

1 Thoroughfare (6)

2 Commercial passenger plane (8)

4 Similar (4)

5 Small pouch for shampoo, etc (6)

6 Printer's mark, indicating an insertion (5)

8 Long strings of pasta (9)

9 Discuss terms of an arrangement (9)

12 Early Christian church (8)

15 Fabric for a painting (6)

16 Brass instrument without valves (5)

17 Relative position (6)

20 Daze (4)

No 62

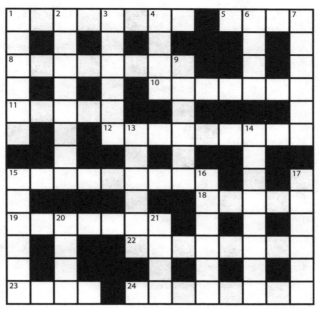

Across

1 Disfiguring (8)
5 Sea vessel (4)
8 Huge South American snake (8)
10 Long, formal letter (7)
11 Lightweight triangular scarf (5)
12 Choice (9)
15 Device consisting of a corrugated surface to scrub clothes on (9)
18 Having the leading position (5)
19 Narrow strip of land connecting two larger land areas (7)
22 Confidently optimistic and cheerful (8)
23 Piquancy (4)
24 Willing to give (8)

Down

1 Makes appear small by comparison (6)
2 Brides-to-be (8)
3 Backing singers (6)
4 Naked (4)
6 Leave out (4)
7 Inn (6)
9 Come into sight (6)
13 Second book of the Old Testament (6)
14 Contagious infection of the skin (8)
15 Heaviness (6)
16 Hang freely (6)
17 Layabouts (6)
20 Slender (4)
21 Replete (4)

No 63

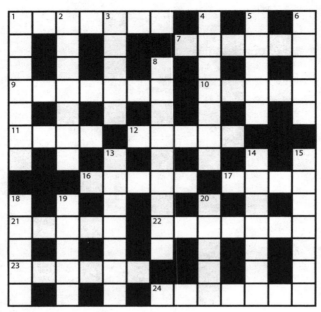

Across

1 Bloated (7)
7 Central American republic (6)
9 Funeral procession (7)
10 Military blockade (5)
11 Waterside plant (4)
12 Burrowing, rabbit-like animal (5)
16 Mother-of-pearl (5)
17 Quiet, serene (4)
21 Commit to memory (5)
22 Small piece of toast served in soup (7)
23 Designating sound transmission from two sources (6)
24 Moves about aimlessly or without any destination (7)

Down

1 Earnest (7)
2 Supervise (7)
3 Defamatory writing (5)
4 Short-tailed burrowing rodent (7)
5 Provide food (5)
6 Projecting edge of a roof (5)
8 Political system (9)
13 Wicker basket (usually one of a pair) (7)
14 Open framework (7)
15 Presaging ill-fortune (7)
18 Embrace (5)
19 Judge's hammer (5)
20 Quantity of twelve items (5)

No 64

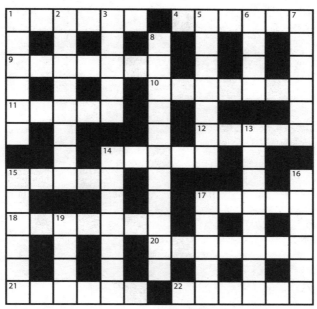

Across

1 Dark purplish red wine (6)
4 Cuts into two equal pieces (6)
9 Wide streets (7)
10 Clergyman's salary (7)
11 Dodge (5)
12 After the expected time (5)
14 Assumed name (5)
15 Fertilized plant ovules (5)
17 Dais (5)
18 Derived by logic, without observed facts (1,6)
20 Opening (7)
21 *The Life and Opinions of Tristram ___, Gentleman*, novel by Laurence Sterne (6)
22 Small couch (6)

Down

1 Swiss cottage (6)
2 Open to persuasion (8)
3 Construe (a meaning) (5)
5 Administers holy oil or ointment (7)
6 Elect (4)
7 Miscellaneous (6)
8 Combination (11)
13 Advocate of the principles of monarchy (8)
14 Astonish (7)
15 Stings (6)
16 Erase (6)
17 Aromatic substance used to add flavoring (5)
19 Roster of names (4)

No 65

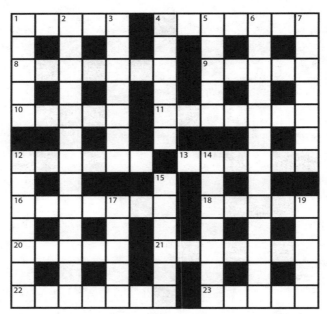

Across

1 Work hastily or carelessly (5)
4 Gloria ___, actress in silent films (7)
8 Mound made by social insects (7)
9 Final drops of a liquid (5)
10 ___ firma, solid ground (5)
11 Impatient especially under restriction or delay (7)
12 Go on a journey (6)
13 Natural flow of ground water (6)
16 Sharp-pointed leaf tip (7)
18 Sharp projections on the paws of an animal (5)
20 Relating to the moon (5)
21 Mass of precious metal (7)
22 Take to a destination (7)
23 Dismal (5)

Down

1 Tip at an angle (5)
2 Between other countries (13)
3 Secret, confidential (7)
4 Income (6)
5 South American mountain range (5)
6 Detailed description of design criteria for a piece of work (13)
7 Fund of money put by as a reserve (4,3)
12 Caused to tumble by pushing (7)
14 Preserved in vinegar (7)
15 Person in a group (6)
17 Russian city on the Vyatka River (5)
19 Bright and pleasant (5)

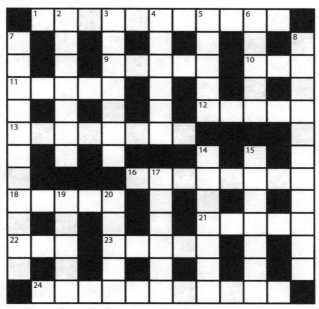

Across

1 Eager to amass material possessions (11)

9 Take by force (5)

10 Form of address (3)

11 Energy supplied (5)

12 Country, capital Madrid (5)

13 Make a labored effort (8)

16 Ranch (8)

18 Mischievous fairies (5)

21 No longer new, uninteresting (5)

22 Health resort (3)

23 Musical half note (5)

24 Murder, especially of socially prominent persons (11)

Down

2 Note the similarities or differences (7)

3 Outshine (7)

4 Relating to the backbone (6)

5 Woody plants (5)

6 Prospect (5)

7 Dairy product, eg Emmantaler or Gruyere (5,6)

8 See-through (11)

14 Male relative (7)

15 Dwell (7)

17 Rectifies (6)

19 Ampoules (5)

20 Lively ballroom dance from Brazil (5)

No 67

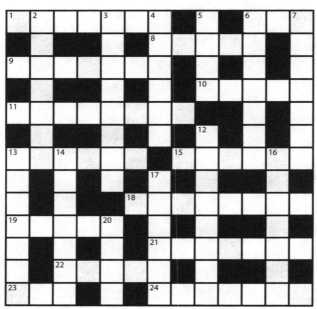

Across

1 Diffusion of liquid through a porous membrane (7)

6 Lip (3)

8 Abnormally fat (5)

9 Seat behind the rider of a motorbike (7)

10 Indicate (5)

11 Roman XIX (8)

13 Unpleasant odor (6)

15 Unorthodox belief (6)

18 Deprived through death (8)

19 Common gastropod (5)

21 Victory (7)

22 Wear away (5)

23 Move the head in agreement (3)

24 No longer active in one's profession (7)

Down

2 Powered conveyance that carries people up a mountain (3,4)

3 Type of neuralgia which affects the hips (8)

4 Poem of fourteen 10- or 11-syllable lines (6)

5 Plant fiber used to make rope (4)

6 Alleviate (7)

7 Baffling thing (7)

12 ___ XVI, the Pope (8)

13 Meeting devoted to a particular activity (7)

14 Affianced (7)

16 Church tower (7)

17 Fool, joker (6)

20 See (4)

No 68

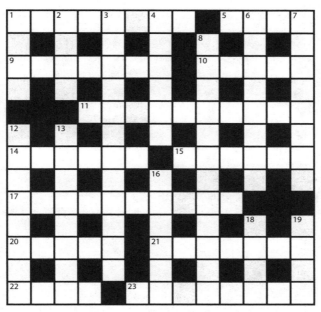

Across

1 Disinherited (8)
5 Jump lightly (4)
9 Edible marine gastropod (7)
10 Fearless (5)
11 Cause to continue (10)
14 Brass musical instrument (6)
15 Showing extreme courage (6)
17 Ship with a reinforced bow to break up frozen waters (10)
20 Leave or strike out, as of vowels (5)
21 Gymnastic garment (7)
22 Garments (4)
23 Curved shape (8)

Down

1 Sketch (4)
2 Blow delivered with an open hand (4)
3 With unconditional and enthusiastic devotion (12)
4 Non-taxable (6)
6 Volcanic island in Indonesia (8)
7 Artful or simulated semblance (8)
8 Noisily and stubbornly defiant (12)
12 Chance event (8)
13 Becoming very cold and icy (8)
16 Seafarer (6)
18 Stick that people can lean on (4)
19 Make changes in text (4)

No 69

Across

1 Of the heart (7)

5 Pulverize (5)

7 Spokes (5)

8 Detection device (7)

9 Cleft (7)

10 Niggling (5)

11 Bicycle seat (6)

13 Stick or hold together (6)

18 Tiny morsel of bread or cake (5)

20 Firmly fastened (7)

21 Whim, sudden desire (7)

22 Find repugnant (5)

23 Repent (5)

24 News (7)

Down

1 Capital of Venezuela (7)

2 Person with bright auburn hair (7)

3 The first letter of a word (7)

4 Small box for holding valuables (6)

5 Very penetrating and clear (5)

6 Place of refuge (7)

12 Alongside each other (7)

14 Fruit garden (7)

15 Made of clay (7)

16 Puts up with (7)

17 Affirm (6)

19 Woman recently married (5)

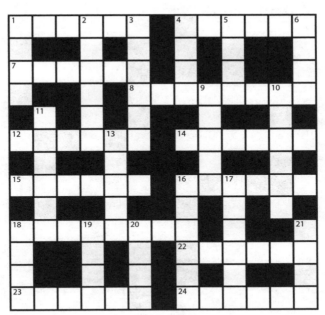

Across

1 Obtuse (6)
4 Able to absorb fluids (6)
7 Ever (6)
8 Organ on the surface of the tongue (5,3)
12 Paleontological relic (6)
14 Vehicle for carrying a coffin (6)
15 Stick of wax with a central wick (6)
16 Hired (6)
18 Investigation (8)
22 Abrade (6)
23 Get at (6)
24 Slowly, in musical tempo (6)

Down

1 Drench (4)
2 Masses of baked bread (6)
3 Extract (6)
4 Clawed feet (4)
5 Journey in a vehicle (4)
6 Exchanged for money (4)
9 In that place (5)
10 Division of Ireland (6)
11 Realm (6)
13 Decoration made by fitting pieces of wood into a surface (5)
16 Country, capital Moscow (6)
17 Aquatic South American rodent (6)
18 Region (4)
19 Interweave (4)
20 Glides over snow (4)
21 Nought (4)

No 71

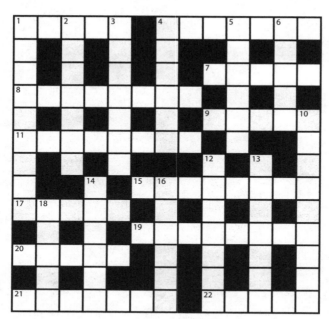

Across

1 Skin covering the top of the head (5)

4 Reach a desired goal (7)

7 Convivial gathering (5)

8 Device that controls the amount of light admitted (8)

9 Provide a brief summary (5)

11 Jeopardize (8)

15 Caution (8)

17 Talk (5)

19 Characterized by charm and generosity of spirit (8)

20 Secret store of valuables (5)

21 Close-fitting garment worn in cold water (3,4)

22 Cut finely (5)

Down

1 Pruning shears (9)

2 Prior to a specified time (7)

3 Sending by mail (7)

4 Change direction abruptly (6)

5 Cowardly (6)

6 Surplus to need (5)

10 Persevered (9)

12 Sticky, syrupy (7)

13 Get over an illness (7)

14 Large northern marine mammal (6)

16 Floating aimlessly (6)

18 Means of communication (5)

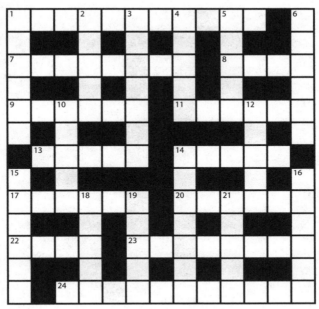

Across

1 Forerunner (11)

7 Coniferous plant (4,4)

8 Turn over and over again (4)

9 Omar ___, star of *Dr Zhivago* (6)

11 Tool used with a mortar (6)

13 Intestine (5)

14 Give form to (5)

17 Large indefinite number (6)

20 Russian wolfhound (6)

22 Primitive chlorophyll-containing, mainly aquatic organisms (4)

23 Tells (a story) (8)

24 Rotating fairground ride (6,5)

Down

1 Roman Catholic (6)

2 Dismal (5)

3 Cautiously attentive (7)

4 Use a broom (5)

5 Fragrant rootstock of various irises (5)

6 Joined by treaty or agreement (6)

10 Love affair (5)

12 Yellow quartz (5)

14 Residential districts on the outskirts of a city (7)

15 Preserve a dead body (6)

16 Threads of metal foil (6)

18 Likeness (5)

19 Person who makes a gift (5)

21 Freshwater fish (5)

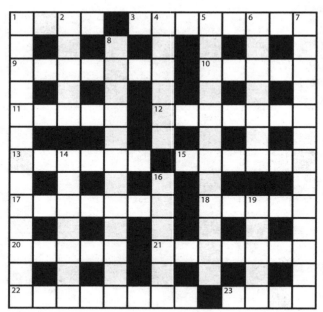

Across

1 Male pig (4)
3 Learned people (8)
9 Hinged airfoil on an aircraft wing (7)
10 Facial expression of dislike (5)
11 Not a soul (2-3)
12 Covered, often columned entrance to a building (7)
13 Putrefied (6)
15 Compares similarities (6)
17 Bearer (7)
18 Advanced slowly (5)
20 Forum in ancient Greece (5)
21 Study of word formation of a language (7)
22 Astronauts (8)
23 Adult male horse kept for breeding (4)

Down

1 Aircraft accommodation between first and economy (8,5)
2 Company which united with BP in 1998 (5)
4 Enter forcibly (6)
5 Former member of the armed forces (2-10)
6 Suffer torment (7)
7 Imprudent (3-10)
8 Not recognized as lawful (12)
14 Framework that supports climbing plants (7)
16 Thick and heavy shoe (6)
19 Whole range (5)

No 74

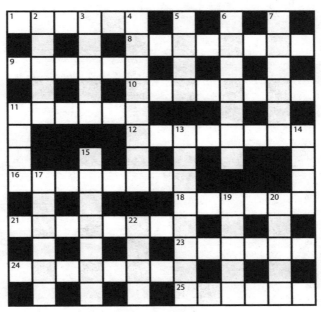

Across

1 Threat (6)
8 Ray of light from Earth's satellite (8)
9 Capital of Croatia (6)
10 Outdated (8)
11 Written stories (6)
12 Closing (8)
16 Acting game, popular at Christmas (8)
18 Dreamlike state (6)
21 Slaughter (8)
23 Quantity (6)
24 Clergyman's title (8)
25 Over there (6)

Down

2 Exercises evaluating skill or knowledge (5)
3 Large artery (5)
4 Embellished with a raised pattern (8)
5 Deprivation (4)
6 Power (7)
7 Secure (6)
11 Actor brother of Julia Roberts (4)
13 Not firmly or solidly positioned (8)
14 Amusement or pastime (4)
15 Gain in wealth (7)
17 Abode of God and the angels (6)
19 Product of the oak tree (5)
20 Small and light boat (5)
22 Organized group of workmen (4)

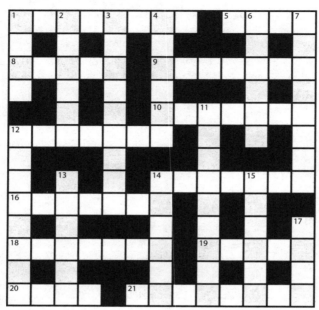

Across

1 Hypothesized (8)
5 Journey for some purpose (4)
8 Those who cannot tell the truth (5)
9 Melodious (7)
10 Chemical used in reactions (7)
12 Close of day (7)
14 Frame supporting the body of a car (7)
16 Style of design popular in the 1920s and 1930s (3,4)
18 Of interest at the present time (7)
19 Above average in size (5)
20 Fine cord of twisted fibers (4)
21 Inhabiting trees (8)

Down

1 Underside of a shoe (4)
2 Roller on a typewriter (6)
3 Building containing a kiln for drying hops (9)
4 Nonresident doctor (6)
6 Roof-supporting beam (6)
7 Profession devoted to governing (8)
11 Small American mammal with a body protected by horny plates (9)
12 Marked by quiet, caution and secrecy (8)
13 Dazed state (6)
14 Neckband (6)
15 Party of people assembled in the evening (6)
17 Metal device which rings when struck (4)

No 76

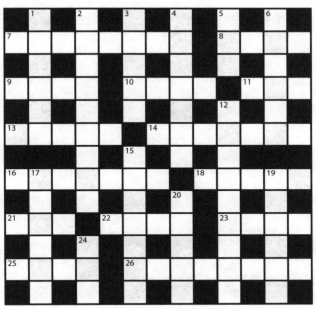

Across

7 Isolated from others (8)

8 Female relative (4)

9 Mr Redding who sang *(Sittin' on) The Dock of the Bay* (4)

10 Gaffe (4)

11 Ventilation device (3)

13 Tool consisting of a rotating shaft with parallel handle (5)

14 Tedious business (7)

16 Move aside (4,3)

18 Adipose (5)

21 Receptacle for ashes (3)

22 Equipment for reproducing sound (2-2)

23 ___ *Lang Syne*, Scottish song (4)

25 Information (4)

26 Adolescent (8)

Down

1 One of two actors who are given the same status in a film (2-4)

2 Employees (9)

3 Drench (5)

4 Meeting for an exchange of ideas (7)

5 Not good (3)

6 If there happens to be need (2,4)

12 Sailing boat with two parallel hulls (9)

15 Assortment (7)

17 Pilot of a plane (6)

19 Lever used to turn the rudder on a boat (6)

20 Animal with two feet (5)

24 Artificial crown for a tooth (3)

Across

1 Scallywag (5)

7 Advocate of political reform (7)

8 In favor of (3)

9 Jewish house of prayer (9)

11 Agitate, waken (5)

12 Someone who lives at a particular place (8)

16 Double-crosser (3-5)

20 Electronic message (5)

21 Movie actors and actresses (4,5)

23 Brick carrier (3)

24 Walter Scott novel (7)

25 Easily irritated (5)

Down

1 Food colorant (7)

2 Type of firearm (3,3)

3 Ship's officer who keeps accounts (6)

4 Press and smooth clothing (4)

5 Refuse to follow orders (7)

6 Group of warships (5)

10 Animated (5)

13 Expel from one's property (5)

14 Statement that expresses a personal opinion (7)

15 Vacation (7)

17 Begrudge (6)

18 Cleanses with soap and water (6)

19 Stick on (5)

22 Pinnacle (4)

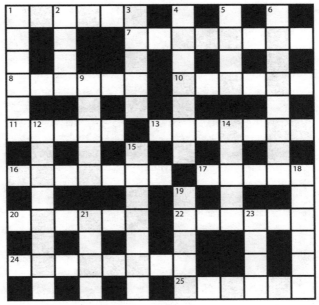

Across

1 Tree with sharp thorns (6)

7 Chief support (8)

8 Slip by (6)

10 Being in the original position (2,4)

11 Having a sharp inclination (5)

13 Cushion for kneeling on (as when praying in church) (7)

16 Glazed and salted cracker (7)

17 Pugilist (5)

20 Identification tags (6)

22 Eating (6)

24 Affected with emotional disorder (8)

25 Canned (6)

Down

1 Mother superior (6)

2 Halo of light (4)

3 Fossilized resin (5)

4 Least possible (7)

5 Egyptian goddess of fertility (4)

6 Tiny piece of anything (8)

9 Make folds in cloth (5)

12 Utter intentions of harm towards (8)

14 Avowed (5)

15 Compactness (7)

18 Observe (6)

19 Legally binding command (5)

21 Basic unit of currency in Germany (4)

23 Man's name, the Russian form of John (4)

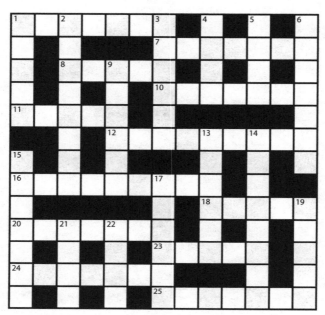

Across

1 Instruction (7)

7 Be fully aware of (7)

8 Darkest part of a shadow (5)

10 Exhausted, spent (4-3)

11 Quizzes (5)

12 Item of equine footwear (9)

16 Alessandro ___, Baroque composer (1660-1725) (9)

18 One stroke over par in golf (5)

20 Cattle-lifter (7)

23 Visitor to whom hospitality is extended (5)

24 Laugh quietly (7)

25 Dominance through threat of punishment (7)

Down

1 Shore of a sea (5)

2 Casserole of eggplant and ground lamb (8)

3 Sliding container in a piece of furniture (6)

4 Traveling show (4)

5 Brand name of a ballpoint pen (4)

6 Colonist (7)

9 Dry measure (6)

13 Comestible (6)

14 Become more extreme (8)

15 African flightless bird (7)

17 Objective (6)

19 Childish word for scrumptious (5)

21 Skim along swiftly and easily (4)

22 Body of water (4)

Mind Puzzles

No 1
Astronomical Wordfit

Can you fit all the listed words into the grid? One is already in place.

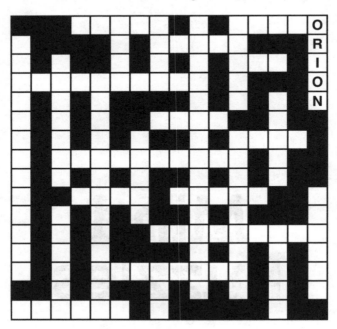

3 letters
ARC
SUN

4 letters
COMA
MARS
MOON
NASA
SETI

5 letters
COMET
EARTH

EPOCH
ORBIT
ORION ✓
PHASE
PLUTO
SOLAR
VENUS

6 letters
EUROPA
PLANET
URANUS

7 letters
MERCURY

8 letters
RED SHIFT

9 letters
METEORITE
SUPERNOVA

10 letters
ABERRATION
RETROGRADE

13 letters
ROTATION
CURVE
STAR
FORMATION

15 letters
POINT OF
APOAPSIS

No 2
Domino Fit

A standard set of twenty-eight dominoes has been laid out as shown. Can you draw in the edges of them all? The check-box is provided as an aid and the dominoes already placed may help.

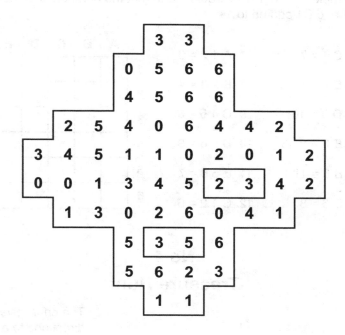

0-0	0-1	0-2	0-3	0-4	0-5	0-6	1-1	1-2

1-3	1-4	1-5	1-6	2-2	2-3	2-4	2-5	2-6	3-3
					✓				

3-4	3-5	3-6	4-4	4-5	4-6	5-5	5-6	6-6
	✓							

No 3
Latin Square

The grid below should be filled with the numbers from 1 to 6, so that each number appears exactly once in every row and every column. The clues refer to the sum of the numbers in the squares mentioned: for example, B C D 1 = 14 would mean that the numbers in squares B1, C1 and D1 add up to 14.

1 B C 1 = 7

2 C D E 2 = 13

3 C D 3 = 10

4 D E F 4 = 13

5 A B 5 = 11

6 B C 6 = 8

7 A 1 2 = 9

8 B 2 3 = 4

9 C 4 5 = 6

10 D 5 6 = 9

11 E 5 6 = 7

12 C 1 2 = 9

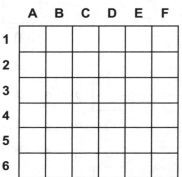

No 4
Treasure Hunt

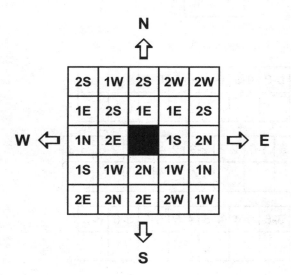

The chart gives directions to a hidden treasure behind the centre black square in the grid. Move the indicated number of spaces north, south, east and west (eg 4N means four squares north) stopping at every square once only, to arrive at the centre.
At which square should you start?

No 5

Spidoku

In the spider's web, each of the eight segments should be filled with a different number from 1 to 8, in such a way that every ring also contains a different number from 1 to 8.

The segments run from the outside of the web to the center, and the rings run all the way around. So that you can see the rings more clearly, we've shaded them gray and white.

Some numbers are already in place. Can you fill in the rest?

1 2 3 4 5 6 7 8

No 6

General Knowledge Spiral

Solve the clues in the normal way and enter them into the grid in a clockwise spiral. The last letter of one answer is the first letter of the next. When finished, the letters in the shaded squares can be rearranged to form the name of a gemstone.

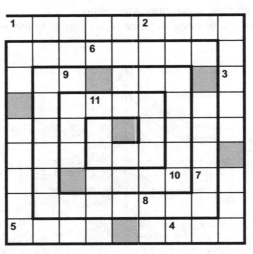

Answer: _____

1 Twelfth sign of the zodiac (6)

2 Winding downhill ski race (6)

3 Highest peak of the Alps (4,5)

4 Clause that modifies a will (7)

5 Common name for nitrous oxide (8,3)

6 Scientific study of earthquakes (10)

7 Unit of length equal to three feet (4)

8 Author of the 1719 novel *Robinson Crusoe* (6,5)

9 Thin outermost layer of the skin (9)

10 Aromatic garden herb, *Mentha spicata* (9)

11 Alternative name for the game of blackjack (6-3)

No 7
Jigword

This crossword has been cut into many pieces. Can you reassemble it? We've placed four pieces to give you a start.

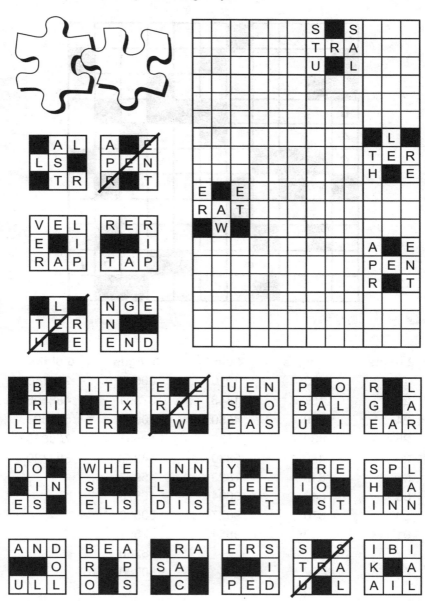

No 8
Numberfit

Can you fit all the listed numbers into the grid? Some are already in place.

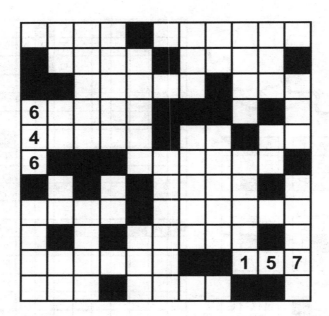

2 digits	3 digits	4 digits	5 digits	6 digits
18	103	1210	30007	281140
20	157 ✓	1843	37591	488506
24	339	4560	40009	594008
25	430	4786	40553	750835
29	489	6830	44377	893780
65	610	7823	45977	
86	646 ✓	9004	46576	
89	870	9027	50500	
91		9854	62509	
			68280	
			80080	

No 9
S-Bend

Place the letters of each word, one per cell, so that every word flows in a clockwise direction around a number. Where the hexagons of one word overlap with those of another, the letter in each cell is common to both.

ABSORB

GASBAG

CALLER

PREACH

ELAPSE

PUNISH

ENGINE

RETURN

RIGGED

SUPPER

TROPHY

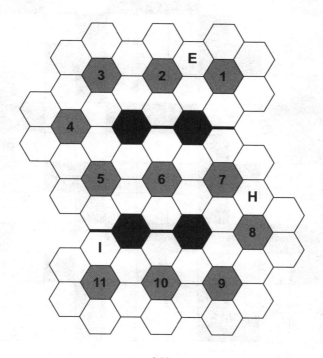

249

No 10
Kakuro

Only the numbers 1, 2, 3, 4, 5, 6, 7, 8 and 9 are used in this puzzle. Place one per blank square so that the numbers reading across total the number to the left of the block, and those reading down total the number above the block. No number appears more than once in a block, as in the example shown here:

No 11
Fill In

Using the list of words below, can you fill in this crossword? Each word is used only once and all are required to fill the grid. One word has been entered to get you started.

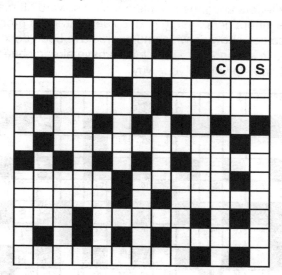

3 letters
COS ✓
NAN

4 letters
CRAB
DUTY
GLUT
MATH
NOVA
OARS

5 letters
ABYSS
ALONG
ANGLE

ANNUL
AVERT
DUSKY
GENIE
HARDY
KENDO
NICER
PANIC
PETER
POKES
RAGGY
RUNNY
SNIPE
SORRY
SPEAK
STALK

STRAW
SWORD
TANGY

7 letters
ASKANCE
GINGHAM
LABORER
POSTMAN
SHELVED
YAWNING

9 letters
CROOKEDLY
MORTALITY
PERTAINED

No 12
Codeword

Every letter in this crossword has been replaced by a number, the number remaining the same for that letter wherever it occurs in the grid. All 26 letters of the alphabet have been used. Can you substitute numbers for letters and thus complete the crossword? It may help to cross off the letters beneath the grid to keep a track of progress, and the reference box showing which numbers have been decoded can also be used to aid solving. Three letters have already been entered into the grid, to help you on your way.

7	18	15	3	3	1	11		19	6	13	26	15	7	17
18		18				12		6		15				25
14	16	14	3	24	8	25	21	24		21	3	6	5	18
3		19		25		24		25		14		19		14
15	22	7	6	22	14		18	3	6	22	9	1	15	12
12				21		7			13			7 **S**		
15		7	26	14	12	14	18	25	22		13	15 **I**	7	11
2		14		3		13		8		21		22 **N**		14
14	6	7	24		6	22	22	14	20	15	22	23		3
		7			11			24		22				5
10	1	15	4	15	14	7	18		7	22	14	14	2	14
14		25		21		18		15		14		12		4
13	15	22	4	14		3	14	7	1	3	3	14	4	18
14				6		6		12				4		12
12	25	24	6	12	18	24		14	19	11	6	18	17	24

A B C D E F G H I J K L M
N O P Q R S T U V W X Y Z

Reference Box

1	2	3	4	5	6	7 **S**	8	9	10	11	12	13
14	15 **I**	16	17	18	19	20	21	22 **N**	23	24	25	26

No 13
One to Nine

Using the numbers below, complete these six equations (three reading across and three reading downwards). Every number from 1 to 9 is used once and one has been entered for you. Calculations should be made in the order in which they appear.

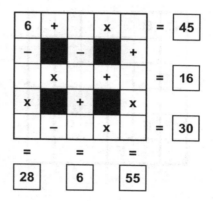

No 14
Total Concentration

The blank squares should be filled with whole numbers between 1 and 20 inclusive, any of which may occur more than once, or not at all. The numbers in every horizontal row add up to the totals on the right; whilst those in every vertical column add up to the totals along the bottom, as do the two long diagonal lines. Can you discover the missing numbers?

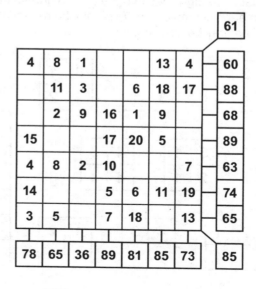

No 15
Logi-6

Every row and column of this grid should contain one each of the letters A, B, C, D, E and F. In addition, each of the shapes (shown marked by thicker lines) should also contain one each of these six letters. Can you complete the grid?

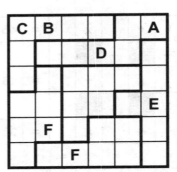

No 16
Tile Twister

Place the eight tiles into the puzzle grid so that all adjacent numbers on each tile match up. Tiles may be rotated through 360 degrees, but none may be flipped over.

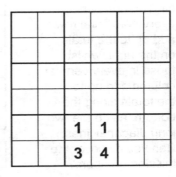

No 17
Bible Characters Wordfit

Can you fit all the listed words into the grid? One is already in place.

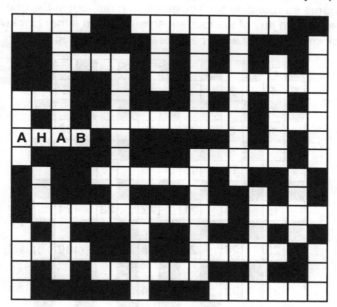

3 letters	LEAH	6 letters	8 letters
EVE	RUTH	AQUILA	BARABBAS
HAM	SAUL	ISRAEL	SHADRACH
JOB	SHEM	NATHAN	
LOT		PILATE	
		SISERA	9 letters
		THOMAS	BATHSHEBA
4 letters	5 letters		ZECHARIAH
ABEL	AARON		
ADAM	LABAN	7 letters	
AHAB ✓	URIAH	ISHMAEL	
BOAZ		LAZARUS	10 letters
ESAU		SOLOMON	BELSHAZZAR
JAEL		TABITHA	

No 18

Around the Squares

The answer to each clue is a four-letter word, to be entered in the four squares surrounding the corresponding number in the grid. The word can start in any of the four squares and read either clockwise or anticlockwise. The first word has already been entered.

	R						
E	1	I	2	3	4	5	6
	T						
	7		8	9	10	11	12
	13		14	15	16	17	18
	19		20	21	22	23	24
	25		26	27	28	29	30
	31		32	33	34	35	36

1 Religious ceremony
2 Vast, imposing
3 Exploit
4 Animal group
5 Pour
6 Sour
7 Elect
8 Pontiff
9 Deceased
10 Unyielding
11 Unglossy
12 Canter, jog
13 Very bad, wicked
14 Pale red hue
15 Like
16 Precipitation
17 Large-headed nail
18 Quip
19 Green citrus fruit
20 Small cut
21 Slither
22 Clock face
23 Sweet foodstuff
24 Back of the foot
25 Repast
26 Tribe
27 Shortly
28 Game played on horseback
29 Coal-derived fuel
30 Turn runny
31 Not at home
32 Three feet
33 Highway
34 Speed
35 Transfer power
36 Alike

No 19
Food and Drink Spiral

Solve the clues in the normal way and enter them into the grid in a clockwise spiral. The last letter of one answer is the first letter of the next. When finished, the letters in the shaded squares can be rearranged to form the name of a French cheese.

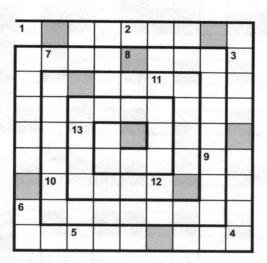

Answer: _____

1 Spicy Mexican sauce or dip (5)

2 Acid found in vinegar (6)

3 White Italian bread, 'slipper' (8)

4 Usual name for an alligator pear (7)

5 Aniseed-flavored Greek spirit (4)

6 Dish of beaten eggs which is fried until set (8)

7 Mild, yellow Dutch cheese (4)

8 Pasta in the form of short, hollow tubes (8)

9 Component part of a recipe (10)

10 Sweet, orange-flavored liqueur (6,3)

11 Thick soup made with seafood (7)

12 Rich French meat and vegetable stew (6)

13 Person who abstains from alcohol (11)

No 20
Wordfit

Can you fit all of the listed words into the grid?

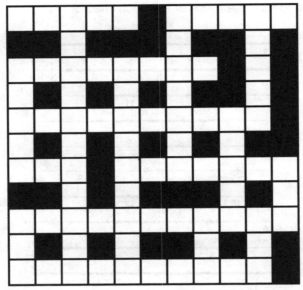

3 letters
AWN
CAT
HOE
PEA
SPY

5 letters
AESOP
ARISE
CLEAR
MAGIC
STOOP

7 letters
CRAYONS
CUSTOMS

8 letters
MAGICIAN

9 letters
CONSCIOUS

10 letters
ASSISTANCE
GREENHOUSE

11 letters
PHOTOGRAPHY
SUGGESTIONS

No 21
Combiku

Each horizontal row and vertical column should contain five different shapes and five different numbers.

Every square will contain one number and one shape and no combination may be repeated anywhere else in the puzzle: for example, if a square has both a 4 and a star, then no other square will contain both a 4 and a star.

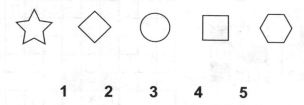

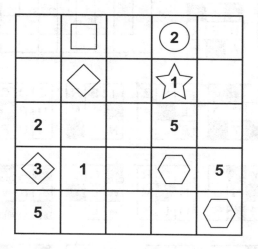

No 22
Jigword

This crossword has been cut into many pieces. Can you reassemble it? We've placed four pieces to give you a start.

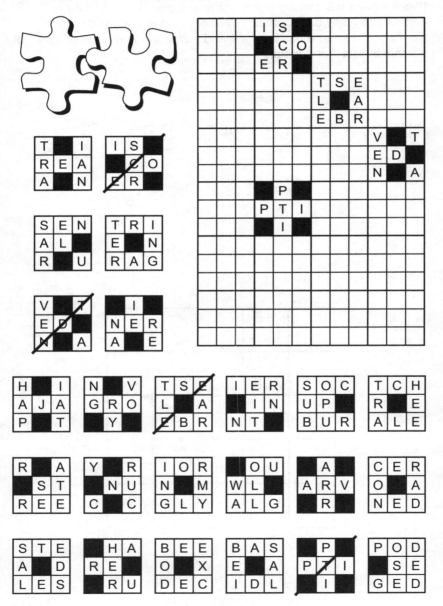

No 23
Domino Fit

A standard set of twenty-eight dominoes has been laid out as shown. Can you draw in the edges of them all? The check-box is provided as an aid and the dominoes already placed may help.

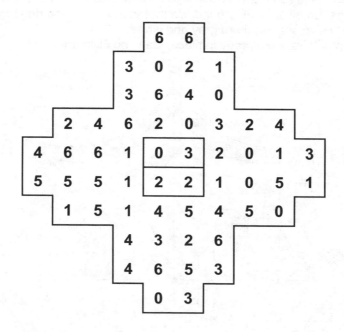

0-0	0-1	0-2	0-3	0-4	0-5	0-6	1-1	1-2
			✔					

1-3	1-4	1-5	1-6	2-2	2-3	2-4	2-5	2-6	3-3
				✔					

3-4	3-5	3-6	4-4	4-5	4-6	5-5	5-6	6-6

No 24
Spidoku

In the spider's web, each of the eight segments should be filled with a different number from 1 to 8, in such a way that every ring also contains a different number from 1 to 8.
The segments run from the outside of the web to the center, and the rings run all the way around. So that you can see the rings more clearly, we've shaded them gray and white.
Some numbers are already in place. Can you fill in the rest?

1 2 3 4 5 6 7 8

No 25
S-Bend

Place the letters of each word, one per cell, so that every word flows in a clockwise direction around a number. Where the hexagons of one word overlap with those of another, the letter in each cell is common to both.

ARCHED

JESTER

SERIAL

BEMUSE

PLASMA

SLOPPY

CAMERA

SNAPPY

REPAIR

HUMANE

WALLET

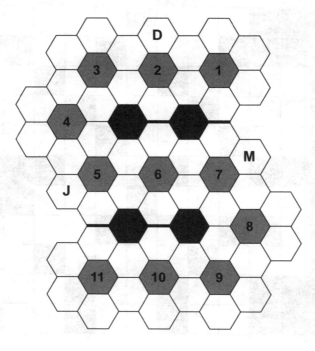

No 26

Kakuro

Only the numbers 1, 2, 3, 4, 5, 6, 7, 8 and 9 are used in this puzzle. Place one per blank square so that the numbers reading across total the number to the left of the block, and those reading down total the number above the block. No number appears more than once in a block, as in the example shown here:

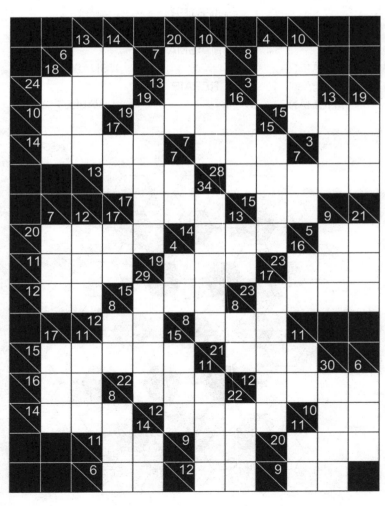

No 27

General Knowledge Spiral

Solve the clues in the normal way and enter them into the grid in a clockwise spiral. The last letter of one answer is the first letter of the next. When finished, the letters in the shaded squares can be rearranged to form the name of a fish.

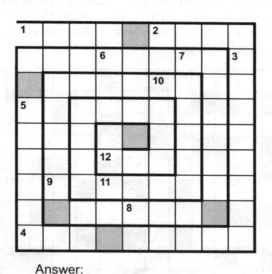

Answer: _____

1 Term for a division in a religion (6)

2 Mediterranean island, capital Valletta (5)

3 Receptacle said to contain the Ten Commandments (3,2,3,8)

4 Better-known name of artist Tiziano Vecelli (6)

5 Capital of the Bahamas (6)

6 Larger of the two forearm bones (4)

7 Group of islands (11)

8 Constellation known as 'the Hunter' (5)

9 Central American country, capital Managua (9)

10 Second-largest country of South America (9)

11 Scientific study of humans (12)

12 Edible potato-like root vegetable (3)

No 28

Codeword

Every letter in this crossword has been replaced by a number, the number remaining the same for that letter wherever it occurs in the grid. All 26 letters of the alphabet have been used. Can you substitute numbers for letters and thus complete the crossword? It may help to cross off the letters beneath the grid to keep a track of progress, and the reference box showing which numbers have been decoded can also be used to aid solving. Three letters have already been entered into the grid, to help you on your way.

Codeword grid (numbers shown per cell). Pre-filled letters: 25 = M, 6 = A, 11 = N.

A	B	C	D	E	F	G	H	I	J	K	L	M
N	O	P	Q	R	S	T	U	V	W	X	Y	Z

Reference Box

1	2	3	4	5	6 A	7	8	9	10	11 N	12	13
14	15	16	17	18	19	20	21	22	23	24	25 M	26

No 29

Fill In

Using the list of words below, can you fill in this crossword? Each word is used only once and all are required to fill the grid. One word has been entered to get you started.

3 letters	PRAY	FUSED	7 letters
DEN	RASP	IDLER	CUTLASS
OUT	SPIN	KHAKI	HEARSAY
	YOKE	NERVY	OBSCENE
		NYLON	PLUMMET
4 letters	5 letters	ODIUM	SUNBEAM
AMEN	ABACK	OKAPI	YEARNED
EPIC	ADORN	OTTER	
FEET	ARISE	PRIZE	
FUEL	CHEST	PUMPS	
GOAD ✓	DITTO	PYGMY	
HIVE	ENTER	SCION	
INTO	EVENS	WAKES	
LOAF	EVICT	WHOLE	

No 30
Treasure Hunt

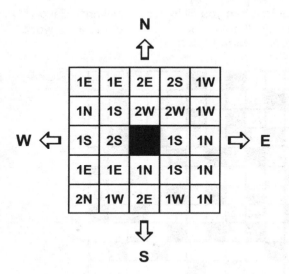

The chart gives directions to a hidden treasure behind the centre black square in the grid. Move the indicated number of spaces north, south, east and west (eg 4N means four squares north) stopping at every square once only, to arrive at the centre.
At which square should you start?

No 31
Latin Square

The grid below should be filled with the numbers from 1 to 6, so that each number appears exactly once in every row and every column. The clues refer to the sum of the numbers in the squares mentioned: for example, B C D 1 = 14 would mean that the numbers in squares B1, C1 and D1 add up to 14.

1 A B C 6 = 14

2 A 2 3 = 7

3 B 3 4 = 3

4 C 1 2 3 = 7

5 D 3 4 = 9

6 E 5 6 = 4

7 F 5 6 = 9

8 D E 1 = 5

9 D E 2 = 10

10 E F 3 = 9

11 E F 4 = 11

12 E F 6 = 5

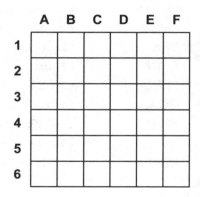

No 32
Jigword

This crossword has been cut into many pieces. Can you reassemble it? We've placed four pieces to give you a start.

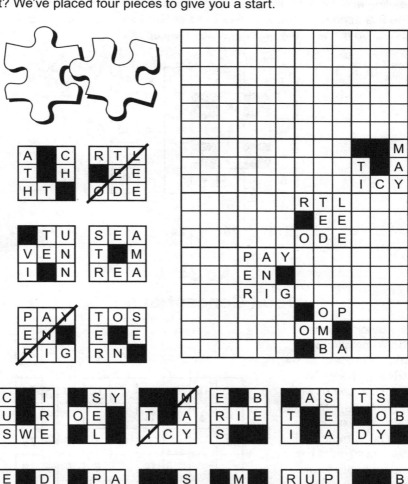

No 33
One to Nine

Using the numbers below, complete these six equations (three reading across and three reading downwards). Every number from 1 to 9 is used once and one has been entered for you. Calculations should be made in the order in which they appear.

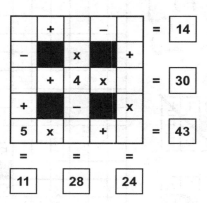

No 34
Total Concentration

The blank squares should be filled with whole numbers between 1 and 20 inclusive, any of which may occur more than once, or not at all. The numbers in every horizontal row add up to the totals on the right; whilst those in every vertical column add up to the totals along the bottom, as do the two long diagonal lines. Can you discover the missing numbers?

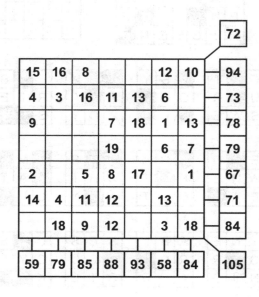

No 35
Kakuro

Only the numbers 1, 2, 3, 4, 5, 6, 7, 8 and 9 are used in this puzzle. Place one per blank square so that the numbers reading across total the number to the left of the block, and those reading down total the number above the block. No number appears more than once in a block, as in the example shown here:

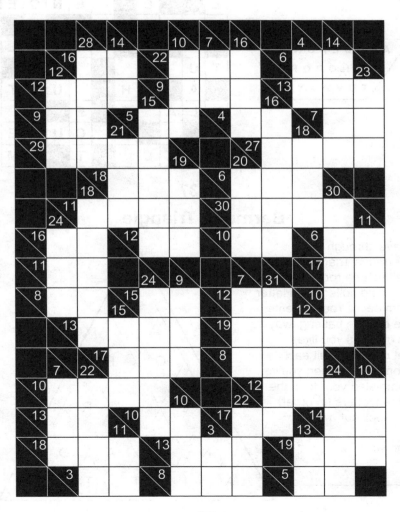

No 36
Alphabet Soup

Ladle the letters from the soup tureen and fit one into each of the 26 empty squares in the grid below, so that the finished result is a complete crossword containing English words. All of the letters in the tureen must be used – thus no letter is used more than once.

A B C D E F G H I J K
L M N O P Q R S
T U V W X Y Z

		M			I		E	R
A			T	E		A		U
L		E		E	N	C		
	S	S		E				
		L						L
T	U						S	
	A		H			U	S	T
B	L	A	E		E			
O			E		C	U	S	E
	H	E	L			T		M

No 37
Bermuda Triangle

Travel through the 'Bermuda Triangle' by visiting one room at a time and collecting a letter from each. You can enter the outside passageway as often as you like, but can only visit each room once. When you've completed your tour, the fifteen letters (in order) will spell out a word.

The word is:

_____

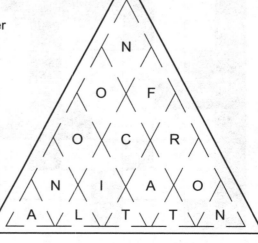

272

No 38
Word Ladders

Change one letter at a time (but not the position of any letter) to make a new word – and move from the word at the top of the ladder to the word at the bottom using the exact number of rungs provided.

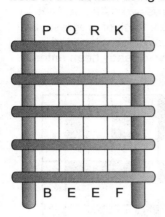

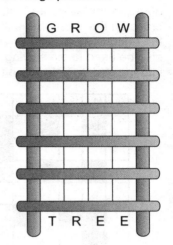

No 39
Couplets

The picture is of a central circle surrounded by shapes, linked to form six sets of three shapes apiece. Can you complete the puzzle by placing each of the two-letter groups below, one per shape, so that every set of three (the central circle, plus the two matching shapes diagonally opposite one another) forms a six-letter word? Whichever pair of letters you place in the central circle will appear in the middle of every word.

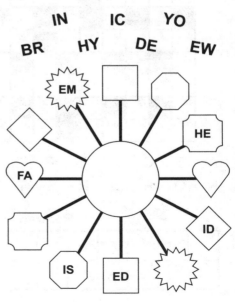

No 40

Codeword

Every letter in this crossword has been replaced by a number, the number remaining the same for that letter wherever it occurs in the grid. All 26 letters of the alphabet have been used. Can you substitute numbers for letters and thus complete the crossword? It may help to cross off the letters beneath the grid to keep a track of progress, and the reference box showing which numbers have been decoded can also be used to aid solving. Three letters have already been entered into the grid, to help you on your way.

22	14	15	24	4	4	8	9	21		10	22	9	17	4
14		1		26		11		22		17		8		17
1	8	10	22	10		6	17	10	17	25	24	4	8	3
17		24		8		22		11		25				22
20	9	25	20	3	2	4	22		2	8	19	19	22	18
19			9		9		12		4		16		11	
15		23	17 A	6	24	9	8	3	17		20	9	8	15
	18		10 R		13		18		14		22		15	
7	17	10	11 M		8	3	22	25	24	14	22	19		3
	15		22		9		9		9		5			24
4	17	6	18	24	21		15	17	19	15	22	7	20	4
24				3		11		4		20		17		24
19	3	17	6	22	21	24	17	15		11	17	9	24	10
22		21		17		19		17		24		21		22
19	3	24	10	9		19	20	10	6	10	8	19	22	18

A B C D E F G H I J K L M
N O P Q R S T U V W X Y Z

Reference Box

1	2	3	4	5	6	7	8	9	10 R	11 M	12	13
14	15	16	17 A	18	19	20	21	22	23	24	25	26

No 41
Logi-6

Every row and column of this grid should contain one each of the letters A, B, C, D, E and F. In addition, each of the shapes (shown marked by thicker lines) should also contain one each of these six letters. Can you complete the grid?

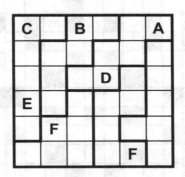

No 42
Pyramid Plus

Every brick in this pyramid contains a number which is the sum of the two numbers below it, so that F=A+B, etc. Just work out the missing numbers!

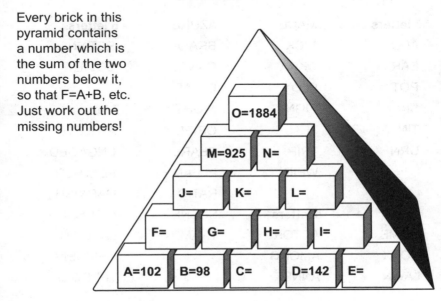

No 43
Fill In

Using the list of words below, can you fill in this crossword? Each word is used only once and all are required to fill the grid. One word has been entered to get you started.

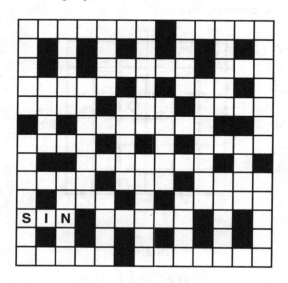

3 letters
ADD
EAR
POT
SIN ✓
TIN
URN

4 letters
BARE
DOME
HOAX
LAWN

MACE
NICK
OKRA
PLOY
SIGN
TEAL
TRIP
WEIR

5 letters
ACTOR
AMONG
ANNEX

AZURE
BRAWL
CANOE
FLEAS
NIGHT
ORIEL
PEARL
PLEAD
RATIO
SCENE
TRAMP

6 letters
RETAIN
SOVIET

7 letters
ATHLETE
ENGAGED
FEATHER
GARNISH
GUMSHOE
LANOLIN
OSMOSIS
THYROID

No 44
Wordfit

Can you fit all of the listed words into the grid?

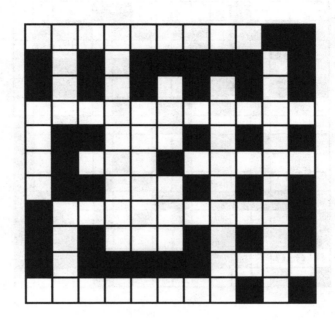

3 letters
BAD
BIT
CUB
LED
SEX
TAX

4 letters
BARN
COWL
ECRU
NONE

5 letters
DIETS

6 letters
NATURE

8 letters
CLARINET

9 letters
ASSISTANT
CHARACTER
DESPERATE
POLITICAL

10 letters
SHELTERING

11 letters
BUSINESSMEN

No 45
Building Wordfit

Can you fit all the listed words into the grid? One is already in place.

3 letters
HUT

4 letters
ARCH
BEAM
DOME
DOOR
HALL
LOFT
MOAT
ROOF ✓

SHED
TILE
WALL
WOOD

5 letters
DEPOT
EXITS
RISER
SHOPS
STAIR
STRUT

6 letters
ESTATE
GRANGE
MORTAR
PLINTH
STONES

7 letters
CELLARS
LANDING
ROTUNDA
SHELTER

TRANSOM
TURRETS

8 letters
BATHROOM
MONUMENT
TRENCHES

9 letters
APARTMENT

278

No 46

Combiku

Each horizontal row and vertical column should contain five different shapes and five different numbers.
Every square will contain one number and one shape and no combination may be repeated anywhere else in the puzzle: for example, if a square has both a 4 and a star, then no other square will contain both a 4 and a star.

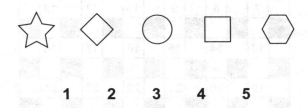

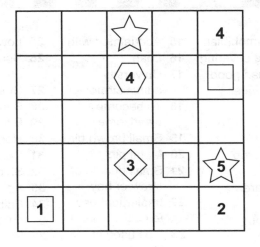

Around the Squares

The answer to each clue is a four-letter word, to be entered in the four squares surrounding the corresponding number in the grid. The word can start in any of the four squares and read either clockwise or anticlockwise. The first word has already been entered.

	F						
G	1	R	2	3	4	5	6
	O						
	7	8	9	10	11	12	
	13	14	15	16	17	18	
	19	20	21	22	23	24	
	25	26	27	28	29	30	
	31	32	33	34	35	36	

1 Small amphibian
2 Building covering
3 Less than good
4 Crude water craft
5 Froth
6 Settled
7 Cereal crop
8 Worry
9 Urban area
10 Gape
11 Numerous
12 Applaud
13 Tailed amphibian
14 Tall vegetable
15 Acquainted with
16 Loan
17 University administrator
18 To become wearisome
19 Small brown bird
20 Metal pin
21 Small bundle of straw or hay
22 Implement used to cultivate land
23 Gas used in lit signs
24 Solely
25 Low value coin
26 South African unit of currency
27 Strut, support
28 Bend out of true
29 Bite away at
30 Horned animal
31 Converse
32 Ship's floor
33 Apiece
34 Edible crustacean
35 Barrier, enclosure
36 High

No 48
Domino Fit

A standard set of twenty-eight dominoes has been laid out as shown. Can you draw in the edges of them all? The check-box is provided as an aid and the dominoes already placed may help.

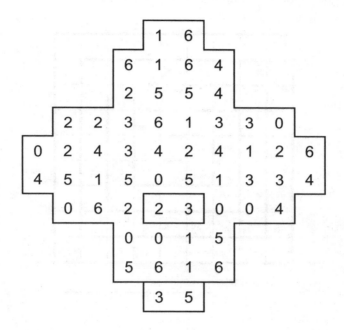

0-0	0-1	0-2	0-3	0-4	0-5	0-6	1-1	1-2

1-3	1-4	1-5	1-6	2-2	2-3	2-4	2-5	2-6	3-3
					✓				

3-4	3-5	3-6	4-4	4-5	4-6	5-5	5-6	6-6
	✓							

No 49

General Knowledge Spiral

Solve the clues in the normal way and enter them into the grid in a clockwise spiral. The last letter of one answer is the first letter of the next. When finished, the letters in the shaded squares can be rearranged to form the name of an English royal house.

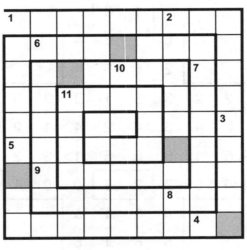

Answer: _____

1 Scottish king who died in 1057 (7)

2 Country, capital Budapest (7)

3 Third color of the rainbow (6)

4 Christian festival seven weeks after Easter (11)

5 Friedrich ___, associate of Karl Marx (6)

6 Capital of Chile (8)

7 Greek mountain known as the 'home of the gods' (7)

8 Young pilchard (7)

9 Charged atomic particle (8)

10 North-easternmost English county (14)

11 Indian town famous for its tea (10)

No 50
Spidoku

In the spider's web, each of the eight segments should be filled with a different number from 1 to 8, in such a way that every ring also contains a different number from 1 to 8.

The segments run from the outside of the web to the center, and the rings run all the way around. So that you can see the rings more clearly, we've shaded them gray and white.

Some numbers are already in place. Can you fill in the rest?

283

No 51
Jigword

This crossword has been cut into many pieces. Can you reassemble it? We've placed four pieces to give you a start.

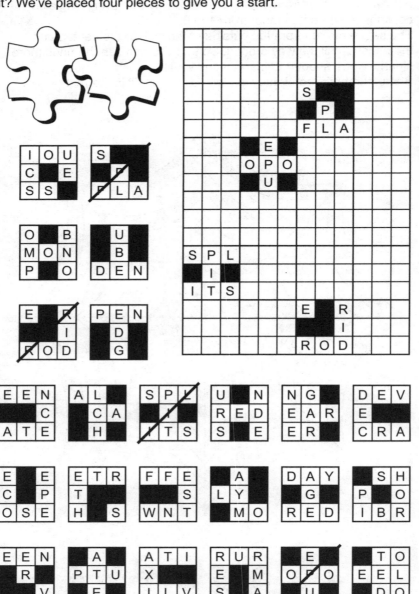

No 52

Kakuro

Only the numbers 1, 2, 3, 4, 5, 6, 7, 8 and 9 are used in this puzzle. Place one per blank square so that the numbers reading across total the number to the left of the block, and those reading down total the number above the block. No number appears more than once in a block, as in the example shown here:

No 53
Latin Square

The grid below should be filled with the numbers from 1 to 6, so that each number appears exactly once in every row and every column. The clues refer to the sum of the numbers in the squares mentioned: for example, B C D 1 = 14 would mean that the numbers in squares B1, C1 and D1 add up to 14.

1 A 5 6 = 3

2 B 2 3 = 4

3 C 3 4 = 7

4 D 2 3 4 = 7

5 E 4 5 = 3

6 F 4 5 = 8

7 C D 1 = 4

8 E F 2 = 11

9 E F 3 = 7

10 A B 4 = 10

11 B C D 5 = 13

12 A B 1 = 11

	A	B	C	D	E	F
1						
2						
3						
4						
5						
6						

No 54
Tile Twister

Place the eight tiles into the puzzle grid so that all adjacent numbers on each tile match up. Tiles may be rotated through 360 degrees, but none may be flipped over.

4	1
3	4

2	1
1	4

2	3
2	3

3	2
3	4

2	4
1	1

3	4
2	1

1	3
2	3

3	1
3	1

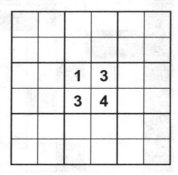

No 55
Total Concentration

The blank squares should be filled with whole numbers between 1 and 20 inclusive, any of which may occur more than once, or not at all. The numbers in every horizontal row add up to the totals on the right; whilst those in every vertical column add up to the totals along the bottom, as do the two long diagonal lines. Can you discover the missing numbers?

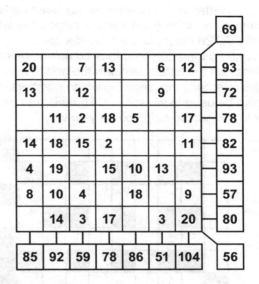

							69
20		7	13		6	12	93
13		12			9		72
	11	2	18	5		17	78
14	18	15	2			11	82
4	19		15	10	13		93
8	10	4		18		9	57
	14	3	17		3	20	80
85	92	59	78	86	51	104	56

No 56
Pyramid Plus

Every brick in this pyramid contains a number which is the sum of the two numbers below it, so that F=A+B, etc. Just work out the missing numbers!

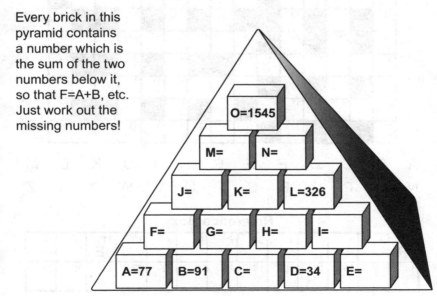

O=1545

M=   N=

J=   K=   L=326

F=   G=   H=   I=

A=77   B=91   C=   D=34   E=

287

Codeword

Every letter in this crossword has been replaced by a number, the
number remaining the same for that letter wherever it occurs in the
grid. All 26 letters of the alphabet have been used. Can you substitute
numbers for letters and thus complete the crossword? It may help to
cross off the letters beneath the grid to keep a track of progress, and
the reference box showing which numbers have been decoded can
also be used to aid solving. Three letters have already been entered
into the grid, to help you on your way.

4	22	20	3	2	18	2	11	14		26		20		9
13			11		6		4		21	1	11	11	5	17
24	11	9	20	25	1	6	7	26		6		15		11
2			3		5			10	13	5	15	7	11	1
13	14	23	13	5	11	24	5	22		11		6		11
5			4		18		17			20		2		19
	5	17 (H)	11 (E)	1 (R)	7	21	2	5		20	5	13	10	11
20			24		10		20		1		10			1
11	13	1	3	17		19	11	16	13	3	2	6	24	
11		2		13			10		14		11			18
14		19		21		11	20	26	2	6	24	13	25	11
5	1	13	12	2	11	1			13		3			24
13		10		3		13	26	13	3	17	11	3	2	5
20	3	1	11	13	8		2		6		10			11
11		22		3		17	11	13	1	3	11	24	11	14

A	B	C	D	E	F	G	H	I	J	K	L	M
N	O	P	Q	R	S	T	U	V	W	X	Y	Z

Reference Box

1 R	2	3	4	5	6	7	8	9	10	11 E	12	13
14	15	16	17 H	18	19	20	21	22	23	24	25	26

No 58
Fill In

Using the list of words below, can you fill in this crossword? Each word is used only once and all are required to fill the grid. One word has been entered to get you started.

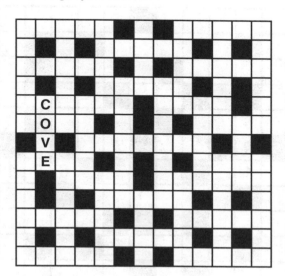

4 letters	5 letters	PENAL	SCAMPI
COVE ✓	ADEPT	ROOST	SETTEE
FELT	AFTER	SCRAP	SPLASH
HOSE	CLEFT	SMART	TRENCH
LINT	DELTA	SOCKS	TSETSE
LYRE	EAGLE	STORY	UTMOST
OATH	EXTOL	WHEAT	YELLOW
STAR	GROWN		
SURF	LITHE	**6 letters**	**7 letters**
TIRE	LUNAR	AZALEA	ELITIST
YETI	MERIT	CANVAS	FISSURE
	OVATE	FENNEL	RISOTTO

No 59
Numberfit

Can you fit all the listed numbers into the grid? Some are already in place.

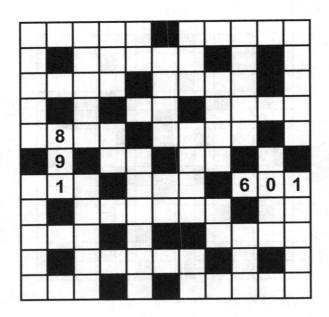

2 digits	3 digits	4 digits	5 digits	6 digits
17	121	1587	11461	250536
27	322	2400	12557	700324
33	340	4532	17304	
43	512	5064	20850	
49	533	5105	27169	
58	601 ✓	7848	38294	
67	685	7872	38772	
89	769	8298	39064	
92	891 ✓	9108	43014	
		9343	49276	
			56137	
			60344	

No 60
Colorful Wordfit

Can you fit all the listed words into the grid? One is already in place.

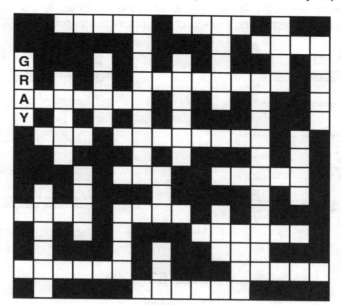

3 letters
ASH
BAY
DUN
JET
RED
TAN

4 letters
DRAB
FAWN
GRAY ✓
HUES
JADE

PINK
PUCE
RUBY
RUST
SAGE
SAND

5 letters
BEIGE
CORAL
EBONY
LEMON
LILAC
WHITE

6 letters
CERISE
CHERRY
COFFEE
PEWTER
SALMON

7 letters
AVOCADO

8 letters
CHESTNUT
LAVENDER

9 letters
CHOCOLATE

11 letters
ULTRAMARINE

No 61
Word Ladders

Change one letter at a time (but not the position of any letter) to make a new word – and move from the word at the top of the ladder to the word at the bottom using the exact number of rungs provided.

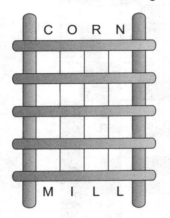

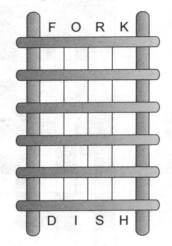

No 62
Couplets

The picture is of a central circle surrounded by shapes, linked to form six sets of three shapes apiece. Can you complete the puzzle by placing each of the two-letter groups below, one per shape, so that every set of three (the central circle, plus the two matching shapes diagonally opposite one another) forms a six-letter word?
Whichever pair of letters you place in the central circle will appear in the middle of every word.

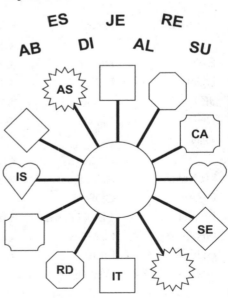

No 63
General Knowledge Spiral

Solve the clues in the normal way and enter them into the grid in a clockwise spiral. The last letter of one answer is the first letter of the next. When finished, the letters in the shaded squares can be rearranged to form the name of a poultry bird.

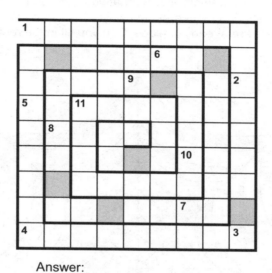

Answer: _____

1 African country, capital Freetown (6,5)

2 ___ complex, strong daughter/father attachment (7)

3 ___ the Great, Greek conqueror (9)

4 Famous Venetian Grand Canal bridge (6)

5 Short, light musical drama (8)

6 Southernmost continent (10)

7 Sir Alan ___, leading British playwright (9)

8 Highly inflammable petroleum jelly (6)

9 Gorgon slain by Perseus (6)

10 English-French battle of 1415 (9)

11 Africa's second-largest lake (10)

No 64

Spidoku

In the spider's web, each of the eight segments should be filled with a different number from 1 to 8, in such a way that every ring also contains a different number from 1 to 8.

The segments run from the outside of the web to the center, and the rings run all the way around. So that you can see the rings more clearly, we've shaded them gray and white.

Some numbers are already in place. Can you fill in the rest?

1 2 3 4 5 6 7 8

No 65
Jigword

This crossword has been cut into many pieces. Can you reassemble it? We've placed four pieces to give you a start.

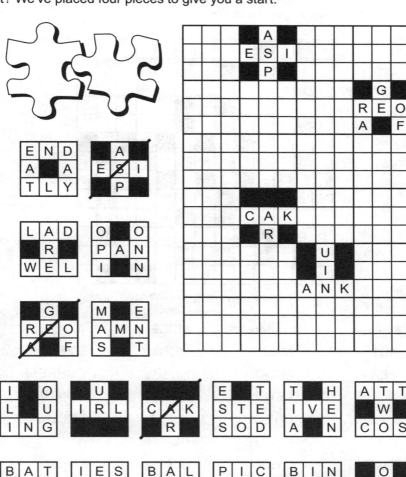

No 66
Fill In

Using the list of words below, can you fill in this crossword? Each word is used only once and all are required to fill the grid. One word has been entered to get you started.

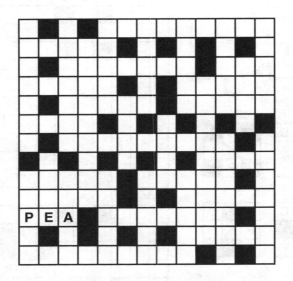

3 letters
ACT
PEA ✓

4 letters
CITY
EMIR
OWNS
SPRY
SUNG
WORE

5 letters
ARENA
ARGON
ASTIR
CHILD
CYCLE
CYNIC
ELATE
EXTRA
HIRED
LEEKS
MAPLE
MODEL
MONEY
NEARS
ORION
PLEAT
RUMEN
SLANG
THETA
YAHOO

7 letters
ADAMANT
AVARICE
EMERGED
EMPRESS
HUNTING
PRUDISH

9 letters
ENSCONCED
EVERGREEN
SHORELINE
SHOWPIECE
TRANSPIRE

No 67
Treasure Hunt

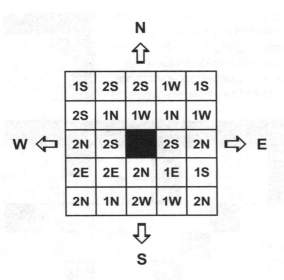

The chart gives directions to a hidden treasure behind the centre black square in the grid. Move the indicated number of spaces north, south, east and west (eg 4N means four squares north) stopping at every square once only, to arrive at the centre.
At which square should you start?

No 68
One to Nine

Using the numbers below, complete these six equations (three reading across and three reading downwards). Every number from 1 to 9 is used once and one has been entered for you. Calculations should be made in the order in which they appear.

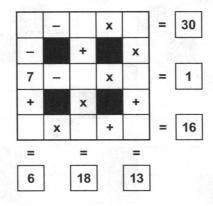

No 69
Kakuro

Only the numbers 1, 2, 3, 4, 5, 6, 7, 8 and 9 are used in this puzzle. Place one per blank square so that the numbers reading across total the number to the left of the block, and those reading down total the number above the block. No number appears more than once in a block, as in the example shown here:

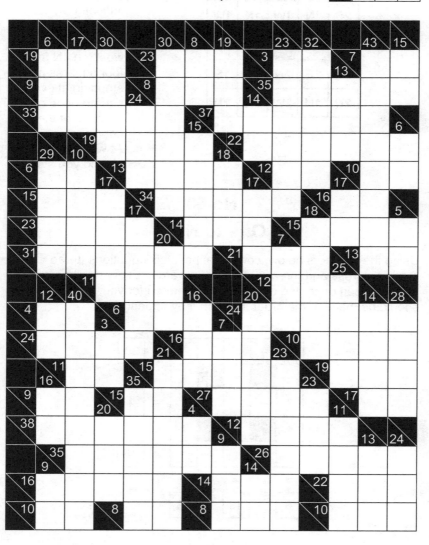

No 70
Wordfit

Can you fit all of the listed words into the grid?

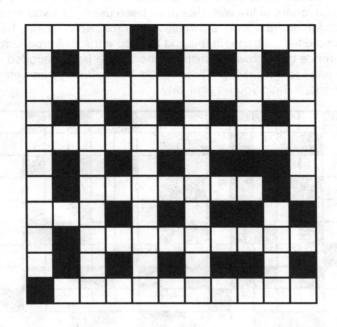

3 letters
GET

4 letters
ECHO
SIDE

5 letters
UNION

6 letters
MUTUAL

7 letters
COMICAL
LINSEED

9 letters
INTRODUCE

10 letters
ARITHMETIC
PERCUSSION
SWIMMINGLY

11 letters
DISTINCTIVE
INSTRUCTION
MAINTENANCE
UNCONSCIOUS

No 71

Codeword

Every letter in this crossword has been replaced by a number, the number remaining the same for that letter wherever it occurs in the grid. All 26 letters of the alphabet have been used. Can you substitute numbers for letters and thus complete the crossword? It may help to cross off the letters beneath the grid to keep a track of progress, and the reference box showing which numbers have been decoded can also be used to aid solving. Three letters have already been entered into the grid, to help you on your way.

	17	7	4	15	2	24	26	15		6		4		6
11			12		12			21	2	7	3	8	4	5
18	5	24	3	6	4	12	15	2		12		13		6
5			8		23			8	18	1	12	24	4	14
25	5	18	19	5	3	24	15	22		12		16		2
8		7			24			8	11	8				7
	13	7	12	4	18	8	14	15		23	8	22	26	7
10		15			16		7		8			8		19
24	18	8	26	23		7	12	23	15	24	9	8	19	
20			4	12	6				23			23		16
			R	**U**	**B**									
5		8		8		25	5	4	24	7	12	15	3	14
23	24	22	26	5	18	24			22		18			26
24		26		15		5	6	4	5	15	24	7	18	15
7	12	23	26	7	15	23			23		7			14
18		14		18		8	20	23	8	4	18	5	3	

A B C D E F G H I J K L M
N O P Q R S T U V W X Y Z

Reference Box

1	2	3	4	5	6	7	8	9	10	11	12	13
			R		**B**						**U**	

14	15	16	17	18	19	20	21	22	23	24	25	26

No 72

Around the Squares

The answer to each clue is a four-letter word, to be entered in the four squares surrounding the corresponding number in the grid. The word can start in any of the four squares and read either clockwise or anticlockwise. The first word has already been entered.

	T						
E	1	T	2	3	4	5	6
	X						
	7		8	9	10	11	12
	13		14	15	16	17	18
	19		20	21	22	23	24
	25		26	27	28	29	30
	31		32	33	34	35	36

1 Written part
2 Time period
3 Genuine
4 Small arrow
5 Concave mark
6 Relieve
7 Tuft-eared wildcat
8 Grinder
9 Chain component
10 Generous
11 Earthwards
12 Young horse

13 Sharp tug
14 Security device
15 As expected
16 Valuable fur
17 Tired, aged
18 Pleat
19 Young deer
20 End of a sleeve
21 Accurate, genuine
22 Rope tie
23 Rotate
24 Draw towards

25 Component
26 Toss, turn over
27 Ran away
28 Comestibles
29 Work implement
30 Trudge
31 Complain loudly
32 Top edge of a cup
33 Movie
34 Argument
35 Pliable
36 Settee

No 73
Farming Wordfit

Can you fit all the listed words into the grid? One is already in place.

3 letters
EWE
HOG
LEA
RYE

4 letters
BYRE ✓
CORN
COWS
CROP
DUCK
EGGS
GOAT
LAMB
PEAR
PIGS

PLUM
RAKE
SHED
YARD

5 letters
APPLE
DAIRY
GOOSE
GRAIN
SHEEP

6 letters
SICKLE
STABLE

7 letters
ACREAGE
ORGANIC
PICKING
TRACTOR

8 letters
CHICKENS
DRAINAGE

9 letters
SCARECROW
10 letters
CULTIVATOR

12 letters
OUTBUILDINGS

No 74

Geography Spiral

Solve the clues in the normal way and enter them into the grid in a clockwise spiral. The last letter of one answer is the first letter of the next. When finished, the letters in the shaded squares can be rearranged to form the name of a country.

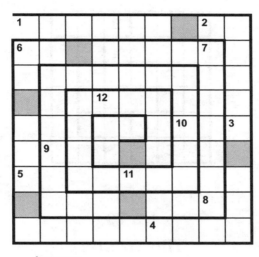

Answer: _____

1 Capital city of Hawaii (8)

2 Republic in east Africa (6)

3 Scotland's third-largest city (8)

4 Arm of the Atlantic Ocean (5,3)

5 The ___, Portuguese islands (6)

6 International London airport (8)

7 Irish county in north-west Ulster (7)

8 Former name of St Petersburg (9)

9 Low-lying region of California (5,6)

10 Town in West Flanders, Belgium (5)

11 Highest mountain in Wales (6)

12 Earth's second-largest island (3,6)

No 75
Logi-6

Every row and column of this grid should contain one each of the letters A, B, C, D, E and F. In addition, each of the shapes (shown marked by thicker lines) should also contain one each of these six letters. Can you complete the grid?

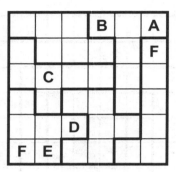

No 76
Tile Twister

Place the eight tiles into the puzzle grid so that all adjacent numbers on each tile match up. Tiles may be rotated through 360 degrees, but none may be flipped over.

Combiku

Each horizontal row and vertical column should contain five different shapes and five different numbers.

Every square will contain one number and one shape and no combination may be repeated anywhere else in the puzzle: for example, if a square has both a 4 and a star, then no other square will contain both a 4 and a star.

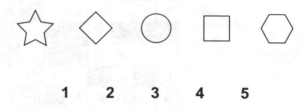

1   2   3   4   5

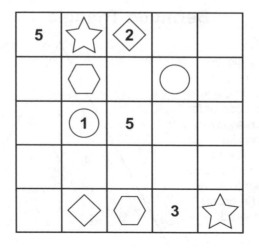

Alphabet Soup

Ladle the letters from the soup tureen and fit one into each of the
26 empty squares in the grid below, so that the finished result is a
complete crossword containing English words. All of the letters in the
tureen must be used – thus no letter is used more than once.

No 79

Bermuda Triangle

Travel through the
'Bermuda Triangle' by
visiting one room at a
time and collecting a letter
from each. You can enter
the outside passageway
as often as you like,
but can only visit each
room once. When you've
completed your tour, the
fifteen letters (in order)
will spell out a word.

The word is:

_____

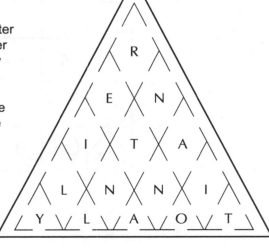

306

No 80
Couplets

The picture is of a central circle surrounded by shapes, linked to form six sets of three shapes apiece.
Can you complete the puzzle by placing each of the two-letter groups below, one per shape, so that every set of three (the central circle, plus the two matching shapes diagonally opposite one another) forms a six-letter word?
Whichever pair of letters you place in the central circle will appear in the middle of every word.

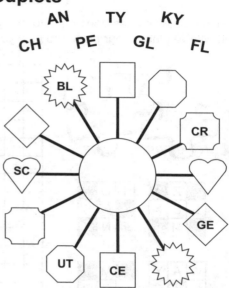

AN   TY   KY

CH   PE   GL   FL

No 81
Pyramid Plus

Every brick in this pyramid contains a number which is the sum of the two numbers below it, so that F=A+B, etc. Just work out the missing numbers!

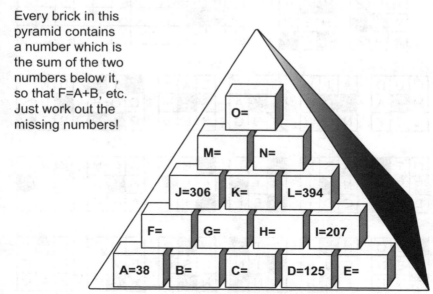

307

No 82
Jigword

This crossword has been cut into many pieces. Can you reassemble it? We've placed four pieces to give you a start.

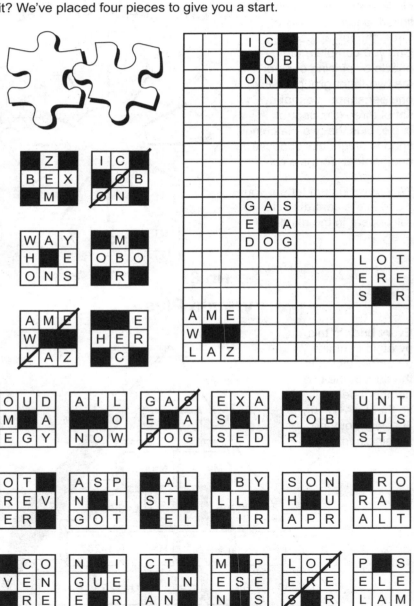

No 83
Kakuro

Only the numbers 1, 2, 3, 4, 5, 6, 7, 8 and 9 are used in this puzzle. Place one per blank square so that the numbers reading across total the number to the left of the block, and those reading down total the number above the block. No number appears more than once in a block, as in the example shown here:

No 84
Codeword

Every letter in this crossword has been replaced by a number, the number remaining the same for that letter wherever it occurs in the grid. All 26 letters of the alphabet have been used. Can you substitute numbers for letters and thus complete the crossword? It may help to cross off the letters beneath the grid to keep a track of progress, and the reference box showing which numbers have been decoded can also be used to aid solving. Three letters have already been entered into the grid, to help you on your way.

24	11	17	10	12	20	15	1		26	7	12	17	26	24
24		26		17			26			19		26		26
26	2	25	11	10	1		7	12	1	25	19	9	20	7
17		12		25		16		7				20		23
26	25	17	5	19	24	20		23	19	17	12	7	19	
		2		17		1		20				1		4
6	5	26	17	10		15	26	21	12	13	25	26	9	20
26			1				25			25				7
13	25	20	8	11	20	7	6	14		12	7	10	11	1
20		9				11		26		18		12		
	2	19	1	1	19	17		10	11	18	18	24	20	23
11		1			2		15		24		9		3	
15	22	12	25	17 **M**	12	15	5		13	12	20	25	6	20
20		15		26 **A**		11			7		12		24	
23	20	17	26	7 **N**	23		2	20	25	9	26	17	19	1

A B C D E F G H I J K L M

N O P Q R S T U V W X Y Z

Reference Box

| 1 | 2 | 3 | 4 | 5 | 6 | 7 **N** | 8 | 9 | 10 | 11 | 12 | 13 |
| 14 | 15 | 16 | 17 **M** | 18 | 19 | 20 | 21 | 22 | 23 | 24 | 25 | 26 **A** |

310

No 85
Domino Fit

A standard set of twenty-eight dominoes has been laid out as shown. Can you draw in the edges of them all? The check-box is provided as an aid and the dominoes already placed may help.

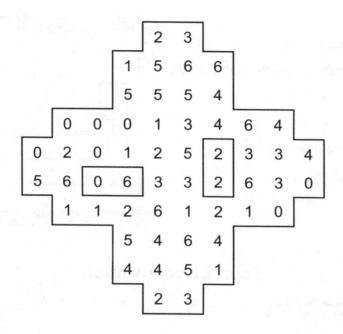

0-0	0-1	0-2	0-3	0-4	0-5	0-6	1-1	1-2
						✔		

1-3	1-4	1-5	1-6	2-2	2-3	2-4	2-5	2-6	3-3
				✔					

3-4	3-5	3-6	4-4	4-5	4-6	5-5	5-6	6-6

No 86
Egg-Timer

Can you complete this puzzle in the time it takes to boil an egg? The answers to the clues are anagrams of the words immediately above and below, plus or minus one letter.

1 Apple grove

2 Muslim woman's head covering

3 Secret stockpile

4 Highway

5 Love intensely

6 Felt hat

7 Prohibited

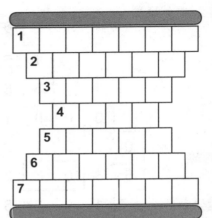

No 87
Total Concentration

The blank squares should be filled with whole numbers between 1 and 20 inclusive, any of which may occur more than once, or not at all. The numbers in every horizontal row add up to the totals on the right; whilst those in every vertical column add up to the totals along the bottom, as do the two long diagonal lines. Can you discover the missing numbers?

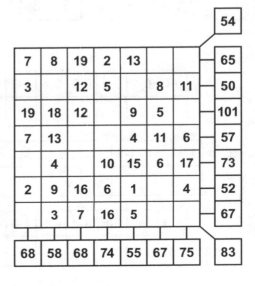

							54
7	8	19	2	13			65
3		12	5		8	11	50
19	18	12		9	5		101
7	13			4	11	6	57
	4		10	15	6	17	73
2	9	16	6	1		4	52
	3	7	16	5			67
68	58	68	74	55	67	75	83

No 88
Fill In

Using the list of words below, can you fill in this crossword? Each word is used only once and all are required to fill the grid. One word has been entered to get you started.

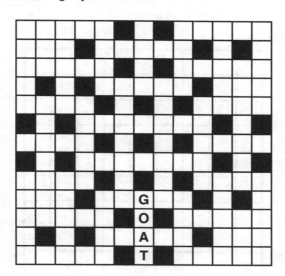

3 letters	GRAY	DAISY	SHRUB
ATE	INCH	HENNA	STAMP
CAN	KIWI	INGOT	SWEPT
HEN	PODS	LEANT	
NAP	RELY	LEAST	**7 letters**
TEA	THIS	LOTUS	AFRICAN
YOU	TOOL	OUNCE	HARPOON
		PLAYS	OPERATE
4 letters	**5 letters**	RAISE	RECIPES
ASPS	ANGST	RAKED	SCORPIO
BETA	ANKLE	REIGN	SOPRANO
BRED	BEECH	REPEL	
CASE	CAROB	SEIZE	
GOAT ✓	COATI	SHARE	

No 89
General Knowledge Spiral

Solve the clues in the normal way and enter them into the grid in a clockwise spiral. The last letter of one answer is the first letter of the next. When finished, the letters in the shaded squares can be rearranged to form the name of a country.

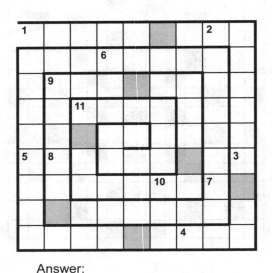

Answer: _____

1 Castel ____, papal summer residence (8)

2 Epic poem attributed to Homer (7)

3 Member of an international gang of Jamaican criminals (6)

4 Extensive marshy area of Florida (10)

5 Serious disease eradicated in the 1970s (8)

6 Hatred of foreigners (10)

7 Spanish-derived word for an ardent fan (10)

8 Group of oil-exporting nations (inits) (4)

9 Usual name for Charles the Great (742-814) (11)

10 Country, capital Tallinn (7)

11 Indigenous people born in a particular place, especially of Australia before the arrival of Europeans (10)

No 90
Fruits and Nuts Wordfit

Can you fit all the listed words into the grid? One is already in place.

3 letters
FIG

4 letters
LIME
PLUM ✓
UGLI

5 letters
GRAPE
LEMON
OLIVE

6 letters
CHERRY
LYCHEE
ORANGE
PAPAYA
QUINCE

7 letters
COCONUT
FILBERT
PUMPKIN
SATSUMA

8 letters
BEECHNUT
EGGPLANT

9 letters
NECTARINE
PINEAPPLE
TANGERINE

10 letters
CLEMENTINE

No 91
Numberfit

Can you fit all the listed numbers into the grid? Some are already in place.

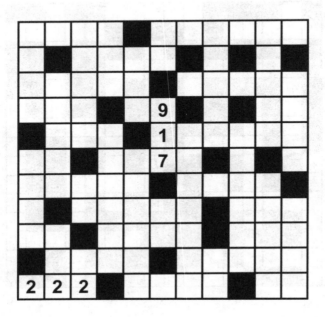

2 digits	3 digits	4 digits	5 digits	6 digits
25	103	2050	10440	157373
45	222 ✓	2506	14017	380718
51	337	2731	30296	561537
65	342	2869	36997	723023
69	522	2871	43048	864018
70	736	2893	49350	
72	826	5004	50936	**7 digits**
84	917 ✓	6304	64522	5150060
91	990	6934	67840	
99		7481	97503	
		8300		

No 92
Spidoku

In the spider's web, each of the eight segments should be filled with a different number from 1 to 8, in such a way that every ring also contains a different number from 1 to 8.

The segments run from the outside of the web to the center, and the rings run all the way around. So that you can see the rings more clearly, we've shaded them gray and white.

Some numbers are already in place. Can you fill in the rest?

1 2 3 4 5 6 7 8

No 93
Pyramid Plus

Every brick in this pyramid contains a number which is the sum of the two numbers below it, so that F=A+B, etc. Just work out the missing numbers!

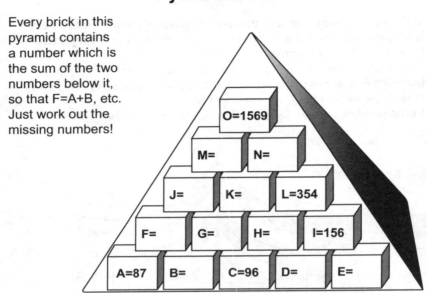

O=1569

M=   N=

J=   K=   L=354

F=   G=   H=   I=156

A=87   B=   C=96   D=   E=

No 94
Wordwheel

How many words of three or more letters can you make from those in the wheel, without using plurals, abbreviations or proper nouns? The central letter must appear once in every word and no letter in a section of the wheel may be used more than once. There is at least one nine-letter word in the wheel.

W N
P   O
  G
R   E
U D

_____
_____
_____
_____
_____
_____
_____
_____

318

Solutions

Solutions

No 1

2	7	4	3	1	5	9	6	8
5	8	9	4	2	6	7	1	3
1	6	3	9	7	8	4	5	2
6	5	7	2	3	1	8	4	9
4	2	8	5	6	9	1	3	7
9	3	1	8	4	7	5	2	6
7	9	2	1	5	3	6	8	4
8	4	5	6	9	2	3	7	1
3	1	6	7	8	4	2	9	5

No 2

1	6	7	8	4	2	3	5	9
5	9	2	6	3	1	8	7	4
8	3	4	9	7	5	6	2	1
7	5	6	3	1	4	9	8	2
4	8	1	5	2	9	7	6	3
3	2	9	7	8	6	1	4	5
6	1	5	4	9	8	2	3	7
2	4	3	1	6	7	5	9	8
9	7	8	2	5	3	4	1	6

No 3

9	5	8	3	4	6	7	1	2
2	1	4	5	7	8	3	6	9
6	3	7	9	1	2	5	4	8
4	2	1	6	9	5	8	7	3
3	9	5	7	8	1	4	2	6
8	7	6	2	3	4	1	9	5
5	8	9	4	6	7	2	3	1
1	4	3	8	2	9	6	5	7
7	6	2	1	5	3	9	8	4

No 4

8	7	1	4	3	6	2	9	5
6	3	2	8	5	9	7	1	4
9	5	4	2	7	1	6	8	3
7	1	5	6	4	8	3	2	9
2	9	8	3	1	5	4	7	6
3	4	6	9	2	7	1	5	8
5	6	3	1	9	2	8	4	7
1	8	7	5	6	4	9	3	2
4	2	9	7	8	3	5	6	1

No 5

7	9	4	2	6	1	8	5	3
1	3	2	5	8	9	7	4	6
6	5	8	3	4	7	9	1	2
4	2	1	9	7	8	6	3	5
5	7	3	6	2	4	1	8	9
8	6	9	1	5	3	2	7	4
3	1	7	4	9	6	5	2	8
2	4	6	8	1	5	3	9	7
9	8	5	7	3	2	4	6	1

No 6

6	1	9	5	4	3	8	7	2
5	7	2	9	6	8	3	1	4
8	3	4	2	7	1	5	9	6
7	8	1	3	2	4	6	5	9
3	4	5	6	8	9	7	2	1
9	2	6	1	5	7	4	8	3
1	9	7	8	3	6	2	4	5
2	6	8	4	1	5	9	3	7
4	5	3	7	9	2	1	6	8

Solutions

No 7

5	6	1	2	4	8	7	9	3
7	9	4	1	5	3	6	2	8
8	3	2	6	7	9	4	1	5
6	5	3	7	9	1	8	4	2
2	4	8	3	6	5	9	7	1
1	7	9	8	2	4	3	5	6
9	2	7	5	3	6	1	8	4
4	8	6	9	1	2	5	3	7
3	1	5	4	8	7	2	6	9

No 8

4	9	7	5	2	1	3	6	8
3	6	5	9	8	4	7	1	2
2	1	8	6	7	3	4	5	9
5	3	2	1	6	7	9	8	4
9	8	1	4	5	2	6	7	3
6	7	4	3	9	8	1	2	5
8	5	9	7	3	6	2	4	1
1	2	6	8	4	9	5	3	7
7	4	3	2	1	5	8	9	6

No 9

7	4	9	1	3	6	2	5	8
8	3	5	7	4	2	6	9	1
2	6	1	5	8	9	4	3	7
3	1	6	8	2	7	5	4	9
4	7	2	3	9	5	8	1	6
9	5	8	4	6	1	3	7	2
1	2	4	9	5	8	7	6	3
6	9	3	2	7	4	1	8	5
5	8	7	6	1	3	9	2	4

No 10

5	6	8	7	3	2	1	9	4
1	4	2	8	9	5	7	6	3
3	9	7	6	4	1	2	8	5
7	8	5	9	1	3	6	4	2
6	3	1	4	2	8	9	5	7
4	2	9	5	6	7	8	3	1
2	5	3	1	8	9	4	7	6
8	1	4	3	7	6	5	2	9
9	7	6	2	5	4	3	1	8

No 11

5	2	6	9	3	4	7	8	1
8	4	3	1	5	7	6	2	9
9	1	7	6	2	8	5	3	4
1	5	9	7	4	2	3	6	8
7	3	4	8	6	9	1	5	2
6	8	2	3	1	5	4	9	7
3	6	8	2	7	1	9	4	5
2	7	5	4	9	6	8	1	3
4	9	1	5	8	3	2	7	6

No 12

3	9	1	7	8	6	2	5	4
5	8	4	1	9	2	7	6	3
6	7	2	4	3	5	1	9	8
9	2	5	8	6	1	4	3	7
8	1	7	9	4	3	6	2	5
4	3	6	5	2	7	8	1	9
7	5	3	2	1	4	9	8	6
1	6	9	3	7	8	5	4	2
2	4	8	6	5	9	3	7	1

4	6	8
3	1	7
5	9	2

Solutions

No 13

1	3	9	6	5	4	7	2	8
6	7	5	8	3	2	1	9	4
2	8	4	9	1	7	6	3	5
7	9	2	5	6	8	3	4	1
3	1	8	2	4	9	5	7	6
5	4	6	1	7	3	2	8	9
4	5	3	7	9	1	8	6	2
8	6	7	4	2	5	9	1	3
9	2	1	3	8	6	4	5	7

No 14

5	9	2	1	7	4	6	8	3
4	3	6	5	2	8	7	1	9
1	7	8	3	6	9	4	5	2
9	6	5	4	3	2	1	7	8
2	1	3	8	5	7	9	4	6
7	8	4	6	9	1	3	2	5
3	5	1	2	4	6	8	9	7
8	2	7	9	1	3	5	6	4
6	4	9	7	8	5	2	3	1

No 15

1	6	4	9	8	7	3	2	5
8	3	7	1	2	5	9	6	4
2	5	9	6	3	4	1	8	7
6	7	2	4	5	3	8	1	9
9	8	5	7	1	2	6	4	3
4	1	3	8	9	6	5	7	2
3	4	6	5	7	8	2	9	1
7	2	1	3	6	9	4	5	8
5	9	8	2	4	1	7	3	6

No 16

2	1	7	8	5	3	9	6	4
5	9	6	4	7	2	8	3	1
3	4	8	9	1	6	2	5	7
8	7	9	3	2	1	5	4	6
1	3	5	6	4	9	7	2	8
6	2	4	7	8	5	1	9	3
4	5	1	2	6	7	3	8	9
7	8	3	5	9	4	6	1	2
9	6	2	1	3	8	4	7	5

No 17

9	2	6	5	3	8	7	1	4
4	3	7	1	9	6	2	5	8
8	1	5	4	7	2	9	6	3
1	5	3	8	6	7	4	2	9
6	8	9	2	4	1	3	7	5
7	4	2	9	5	3	1	8	6
2	9	4	7	8	5	6	3	1
5	6	1	3	2	9	8	4	7
3	7	8	6	1	4	5	9	2

No 18

6	5	2	9	7	3	4	1	8
4	8	7	5	6	1	3	9	2
3	1	9	8	2	4	6	7	5
9	2	8	4	1	6	5	3	7
5	7	6	2	3	9	8	4	1
1	3	4	7	8	5	9	2	6
2	4	3	6	5	7	1	8	9
7	6	1	3	9	8	2	5	4
8	9	5	1	4	2	7	6	3

Solutions

No 19

8	3	6	7	9	1	4	5	2
5	2	9	6	4	3	1	8	7
4	1	7	2	8	5	3	9	6
3	7	2	1	6	8	9	4	5
6	8	4	9	5	2	7	1	3
1	9	5	3	7	4	2	6	8
2	5	8	4	3	9	6	7	1
7	4	1	8	2	6	5	3	9
9	6	3	5	1	7	8	2	4

No 20

4	1	2	3	8	6	5	7	9
9	5	3	2	4	7	6	1	8
8	7	6	9	1	5	3	4	2
3	4	7	8	2	1	9	5	6
6	9	1	5	3	4	2	8	7
2	8	5	6	7	9	1	3	4
1	3	9	7	6	8	4	2	5
7	6	4	1	5	2	8	9	3
5	2	8	4	9	3	7	6	1

No 21

6	1	9	8	3	7	2	5	4
4	7	2	6	5	1	9	3	8
3	5	8	9	4	2	1	7	6
8	4	1	2	7	6	5	9	3
2	6	5	1	9	3	8	4	7
9	3	7	4	8	5	6	1	2
1	8	4	3	6	9	7	2	5
5	9	6	7	2	4	3	8	1
7	2	3	5	1	8	4	6	9

No 22

9	4	3	7	6	1	2	8	5
2	7	5	9	4	8	6	3	1
1	6	8	2	3	5	4	7	9
5	1	2	3	8	6	7	9	4
6	3	9	4	5	7	1	2	8
4	8	7	1	9	2	3	5	6
8	9	4	6	7	3	5	1	2
3	2	6	5	1	9	8	4	7
7	5	1	8	2	4	9	6	3

No 23

4	3	2	9	8	7	5	1	6
5	8	6	4	1	3	7	9	2
7	1	9	6	5	2	4	3	8
2	7	1	3	9	4	8	6	5
8	9	5	7	6	1	2	4	3
6	4	3	5	2	8	1	7	9
3	5	4	2	7	9	6	8	1
1	2	7	8	3	6	9	5	4
9	6	8	1	4	5	3	2	7

No 24

3	2	4	9	8	5	7	6	1
6	1	5	2	7	3	9	4	8
9	7	8	1	4	6	2	5	3
4	6	2	7	3	8	1	9	5
8	9	3	6	5	1	4	2	7
7	5	1	4	9	2	3	8	6
2	3	6	8	1	9	5	7	4
5	8	7	3	2	4	6	1	9
1	4	9	5	6	7	8	3	2

4	6	8
3	1	7
5	9	2

1	9	8
3	5	2
4	6	7

Solutions

No 25

9	2	5	1	3	6	7	8	4
7	4	3	2	8	9	6	1	5
8	6	1	4	5	7	9	3	2
1	8	2	5	9	4	3	7	6
5	3	7	6	1	8	4	2	9
6	9	4	3	7	2	1	5	8
2	5	9	7	6	3	8	4	1
4	7	8	9	2	1	5	6	3
3	1	6	8	4	5	2	9	7

No 26

9	1	4	8	2	5	7	3	6
5	3	8	7	6	4	9	2	1
6	2	7	3	1	9	4	8	5
7	8	5	2	9	6	3	1	4
3	6	9	1	4	8	2	5	7
1	4	2	5	3	7	8	6	9
4	5	6	9	8	2	1	7	3
2	7	3	4	5	1	6	9	8
8	9	1	6	7	3	5	4	2

No 27

1	9	6	8	5	4	2	3	7
7	2	4	6	3	9	5	8	1
3	5	8	2	1	7	9	4	6
9	4	1	7	6	2	3	5	8
6	3	5	9	8	1	4	7	2
2	8	7	5	4	3	1	6	9
4	1	9	3	7	8	6	2	5
8	6	3	1	2	5	7	9	4
5	7	2	4	9	6	8	1	3

No 28

4	3	1	7	8	5	6	9	2
5	7	2	9	6	3	4	1	8
6	8	9	1	2	4	5	3	7
9	5	8	4	3	6	7	2	1
1	4	3	2	5	7	9	8	6
7	2	6	8	1	9	3	5	4
3	1	7	6	9	8	2	4	5
2	9	4	5	7	1	8	6	3
8	6	5	3	4	2	1	7	9

No 29

9	2	6	3	8	5	4	1	7
3	1	4	9	2	7	6	5	8
7	8	5	6	4	1	9	2	3
8	4	2	7	1	6	5	3	9
1	7	9	4	5	3	2	8	6
6	5	3	2	9	8	1	7	4
2	6	7	1	3	9	8	4	5
5	3	1	8	6	4	7	9	2
4	9	8	5	7	2	3	6	1

No 30

1	4	8	9	7	5	2	6	3
9	2	7	3	4	6	5	1	8
3	6	5	1	2	8	9	7	4
7	5	6	8	9	2	3	4	1
2	8	1	4	6	3	7	9	5
4	3	9	5	1	7	8	2	6
8	9	4	7	3	1	6	5	2
5	7	2	6	8	4	1	3	9
6	1	3	2	5	9	4	8	7

5	1	4
8	3	6
9	2	7

Solutions

No 31

7	4	8	2	3	1	5	9	6
3	1	6	4	9	5	8	2	7
5	9	2	8	7	6	1	3	4
8	2	7	5	1	9	4	6	3
4	6	5	3	2	7	9	8	1
1	3	9	6	4	8	2	7	5
9	7	4	1	8	3	6	5	2
6	8	1	7	5	2	3	4	9
2	5	3	9	6	4	7	1	8

No 32

8	5	9	1	7	6	3	4	2
3	1	2	4	8	5	9	6	7
6	7	4	3	9	2	5	8	1
7	6	1	9	4	8	2	3	5
9	2	8	5	1	3	4	7	6
4	3	5	2	6	7	1	9	8
2	4	6	7	3	1	8	5	9
1	9	7	8	5	4	6	2	3
5	8	3	6	2	9	7	1	4

No 33

1	2	8	5	9	6	7	4	3
7	4	6	3	2	1	9	5	8
9	5	3	7	4	8	2	1	6
8	3	7	9	5	4	6	2	1
5	1	4	6	3	2	8	9	7
6	9	2	8	1	7	5	3	4
3	6	9	4	8	5	1	7	2
2	8	5	1	7	3	4	6	9
4	7	1	2	6	9	3	8	5

No 34

6	1	2	3	7	5	9	8	4
8	4	5	2	6	9	7	1	3
7	9	3	4	8	1	6	2	5
4	7	8	5	9	2	3	6	1
3	5	1	7	4	6	2	9	8
9	2	6	8	1	3	5	4	7
2	6	7	1	3	4	8	5	9
1	3	9	6	5	8	4	7	2
5	8	4	9	2	7	1	3	6

No 35

8	7	2	6	9	5	3	4	1
1	5	6	7	3	4	2	9	8
9	3	4	1	2	8	7	6	5
6	2	5	3	4	7	8	1	9
3	4	8	9	1	2	5	7	6
7	1	9	8	5	6	4	2	3
2	9	3	4	8	1	6	5	7
4	8	7	5	6	9	1	3	2
5	6	1	2	7	3	9	8	4

No 36

2	4	6	7	3	1	9	5	8
8	7	1	9	6	5	3	4	2
9	3	5	2	4	8	6	1	7
1	6	9	5	8	7	4	2	3
7	2	3	4	9	6	5	8	1
5	8	4	3	1	2	7	6	9
4	1	2	6	7	3	8	9	5
6	5	7	8	2	9	1	3	4
3	9	8	1	5	4	2	7	6

4	6	8
3	1	7
5	9	2

Solutions

No 37

9	7	2	5	3	8	1	4	6
3	6	8	9	4	1	5	7	2
1	4	5	7	2	6	3	9	8
2	1	9	6	8	5	4	3	7
4	3	6	2	1	7	8	5	9
5	8	7	4	9	3	6	2	1
6	5	1	3	7	9	2	8	4
7	2	3	8	6	4	9	1	5
8	9	4	1	5	2	7	6	3

No 38

9	1	8	5	6	4	3	2	7
2	5	4	1	7	3	6	8	9
6	7	3	8	2	9	1	4	5
3	2	6	7	4	1	5	9	8
4	8	7	3	9	5	2	1	6
1	9	5	6	8	2	7	3	4
7	4	9	2	1	6	8	5	3
5	6	1	9	3	8	4	7	2
8	3	2	4	5	7	9	6	1

No 39

7	5	8	2	1	3	6	9	4
9	4	2	8	7	6	3	1	5
6	1	3	9	5	4	2	8	7
1	8	4	7	3	2	5	6	9
2	3	7	5	6	9	8	4	1
5	6	9	1	4	8	7	2	3
8	9	1	3	2	5	4	7	6
3	7	6	4	8	1	9	5	2
4	2	5	6	9	7	1	3	8

No 40

8	9	3	4	6	7	1	2	5
2	5	4	3	1	8	6	7	9
1	7	6	5	9	2	4	8	3
3	2	1	9	8	6	7	5	4
7	4	8	1	3	5	2	9	6
9	6	5	7	2	4	8	3	1
5	8	2	6	4	9	3	1	7
4	1	7	2	5	3	9	6	8
6	3	9	8	7	1	5	4	2

No 41

4	3	7	2	6	9	1	8	5
2	1	6	8	5	7	9	3	4
8	9	5	3	4	1	2	7	6
7	5	9	6	2	4	8	1	3
1	4	2	9	3	8	6	5	7
3	6	8	1	7	5	4	9	2
9	7	3	4	8	6	5	2	1
6	2	1	5	9	3	7	4	8
5	8	4	7	1	2	3	6	9

No 42

1	7	6	5	8	4	9	2	3
3	5	9	1	6	2	7	4	8
2	4	8	7	3	9	5	6	1
4	9	3	6	2	8	1	5	7
5	6	2	3	7	1	8	9	4
7	8	1	9	4	5	2	3	6
6	2	5	4	1	7	3	8	9
9	1	4	8	5	3	6	7	2
8	3	7	2	9	6	4	1	5

Solutions

No 43

7	3	1	9	2	8	6	4	5
5	4	6	7	1	3	9	8	2
2	9	8	4	5	6	1	7	3
4	5	9	8	6	2	3	1	7
6	8	3	1	4	7	2	5	9
1	2	7	3	9	5	8	6	4
9	7	4	2	8	1	5	3	6
3	1	5	6	7	9	4	2	8
8	6	2	5	3	4	7	9	1

No 44

2	9	5	3	7	8	1	4	6
7	6	8	9	1	4	5	2	3
1	3	4	2	6	5	9	8	7
8	5	3	6	2	9	4	7	1
9	2	1	4	5	7	6	3	8
6	4	7	8	3	1	2	5	9
5	8	6	7	9	2	3	1	4
4	1	9	5	8	3	7	6	2
3	7	2	1	4	6	8	9	5

No 45

4	2	1	3	9	8	6	5	7
5	7	6	4	1	2	9	3	8
3	8	9	5	6	7	1	4	2
7	9	3	2	5	6	4	8	1
8	1	4	7	3	9	5	2	6
2	6	5	8	4	1	3	7	9
1	5	2	9	8	4	7	6	3
6	3	7	1	2	5	8	9	4
9	4	8	6	7	3	2	1	5

No 46

5	1	8	4	2	7	9	3	6
9	2	6	1	3	8	4	5	7
7	4	3	6	9	5	1	8	2
4	3	5	8	6	1	7	2	9
1	6	2	7	5	9	8	4	3
8	9	7	2	4	3	6	1	5
2	8	9	5	7	4	3	6	1
6	7	1	3	8	2	5	9	4
3	5	4	9	1	6	2	7	8

No 47

2	5	4	3	8	7	1	6	9
9	8	1	6	2	5	3	7	4
7	6	3	4	9	1	2	5	8
4	2	5	9	1	8	6	3	7
8	1	9	7	3	6	5	4	2
3	7	6	2	5	4	8	9	1
5	4	8	1	6	9	7	2	3
1	3	7	5	4	2	9	8	6
6	9	2	8	7	3	4	1	5

No 48

6	4	2	7	9	8	5	3	1
9	8	7	1	5	3	2	4	6
3	1	5	4	6	2	8	7	9
4	2	8	3	7	6	1	9	5
7	6	9	5	4	1	3	8	2
1	5	3	8	2	9	7	6	4
2	3	6	9	8	5	4	1	7
8	9	4	2	1	7	6	5	3
5	7	1	6	3	4	9	2	8

4 6 8
3 1 7
5 9 2

Solutions

No 49

2	4	6	3	5	8	9	7	1
8	9	1	4	7	6	3	5	2
3	5	7	9	2	1	8	4	6
9	1	2	7	8	3	4	6	5
5	3	4	1	6	9	7	2	8
7	6	8	2	4	5	1	3	9
1	2	9	6	3	7	5	8	4
4	8	3	5	1	2	6	9	7
6	7	5	8	9	4	2	1	3

No 50

8	1	4	9	5	3	6	2	7
2	6	5	8	1	7	9	4	3
3	9	7	6	4	2	5	1	8
5	3	6	4	2	9	8	7	1
4	2	8	1	7	6	3	9	5
9	7	1	5	3	8	2	6	4
1	8	3	2	6	4	7	5	9
6	5	9	7	8	1	4	3	2
7	4	2	3	9	5	1	8	6

No 51

3	4	5	8	1	2	9	7	6
8	2	7	9	5	6	1	3	4
9	6	1	3	7	4	8	2	5
1	8	4	6	3	5	2	9	7
7	5	2	4	9	1	6	8	3
6	9	3	2	8	7	4	5	1
2	1	9	5	4	3	7	6	8
5	7	6	1	2	8	3	4	9
4	3	8	7	6	9	5	1	2

No 52

5	7	1	2	3	6	9	8	4
9	3	2	5	4	8	1	6	7
6	8	4	7	1	9	5	3	2
2	6	9	4	8	5	3	7	1
4	5	8	3	7	1	2	9	6
7	1	3	9	6	2	8	4	5
3	2	6	1	9	7	4	5	8
1	4	7	8	5	3	6	2	9
8	9	5	6	2	4	7	1	3

No 53

1	2	9	6	4	7	8	3	5
4	6	3	9	8	5	7	1	2
5	7	8	3	1	2	4	9	6
3	8	2	7	6	1	5	4	9
9	1	6	5	3	4	2	8	7
7	4	5	2	9	8	1	6	3
2	3	1	8	5	9	6	7	4
6	5	4	1	7	3	9	2	8
8	9	7	4	2	6	3	5	1

No 54

8	5	1	6	2	3	7	9	4
2	3	4	7	5	9	1	6	8
9	6	7	4	8	1	2	3	5
4	2	3	8	1	5	6	7	9
5	1	8	9	7	6	3	4	2
7	9	6	2	3	4	5	8	1
3	4	5	1	6	8	9	2	7
6	8	2	5	9	7	4	1	3
1	7	9	3	4	2	8	5	6

Solutions

No 55

5	7	2	9	4	6	8	1	3
4	9	1	3	7	8	5	2	6
3	6	8	1	2	5	9	4	7
7	5	9	8	3	4	2	6	1
8	4	3	6	1	2	7	5	9
2	1	6	5	9	7	3	8	4
9	8	5	7	6	1	4	3	2
6	3	4	2	8	9	1	7	5
1	2	7	4	5	3	6	9	8

No 56

9	1	6	5	4	8	3	2	7
5	2	4	7	9	3	1	6	8
3	7	8	6	1	2	5	9	4
6	3	1	4	5	7	2	8	9
2	4	5	8	6	9	7	1	3
7	8	9	2	3	1	4	5	6
1	5	7	9	8	4	6	3	2
8	6	2	3	7	5	9	4	1
4	9	3	1	2	6	8	7	5

No 57

6	9	3	4	7	5	2	1	8
2	1	8	3	6	9	5	4	7
7	5	4	1	8	2	6	9	3
8	2	1	9	3	6	7	5	4
3	6	9	5	4	7	8	2	1
4	7	5	2	1	8	3	6	9
1	8	2	6	9	3	4	7	5
5	4	7	8	2	1	9	3	6
9	3	6	7	5	4	1	8	2

No 58

6	5	8	4	7	2	1	3	9
1	2	4	9	5	3	7	6	8
3	9	7	8	1	6	5	2	4
5	8	2	6	9	1	3	4	7
9	4	6	3	8	7	2	1	5
7	1	3	2	4	5	9	8	6
8	3	9	7	2	4	6	5	1
4	6	5	1	3	9	8	7	2
2	7	1	5	6	8	4	9	3

No 59

5	3	4	6	1	2	8	7	9
6	9	7	5	8	3	1	2	4
2	1	8	4	9	7	5	6	3
7	5	9	2	3	6	4	1	8
1	6	3	8	5	4	7	9	2
8	4	2	1	7	9	6	3	5
4	7	6	3	2	8	9	5	1
9	2	1	7	4	5	3	8	6
3	8	5	9	6	1	2	4	7

No 60

4	3	5	9	8	2	7	6	1
1	7	9	3	5	6	8	2	4
2	8	6	7	1	4	5	9	3
7	5	3	4	9	1	2	8	6
8	9	2	5	6	3	4	1	7
6	4	1	2	7	8	3	5	9
3	1	4	6	2	5	9	7	8
5	6	7	8	4	9	1	3	2
9	2	8	1	3	7	6	4	5

4	6	8
3	1	7
5	9	2

1	9	8
3	5	2
4	6	7

Solutions

No 61

3	4	2	6	5	7	9	8	1
8	6	9	3	4	1	2	7	5
7	1	5	9	8	2	3	4	6
6	2	4	8	7	9	5	1	3
9	7	3	1	2	5	8	6	4
1	5	8	4	6	3	7	2	9
2	9	6	7	3	4	1	5	8
5	8	1	2	9	6	4	3	7
4	3	7	5	1	8	6	9	2

No 62

6	4	1	8	5	9	2	3	7
2	7	9	4	1	3	5	6	8
5	8	3	2	7	6	4	1	9
9	6	5	3	4	2	8	7	1
8	2	4	7	9	1	3	5	6
3	1	7	5	6	8	9	2	4
7	3	6	9	8	5	1	4	2
1	9	2	6	3	4	7	8	5
4	5	8	1	2	7	6	9	3

No 63

3	2	8	4	5	7	1	9	6
5	9	6	8	1	2	7	4	3
1	7	4	6	3	9	2	5	8
4	8	2	9	6	5	3	1	7
9	1	5	7	8	3	4	6	2
7	6	3	2	4	1	5	8	9
6	4	7	5	2	8	9	3	1
2	5	1	3	9	6	8	7	4
8	3	9	1	7	4	6	2	5

No 64

5	4	9	7	2	1	6	3	8
3	7	8	9	6	5	4	1	2
2	1	6	3	4	8	5	9	7
8	2	7	4	1	6	9	5	3
9	5	4	2	7	3	1	8	6
6	3	1	8	5	9	7	2	4
4	6	3	5	9	2	8	7	1
7	9	2	1	8	4	3	6	5
1	8	5	6	3	7	2	4	9

No 65

9	2	8	1	4	5	7	6	3
6	4	7	3	2	9	5	8	1
3	1	5	6	7	8	2	4	9
1	9	2	7	8	4	3	5	6
5	6	4	2	1	3	9	7	8
7	8	3	5	9	6	4	1	2
4	7	1	9	6	2	8	3	5
8	3	9	4	5	1	6	2	7
2	5	6	8	3	7	1	9	4

No 66

9	2	8	3	1	6	7	5	4
3	1	5	9	7	4	2	8	6
6	4	7	8	5	2	9	1	3
5	9	2	6	3	7	1	4	8
4	8	1	2	9	5	6	3	7
7	6	3	4	8	1	5	9	2
8	7	9	5	6	3	4	2	1
2	5	6	1	4	8	3	7	9
1	3	4	7	2	9	8	6	5

5	1	4
8	3	6
9	2	7

Solutions

No 67

2	8	1	7	3	5	9	6	4
3	6	9	1	4	8	5	2	7
4	5	7	6	9	2	3	8	1
9	1	2	4	8	6	7	3	5
6	3	5	9	2	7	1	4	8
7	4	8	3	5	1	2	9	6
1	7	4	2	6	9	8	5	3
5	2	3	8	1	4	6	7	9
8	9	6	5	7	3	4	1	2

No 68

4	6	9	7	8	3	5	1	2
7	3	1	2	4	5	6	8	9
5	8	2	9	1	6	3	4	7
6	7	4	1	5	9	8	2	3
3	9	5	8	6	2	4	7	1
1	2	8	4	3	7	9	5	6
2	5	6	3	7	8	1	9	4
9	4	3	5	2	1	7	6	8
8	1	7	6	9	4	2	3	5

No 69

5	9	6	1	3	2	8	7	4
1	3	2	8	7	4	9	6	5
8	7	4	9	6	5	3	2	1
7	4	8	6	5	9	2	1	3
3	2	1	7	4	8	6	5	9
9	6	5	3	2	1	7	4	8
6	5	9	2	1	3	4	8	7
2	1	3	4	8	7	5	9	6
4	8	7	5	9	6	1	3	2

No 70

9	1	8	6	2	4	5	3	7
2	4	7	3	9	5	8	6	1
3	6	5	1	8	7	2	4	9
7	8	6	5	4	1	9	2	3
1	5	9	2	3	6	4	7	8
4	3	2	8	7	9	6	1	5
8	9	3	4	1	2	7	5	6
5	2	1	7	6	8	3	9	4
6	7	4	9	5	3	1	8	2

No 71

5	6	7	8	4	3	9	1	2
9	1	4	6	2	7	8	3	5
8	2	3	9	5	1	6	7	4
7	4	5	1	9	2	3	8	6
3	9	6	7	8	5	2	4	1
1	8	2	3	6	4	5	9	7
4	5	1	2	3	8	7	6	9
2	3	9	4	7	6	1	5	8
6	7	8	5	1	9	4	2	3

No 72

5	2	6	3	4	8	1	7	9
3	7	1	6	2	9	4	5	8
4	9	8	5	7	1	2	3	6
6	4	3	8	5	7	9	1	2
7	8	9	1	3	2	5	6	4
2	1	5	9	6	4	3	8	7
8	5	7	4	9	3	6	2	1
1	3	4	2	8	6	7	9	5
9	6	2	7	1	5	8	4	3

Solutions

No 73

6	4	7	2	8	3	5	9	1
8	1	5	4	6	9	7	3	2
9	3	2	5	1	7	8	4	6
2	7	3	8	4	6	1	5	9
1	5	9	7	3	2	4	6	8
4	8	6	9	5	1	2	7	3
7	6	8	1	9	5	3	2	4
3	2	1	6	7	4	9	8	5
5	9	4	3	2	8	6	1	7

No 74

1	8	2	4	5	6	3	9	7
6	9	7	8	2	3	1	5	4
3	5	4	1	7	9	2	6	8
8	2	5	3	6	4	9	7	1
7	1	9	5	8	2	4	3	6
4	6	3	7	9	1	5	8	2
2	7	8	9	1	5	6	4	3
5	4	6	2	3	8	7	1	9
9	3	1	6	4	7	8	2	5

No 75

5	4	3	8	6	7	1	2	9
9	1	7	3	2	5	8	6	4
2	6	8	9	1	4	3	5	7
6	8	5	7	3	2	4	9	1
3	7	2	1	4	9	5	8	6
1	9	4	6	5	8	2	7	3
8	2	9	4	7	3	6	1	5
4	5	6	2	9	1	7	3	8
7	3	1	5	8	6	9	4	2

No 76

3	4	1	6	5	9	2	7	8
6	5	8	7	2	1	3	4	9
9	7	2	3	8	4	5	1	6
4	9	3	8	7	2	1	6	5
1	6	5	9	4	3	8	2	7
2	8	7	1	6	5	4	9	3
7	1	6	4	3	8	9	5	2
5	3	4	2	9	7	6	8	1
8	2	9	5	1	6	7	3	4

No 77

6	2	4	1	9	3	5	8	7
7	9	5	8	6	4	1	3	2
3	1	8	2	5	7	4	6	9
4	8	6	9	1	2	7	5	3
1	7	9	3	4	5	6	2	8
5	3	2	7	8	6	9	1	4
9	4	1	6	3	8	2	7	5
2	6	3	5	7	9	8	4	1
8	5	7	4	2	1	3	9	6

No 78

9	4	8	2	3	7	5	6	1
1	3	6	5	9	4	2	8	7
7	2	5	8	1	6	4	3	9
6	9	7	3	4	2	1	5	8
5	1	4	9	6	8	3	7	2
2	8	3	7	5	1	6	9	4
4	5	1	6	8	9	7	2	3
8	6	2	4	7	3	9	1	5
3	7	9	1	2	5	8	4	6

Solutions

No 79

4	6	1	2	5	9	3	8	7
8	5	2	7	3	4	1	9	6
7	3	9	6	8	1	2	5	4
3	9	7	8	2	5	4	6	1
2	8	5	4	1	6	7	3	9
6	1	4	9	7	3	8	2	5
5	4	3	1	6	8	9	7	2
1	2	6	3	9	7	5	4	8
9	7	8	5	4	2	6	1	3

No 80

2	7	8	1	5	3	4	9	6
5	6	1	4	8	9	7	2	3
3	4	9	7	6	2	1	8	5
9	8	5	3	4	1	2	6	7
7	1	3	9	2	6	8	5	4
6	2	4	5	7	8	9	3	1
1	3	6	2	9	4	5	7	8
4	9	7	8	3	5	6	1	2
8	5	2	6	1	7	3	4	9

No 81

2	1	6	9	5	4	7	3	8
8	3	9	7	1	6	2	4	5
4	7	5	2	8	3	6	9	1
9	6	7	5	4	8	1	2	3
3	4	8	1	2	9	5	7	6
1	5	2	3	6	7	4	8	9
7	8	1	6	9	2	3	5	4
6	2	4	8	3	5	9	1	7
5	9	3	4	7	1	8	6	2

No 82

4	3	2	6	5	8	1	9	7
5	8	7	2	1	9	4	6	3
6	1	9	3	4	7	5	8	2
8	7	1	4	9	2	3	5	6
3	9	5	8	6	1	7	2	4
2	6	4	5	7	3	8	1	9
9	5	8	7	2	4	6	3	1
1	4	6	9	3	5	2	7	8
7	2	3	1	8	6	9	4	5

No 83

9	6	7	2	3	1	8	4	5
3	4	8	5	9	7	2	6	1
2	5	1	4	8	6	3	7	9
4	9	6	7	2	8	5	1	3
8	7	2	1	5	3	4	9	6
1	3	5	6	4	9	7	2	8
7	8	4	9	1	5	6	3	2
6	1	3	8	7	2	9	5	4
5	2	9	3	6	4	1	8	7

No 84

2	8	3	6	9	4	5	1	7
7	1	4	5	8	2	9	6	3
9	5	6	7	3	1	8	2	4
8	4	5	2	6	3	1	7	9
1	7	9	4	5	8	2	3	6
3	6	2	1	7	9	4	8	5
4	9	7	8	1	6	3	5	2
6	2	1	3	4	5	7	9	8
5	3	8	9	2	7	6	4	1

4	6	8
3	1	7
5	9	2

Solutions

No 85

9	8	4	7	2	5	6	1	3
2	6	7	8	1	3	9	5	4
3	1	5	6	9	4	8	2	7
6	4	1	5	7	9	2	3	8
8	7	9	3	6	2	1	4	5
5	3	2	4	8	1	7	9	6
4	9	6	1	3	8	5	7	2
7	2	3	9	5	6	4	8	1
1	5	8	2	4	7	3	6	9

No 86

4	9	2	3	5	1	6	8	7
1	5	8	2	7	6	9	3	4
6	7	3	9	8	4	1	5	2
3	1	4	8	9	2	5	7	6
7	2	9	6	4	5	3	1	8
5	8	6	1	3	7	4	2	9
8	4	1	5	2	9	7	6	3
2	6	7	4	1	3	8	9	5
9	3	5	7	6	8	2	4	1

No 87

4	1	7	6	3	9	2	8	5
3	5	2	8	4	1	6	9	7
8	6	9	7	2	5	1	3	4
7	8	3	4	6	2	5	1	9
1	2	6	5	9	3	4	7	8
5	9	4	1	7	8	3	6	2
2	4	8	3	1	7	9	5	6
9	7	1	2	5	6	8	4	3
6	3	5	9	8	4	7	2	1

No 88

6	8	3	2	1	9	7	5	4
4	2	5	8	7	6	1	9	3
1	9	7	5	4	3	8	2	6
7	1	8	6	9	5	3	4	2
9	3	4	1	8	2	5	6	7
2	5	6	4	3	7	9	8	1
3	6	2	9	5	1	4	7	8
8	7	9	3	2	4	6	1	5
5	4	1	7	6	8	2	3	9

No 89

3	2	5	9	8	4	7	1	6
6	4	1	5	3	7	2	8	9
7	8	9	2	1	6	4	5	3
9	3	8	1	6	2	5	4	7
4	5	7	3	9	8	1	6	2
1	6	2	4	7	5	9	3	8
5	7	4	6	2	3	8	9	1
8	9	3	7	5	1	6	2	4
2	1	6	8	4	9	3	7	5

No 90

5	6	3	4	2	9	8	1	7
1	4	2	7	8	6	5	3	9
8	9	7	3	5	1	2	4	6
3	8	4	9	1	5	7	6	2
7	2	9	6	4	3	1	5	8
6	5	1	8	7	2	4	9	3
9	7	8	5	6	4	3	2	1
2	3	5	1	9	7	6	8	4
4	1	6	2	3	8	9	7	5

Solutions

7	8	5
2	9	6
4	3	1

No 91

2	8	3	1	7	4	6	5	9
7	5	9	8	6	3	1	4	2
6	1	4	5	2	9	8	7	3
1	9	2	6	4	8	7	3	5
5	6	7	2	3	1	4	9	8
4	3	8	7	9	5	2	6	1
9	4	1	3	8	7	5	2	6
8	7	6	9	5	2	3	1	4
3	2	5	4	1	6	9	8	7

No 92

7	8	9	3	1	4	6	2	5
5	4	2	9	6	7	1	8	3
3	6	1	2	8	5	7	9	4
8	9	5	6	7	2	4	3	1
6	3	7	1	4	9	2	5	8
2	1	4	8	5	3	9	7	6
4	7	6	5	2	8	3	1	9
1	5	3	7	9	6	8	4	2
9	2	8	4	3	1	5	6	7

No 93

7	1	5	6	3	9	8	2	4
6	4	8	1	7	2	5	9	3
2	3	9	4	8	5	1	6	7
1	7	4	5	6	8	2	3	9
9	6	3	7	2	1	4	8	5
8	5	2	9	4	3	6	7	1
5	8	1	2	9	7	3	4	6
4	2	7	3	5	6	9	1	8
3	9	6	8	1	4	7	5	2

No 94

2	9	6	7	8	4	1	3	5
7	4	3	1	9	5	2	8	6
8	5	1	2	3	6	7	9	4
9	2	8	3	5	1	4	6	7
6	7	5	9	4	2	8	1	3
3	1	4	8	6	7	5	2	9
5	3	7	6	2	8	9	4	1
1	8	9	4	7	3	6	5	2
4	6	2	5	1	9	3	7	8

No 95

4	2	8	1	3	6	5	7	9
5	6	3	7	2	9	8	1	4
7	1	9	8	5	4	2	3	6
9	4	5	2	6	7	1	8	3
1	3	6	4	8	5	7	9	2
8	7	2	3	9	1	4	6	5
6	9	4	5	7	8	3	2	1
2	8	1	9	4	3	6	5	7
3	5	7	6	1	2	9	4	8

No 96

5	6	1	4	2	7	9	8	3
2	3	8	6	9	1	7	5	4
9	4	7	3	5	8	6	1	2
6	8	3	7	4	9	5	2	1
7	9	5	1	3	2	4	6	8
1	2	4	8	6	5	3	9	7
8	5	9	2	7	4	1	3	6
3	7	2	5	1	6	8	4	9
4	1	6	9	8	3	2	7	5

4	6	8
3	1	7
5	9	2

Solutions

No 97

6	9	7	1	2	8	4	3	5
3	2	5	6	4	9	7	1	8
4	8	1	7	3	5	2	9	6
1	7	9	8	6	2	5	4	3
5	6	8	3	1	4	9	7	2
2	4	3	5	9	7	6	8	1
7	5	2	9	8	1	3	6	4
8	3	4	2	7	6	1	5	9
9	1	6	4	5	3	8	2	7

No 98

4	5	1	7	8	2	3	6	9
8	6	9	3	5	4	7	2	1
7	2	3	1	6	9	4	5	8
1	7	8	2	3	6	9	4	5
6	3	4	5	9	1	8	7	2
5	9	2	8	4	7	6	1	3
3	4	6	9	1	5	2	8	7
9	1	7	4	2	8	5	3	6
2	8	5	6	7	3	1	9	4

No 99

8	4	3	2	7	9	1	6	5
1	6	7	5	3	8	4	9	2
2	5	9	6	1	4	8	7	3
3	9	2	7	8	1	6	5	4
4	7	1	3	5	6	9	2	8
6	8	5	9	4	2	7	3	1
5	2	4	1	9	7	3	8	6
7	3	8	4	6	5	2	1	9
9	1	6	8	2	3	5	4	7

No 100

9	6	7	2	1	4	8	3	5
1	4	2	8	3	5	7	6	9
8	3	5	6	9	7	4	2	1
7	2	6	9	4	8	1	5	3
4	1	9	5	7	3	2	8	6
5	8	3	1	6	2	9	4	7
6	9	8	3	2	1	5	7	4
2	7	1	4	5	6	3	9	8
3	5	4	7	8	9	6	1	2

No 101

7	6	4	8	1	9	5	2	3
5	9	3	2	4	7	6	1	8
2	8	1	6	3	5	9	4	7
4	2	8	1	5	6	3	7	9
6	1	9	7	2	3	4	8	5
3	5	7	4	9	8	1	6	2
9	7	6	5	8	4	2	3	1
1	4	5	3	7	2	8	9	6
8	3	2	9	6	1	7	5	4

No 102

7	4	1	5	8	9	2	6	3
6	2	9	3	7	1	4	8	5
5	3	8	6	2	4	9	1	7
9	6	7	4	1	3	5	2	8
2	8	3	7	6	5	1	9	4
1	5	4	8	9	2	7	3	6
3	1	5	9	4	6	8	7	2
4	7	2	1	3	8	6	5	9
8	9	6	2	5	7	3	4	1

Solutions

No 103

7	5	3	1	6	2	4	8	9
6	1	8	4	5	9	7	2	3
9	4	2	3	8	7	1	6	5
2	9	6	8	7	1	5	3	4
3	7	5	9	4	6	8	1	2
4	8	1	5	2	3	6	9	7
1	2	7	6	9	4	3	5	8
5	3	4	2	1	8	9	7	6
8	6	9	7	3	5	2	4	1

No 104

3	1	2	9	5	7	4	6	8
9	8	6	4	1	2	7	3	5
5	7	4	8	6	3	2	9	1
6	9	1	7	3	5	8	2	4
8	2	7	6	4	9	1	5	3
4	3	5	2	8	1	6	7	9
7	5	8	1	9	6	3	4	2
2	4	3	5	7	8	9	1	6
1	6	9	3	2	4	5	8	7

No 105

7	3	2	1	8	5	9	6	4
4	8	5	9	6	3	1	2	7
9	1	6	4	7	2	3	8	5
2	5	8	7	3	4	6	9	1
6	9	3	5	1	8	7	4	2
1	7	4	6	2	9	8	5	3
5	4	7	8	9	1	2	3	6
3	6	9	2	5	7	4	1	8
8	2	1	3	4	6	5	7	9

No 106

9	5	2	1	4	7	6	3	8
1	3	7	6	2	8	9	4	5
4	6	8	3	9	5	7	2	1
2	9	4	5	7	3	8	1	6
5	8	1	9	6	4	3	7	2
6	7	3	8	1	2	4	5	9
3	2	5	7	8	6	1	9	4
7	1	6	4	5	9	2	8	3
8	4	9	2	3	1	5	6	7

No 107

1	2	3	4	7	6	5	9	8
7	6	8	5	2	9	3	4	1
9	4	5	8	1	3	7	6	2
8	7	6	1	3	2	4	5	9
2	3	1	9	5	4	6	8	7
5	9	4	7	6	8	2	1	3
6	8	2	3	4	1	9	7	5
4	1	7	2	9	5	8	3	6
3	5	9	6	8	7	1	2	4

No 108

8	1	9	6	3	5	4	2	7
2	7	6	1	9	4	8	5	3
4	5	3	8	7	2	1	6	9
7	4	5	9	2	8	6	3	1
3	2	1	5	6	7	9	8	4
9	6	8	3	4	1	2	7	5
6	9	7	2	1	3	5	4	8
5	3	2	4	8	9	7	1	6
1	8	4	7	5	6	3	9	2

4	6	8
3	1	7
5	9	2

1	9	8
3	5	2
4	6	7

Solutions

No 109

1	5	3	7	4	8	6	9	2
7	8	4	6	2	9	3	1	5
2	6	9	1	3	5	4	8	7
5	4	8	3	7	1	9	2	6
6	1	7	9	8	2	5	4	3
9	3	2	4	5	6	8	7	1
3	7	1	8	6	4	2	5	9
4	2	6	5	9	7	1	3	8
8	9	5	2	1	3	7	6	4

No 110

2	5	6	3	8	9	1	7	4
9	4	3	6	7	1	8	5	2
1	8	7	5	4	2	6	9	3
7	6	5	8	1	3	2	4	9
8	3	9	2	5	4	7	1	6
4	2	1	7	9	6	3	8	5
6	7	8	4	3	5	9	2	1
5	9	2	1	6	8	4	3	7
3	1	4	9	2	7	5	6	8

No 111

7	9	4	2	6	5	8	1	3
6	2	1	9	3	8	5	4	7
5	3	8	4	1	7	9	6	2
9	8	5	3	2	1	4	7	6
2	4	7	8	5	6	1	3	9
3	1	6	7	9	4	2	5	8
1	5	9	6	7	2	3	8	4
8	6	2	1	4	3	7	9	5
4	7	3	5	8	9	6	2	1

No 112

4	7	9	1	5	2	8	6	3
6	1	2	9	8	3	7	5	4
5	3	8	7	4	6	2	1	9
9	2	3	6	7	1	4	8	5
8	5	1	3	2	4	9	7	6
7	6	4	5	9	8	1	3	2
3	9	7	2	1	5	6	4	8
2	4	5	8	6	7	3	9	1
1	8	6	4	3	9	5	2	7

No 113

2	7	6	4	9	8	5	1	3
1	4	3	6	5	7	8	2	9
8	9	5	2	3	1	4	6	7
3	5	4	1	7	2	9	8	6
9	1	8	5	6	4	7	3	2
7	6	2	3	8	9	1	5	4
4	8	1	9	2	3	6	7	5
5	2	7	8	4	6	3	9	1
6	3	9	7	1	5	2	4	8

No 114

5	1	8	2	4	7	9	6	3
4	2	6	9	3	8	5	7	1
9	3	7	6	5	1	2	4	8
6	7	3	1	8	9	4	2	5
8	5	9	4	6	2	3	1	7
2	4	1	5	7	3	8	9	6
7	9	5	3	2	6	1	8	4
3	8	2	7	1	4	6	5	9
1	6	4	8	9	5	7	3	2

5	1	4
8	3	6
9	2	7

Solutions

No 115

5	8	3	1	7	9	4	2	6
1	4	7	8	2	6	9	5	3
6	9	2	4	3	5	7	8	1
4	5	8	3	6	1	2	9	7
2	1	9	7	8	4	6	3	5
3	7	6	5	9	2	8	1	4
8	2	5	6	4	3	1	7	9
7	6	1	9	5	8	3	4	2
9	3	4	2	1	7	5	6	8

No 116

8	3	6	9	7	4	5	2	1
4	1	5	2	8	3	6	7	9
2	9	7	6	1	5	3	4	8
6	4	8	5	9	1	7	3	2
9	5	3	7	6	2	1	8	4
7	2	1	3	4	8	9	5	6
5	6	4	8	3	9	2	1	7
1	7	2	4	5	6	8	9	3
3	8	9	1	2	7	4	6	5

No 117

9	1	3	7	5	8	6	2	4
2	6	8	9	1	4	7	5	3
5	7	4	3	6	2	9	8	1
1	9	2	6	4	5	8	3	7
6	8	7	1	3	9	5	4	2
4	3	5	2	8	7	1	6	9
7	4	6	5	9	3	2	1	8
3	2	1	8	7	6	4	9	5
8	5	9	4	2	1	3	7	6

No 118

7	9	5	8	1	6	2	4	3
6	8	3	9	4	2	7	1	5
1	4	2	5	3	7	6	9	8
3	5	4	2	7	9	8	6	1
2	6	9	1	8	5	3	7	4
8	1	7	3	6	4	5	2	9
5	7	6	4	9	3	1	8	2
4	3	8	6	2	1	9	5	7
9	2	1	7	5	8	4	3	6

No 119

3	1	4	2	9	7	6	8	5
6	7	8	4	3	5	1	9	2
9	2	5	8	6	1	3	7	4
2	3	9	5	1	8	4	6	7
4	5	7	3	2	6	8	1	9
1	8	6	9	7	4	5	2	3
7	4	1	6	5	9	2	3	8
5	9	2	1	8	3	7	4	6
8	6	3	7	4	2	9	5	1

No 120

2	4	8	7	6	1	9	3	5
7	1	3	8	5	9	6	2	4
6	5	9	4	2	3	7	1	8
1	2	7	5	4	6	3	8	9
5	8	6	9	3	2	1	4	7
3	9	4	1	8	7	2	5	6
4	6	2	3	9	8	5	7	1
8	3	1	6	7	5	4	9	2
9	7	5	2	1	4	8	6	3

4 6 8
3 1 7
5 9 2

Solutions

No 121

9	5	6	4	8	7	1	2	3
8	4	3	2	1	6	9	7	5
2	7	1	3	5	9	8	4	6
6	8	5	1	3	2	7	9	4
4	2	9	6	7	5	3	8	1
3	1	7	8	9	4	6	5	2
1	9	2	5	6	8	4	3	7
5	6	8	7	4	3	2	1	9
7	3	4	9	2	1	5	6	8

No 122

7	9	3	5	4	1	2	8	6
5	4	2	9	6	8	3	7	1
8	1	6	3	7	2	5	4	9
9	2	4	7	8	3	6	1	5
3	8	5	1	2	6	7	9	4
1	6	7	4	9	5	8	2	3
2	3	9	8	5	4	1	6	7
4	5	8	6	1	7	9	3	2
6	7	1	2	3	9	4	5	8

No 123

8	2	1	7	6	4	5	3	9
4	3	6	1	9	5	7	8	2
7	5	9	3	2	8	4	1	6
3	9	4	5	1	7	2	6	8
2	1	5	9	8	6	3	7	4
6	8	7	4	3	2	9	5	1
1	7	2	8	4	3	6	9	5
5	6	8	2	7	9	1	4	3
9	4	3	6	5	1	8	2	7

No 124

8	7	9	4	3	6	2	1	5
1	5	4	2	8	9	3	7	6
3	2	6	7	1	5	8	9	4
5	3	1	9	2	4	6	8	7
6	4	7	8	5	3	9	2	1
2	9	8	6	7	1	4	5	3
9	8	3	5	6	7	1	4	2
7	6	2	1	4	8	5	3	9
4	1	5	3	9	2	7	6	8

No 125

8	6	4	9	5	7	2	1	3
7	2	9	8	1	3	5	4	6
5	3	1	4	2	6	7	9	8
2	1	7	3	6	5	4	8	9
4	8	6	7	9	2	1	3	5
9	5	3	1	8	4	6	7	2
6	7	8	5	3	1	9	2	4
3	4	2	6	7	9	8	5	1
1	9	5	2	4	8	3	6	7

No 126

4	1	6	7	5	9	3	8	2
3	9	2	1	6	8	7	5	4
8	7	5	3	2	4	9	6	1
5	2	3	9	8	1	4	7	6
9	4	7	5	3	6	2	1	8
1	6	8	2	4	7	5	9	3
6	5	1	4	7	3	8	2	9
7	8	4	6	9	2	1	3	5
2	3	9	8	1	5	6	4	7

Solutions

7	8	5
2	9	6
4	3	1

No 127

7	9	5	3	8	2	1	6	4
4	8	6	7	1	9	2	5	3
3	2	1	6	4	5	9	7	8
9	1	7	8	5	6	4	3	2
6	3	4	9	2	7	5	8	1
2	5	8	1	3	4	7	9	6
8	4	2	5	7	3	6	1	9
1	7	9	2	6	8	3	4	5
5	6	3	4	9	1	8	2	7

No 128

1	2	5	9	6	4	8	7	3
7	9	6	8	3	2	5	4	1
4	3	8	7	1	5	9	2	6
2	5	4	3	7	9	6	1	8
8	6	9	4	2	1	3	5	7
3	7	1	5	8	6	4	9	2
9	8	2	1	5	3	7	6	4
6	4	3	2	9	7	1	8	5
5	1	7	6	4	8	2	3	9

No 129

7	5	1	9	4	3	6	2	8
6	8	9	2	7	5	3	1	4
2	3	4	6	8	1	9	7	5
8	7	5	3	2	6	4	9	1
9	4	3	5	1	8	7	6	2
1	6	2	7	9	4	8	5	3
4	2	6	1	3	7	5	8	9
5	1	8	4	6	9	2	3	7
3	9	7	8	5	2	1	4	6

No 130

7	6	5	4	1	8	3	9	2
4	9	2	5	6	3	7	8	1
3	8	1	7	9	2	4	5	6
2	3	7	9	8	1	5	6	4
9	5	8	6	3	4	2	1	7
6	1	4	2	5	7	9	3	8
1	4	3	8	7	9	6	2	5
8	7	6	3	2	5	1	4	9
5	2	9	1	4	6	8	7	3

No 131

2	6	7	3	9	4	5	1	8
8	3	4	5	1	2	9	7	6
9	5	1	6	7	8	4	2	3
7	8	2	9	5	3	6	4	1
4	9	3	1	2	6	7	8	5
5	1	6	4	8	7	2	3	9
6	4	9	2	3	1	8	5	7
3	7	5	8	4	9	1	6	2
1	2	8	7	6	5	3	9	4

No 132

2	6	1	7	9	5	4	3	8
4	5	8	3	6	1	2	7	9
3	9	7	8	2	4	6	5	1
5	1	9	4	7	8	3	2	6
8	3	6	2	5	9	1	4	7
7	2	4	6	1	3	9	8	5
9	4	3	1	8	7	5	6	2
6	8	5	9	3	2	7	1	4
1	7	2	5	4	6	8	9	3

4	6	8
3	1	7
5	9	2

Solutions

No 133

7	2	4	6	5	3	9	1	8
3	1	8	9	4	2	7	5	6
9	5	6	1	8	7	3	4	2
2	4	7	8	1	5	6	9	3
6	8	3	7	9	4	5	2	1
5	9	1	3	2	6	4	8	7
1	3	9	4	7	8	2	6	5
8	7	5	2	6	9	1	3	4
4	6	2	5	3	1	8	7	9

No 134

7	8	6	9	3	2	4	1	5
2	9	1	4	5	8	7	6	3
4	5	3	7	1	6	2	9	8
9	4	7	3	6	1	8	5	2
1	2	5	8	9	4	3	7	6
6	3	8	2	7	5	1	4	9
5	6	4	1	8	3	9	2	7
3	1	9	5	2	7	6	8	4
8	7	2	6	4	9	5	3	1

No 135

8	7	9	5	2	4	3	6	1
4	2	3	6	1	7	9	8	5
6	1	5	8	9	3	7	2	4
1	8	7	9	5	2	6	4	3
3	4	2	7	6	1	8	5	9
9	5	6	4	3	8	1	7	2
2	6	8	1	4	9	5	3	7
5	3	1	2	7	6	4	9	8
7	9	4	3	8	5	2	1	6

No 136

4	5	9	7	8	6	3	1	2
1	7	2	5	9	3	6	4	8
3	8	6	4	1	2	9	7	5
6	4	5	1	7	8	2	9	3
8	3	1	6	2	9	4	5	7
2	9	7	3	5	4	8	6	1
5	6	3	2	4	7	1	8	9
9	1	4	8	3	5	7	2	6
7	2	8	9	6	1	5	3	4

No 137

3	6	9	4	8	1	5	2	7
4	8	5	7	6	2	3	9	1
2	7	1	5	3	9	8	4	6
5	3	2	1	4	8	6	7	9
9	4	7	3	5	6	1	8	2
8	1	6	2	9	7	4	3	5
1	2	3	8	7	5	9	6	4
6	5	8	9	2	4	7	1	3
7	9	4	6	1	3	2	5	8

No 138

6	5	2	3	8	1	7	9	4
8	7	3	9	6	4	5	2	1
1	4	9	2	7	5	3	6	8
9	6	4	1	2	3	8	7	5
2	8	7	5	4	6	1	3	9
3	1	5	8	9	7	2	4	6
4	3	6	7	1	8	9	5	2
7	9	8	4	5	2	6	1	3
5	2	1	6	3	9	4	8	7

Solutions

No 139

9	8	4	5	1	3	2	6	7
6	1	7	4	2	9	8	5	3
3	5	2	6	7	8	4	9	1
4	9	1	8	6	7	5	3	2
5	7	3	2	4	1	9	8	6
8	2	6	9	3	5	1	7	4
7	4	8	3	9	2	6	1	5
1	6	5	7	8	4	3	2	9
2	3	9	1	5	6	7	4	8

No 140

1	6	4	3	2	8	9	5	7
3	5	9	6	7	1	4	2	8
2	8	7	4	5	9	1	3	6
5	1	6	2	8	3	7	9	4
8	9	2	7	4	5	6	1	3
4	7	3	9	1	6	2	8	5
7	2	5	8	9	4	3	6	1
6	4	1	5	3	2	8	7	9
9	3	8	1	6	7	5	4	2

No 141

6	4	5	9	3	8	1	7	2
2	9	8	7	1	4	5	3	6
3	1	7	6	5	2	4	8	9
8	5	9	4	7	1	6	2	3
1	7	6	5	2	3	9	4	8
4	2	3	8	9	6	7	5	1
5	3	1	2	6	7	8	9	4
7	6	4	3	8	9	2	1	5
9	8	2	1	4	5	3	6	7

No 142

7	5	2	3	9	6	8	4	1
1	9	3	8	4	2	7	6	5
4	6	8	5	1	7	3	9	2
5	4	6	9	3	1	2	8	7
3	2	7	6	8	4	5	1	9
9	8	1	2	7	5	6	3	4
8	7	9	1	5	3	4	2	6
6	1	5	4	2	8	9	7	3
2	3	4	7	6	9	1	5	8

No 143

6	8	5	3	7	9	4	2	1
2	1	7	5	8	4	3	6	9
3	9	4	1	2	6	5	8	7
4	7	6	9	3	5	2	1	8
1	5	2	8	4	7	9	3	6
8	3	9	6	1	2	7	5	4
5	6	1	7	9	3	8	4	2
7	2	8	4	5	1	6	9	3
9	4	3	2	6	8	1	7	5

No 144

1	6	3	2	9	7	5	8	4
5	8	7	6	3	4	2	1	9
4	2	9	8	1	5	3	6	7
7	1	4	3	2	9	8	5	6
3	5	6	7	4	8	1	9	2
2	9	8	5	6	1	4	7	3
8	3	1	9	7	2	6	4	5
6	7	5	4	8	3	9	2	1
9	4	2	1	5	6	7	3	8

4	6	8
3	1	7
5	9	2

Solutions

No 145

9	3	1	4	8	7	6	2	5
8	6	5	9	3	2	7	1	4
4	2	7	5	1	6	8	9	3
3	8	4	7	2	9	1	5	6
5	7	2	1	6	4	9	3	8
6	1	9	8	5	3	2	4	7
1	4	3	6	9	8	5	7	2
7	5	6	2	4	1	3	8	9
2	9	8	3	7	5	4	6	1

No 146

5	4	8	1	3	6	9	7	2
2	1	6	9	7	5	4	3	8
9	7	3	4	2	8	5	1	6
4	8	2	3	5	9	1	6	7
7	9	1	8	6	4	3	2	5
3	6	5	2	1	7	8	9	4
8	2	4	6	9	3	7	5	1
6	3	7	5	4	1	2	8	9
1	5	9	7	8	2	6	4	3

No 147

1	9	3	5	7	2	4	8	6
6	2	7	4	3	8	1	5	9
5	4	8	1	9	6	2	3	7
4	6	9	7	2	5	8	1	3
8	1	2	3	6	9	7	4	5
3	7	5	8	1	4	9	6	2
9	5	4	6	8	7	3	2	1
7	3	6	2	4	1	5	9	8
2	8	1	9	5	3	6	7	4

No 148

9	6	2	1	3	4	5	7	8
8	1	3	5	7	9	2	6	4
7	4	5	6	8	2	1	3	9
3	5	8	2	4	1	7	9	6
4	7	6	8	9	5	3	1	2
2	9	1	7	6	3	8	4	5
6	3	7	4	2	8	9	5	1
1	2	4	9	5	7	6	8	3
5	8	9	3	1	6	4	2	7

No 149

6	2	4	8	7	5	1	3	9
9	8	1	3	4	6	7	5	2
5	3	7	9	1	2	4	6	8
3	4	6	7	9	1	2	8	5
8	5	9	4	2	3	6	1	7
1	7	2	6	5	8	3	9	4
4	1	8	2	3	9	5	7	6
7	9	3	5	6	4	8	2	1
2	6	5	1	8	7	9	4	3

No 150

9	2	1	6	4	3	7	8	5
4	7	3	9	5	8	6	2	1
6	8	5	1	2	7	4	3	9
8	5	4	7	1	6	3	9	2
1	6	9	8	3	2	5	4	7
2	3	7	4	9	5	8	1	6
3	9	8	5	7	1	2	6	4
7	1	6	2	8	4	9	5	3
5	4	2	3	6	9	1	7	8

Solutions

No 1

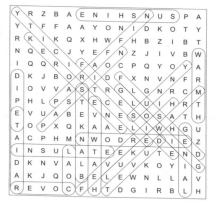

No 2

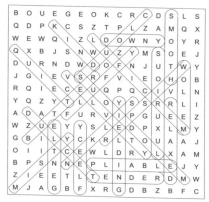

No 3

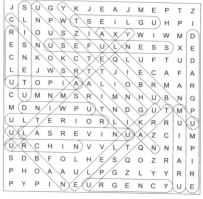

No 4

No 5

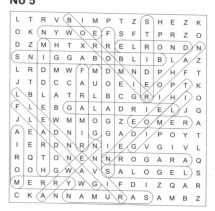

No 6

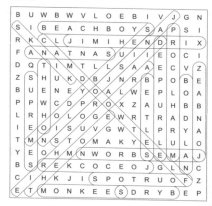

Solutions

No 7

No 8

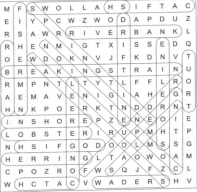

No 9

No 10

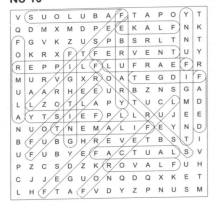

No 11

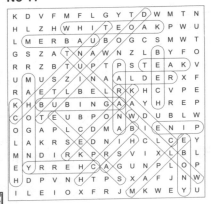

No 12

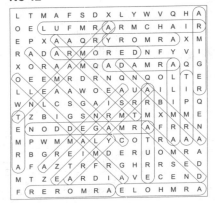

Solutions

No 13

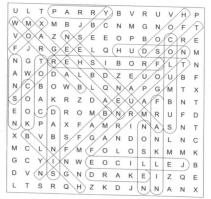

No 14

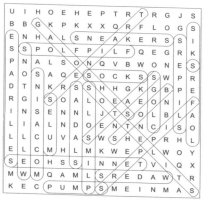

No 15

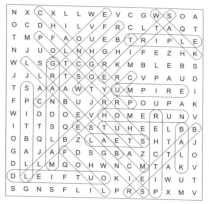

No 16

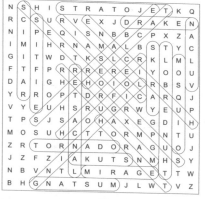

No 17

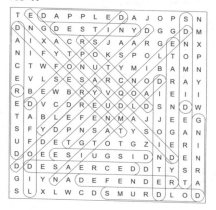

No 18

Solutions

No 19

No 20

No 21

No 22

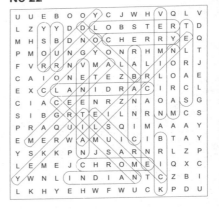

No 23

No 24

Solutions

No 25

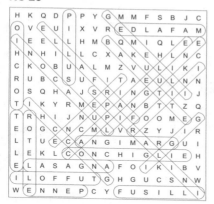

No 26

No 27

No 28

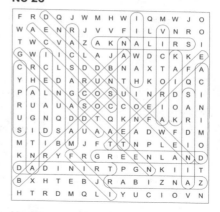

No 29

No 30

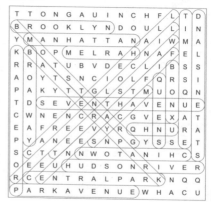

Solutions

No 31

No 32

No 33

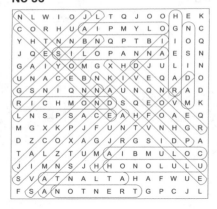

No 34

No 35

No 36

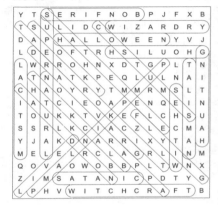

Solutions

No 37

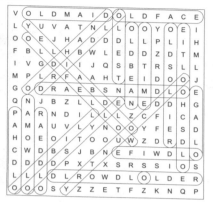

No 38

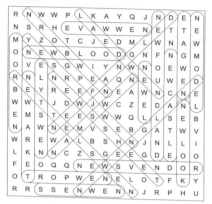

No 39

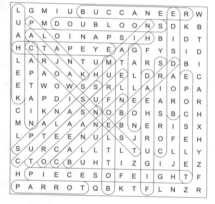

No 40

No 41

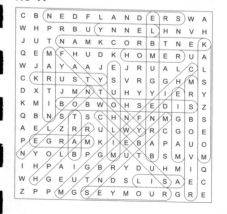

No 42

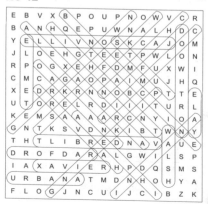

Solutions

No 43

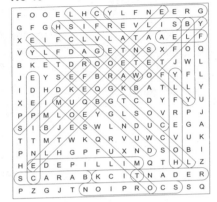

No 44

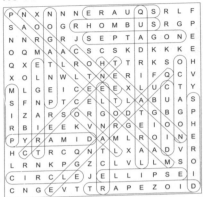

No 45

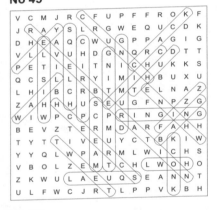

No 46

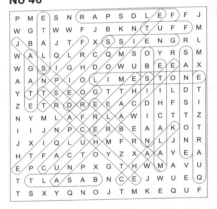

No 47

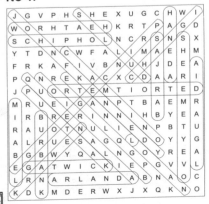

No 48

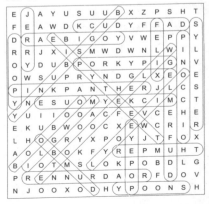

Solutions

No 49

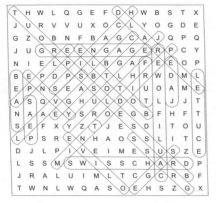

No 50

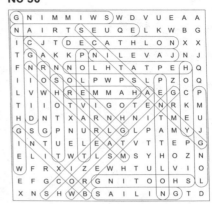

No 51

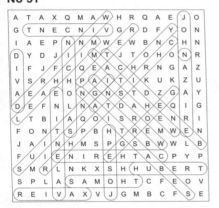

No 52

No 53

No 54

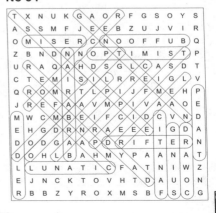

Solutions

No 55

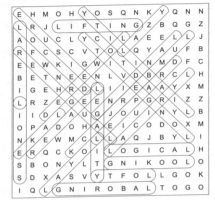

No 56

No 57

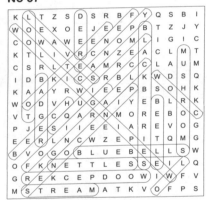

No 58

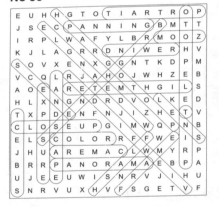

No 59

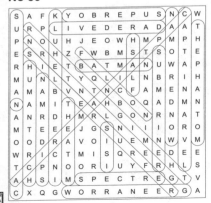

No 60

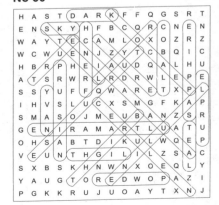

Solutions

No 61

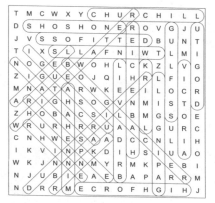

No 62

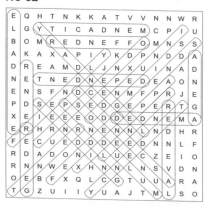

No 63

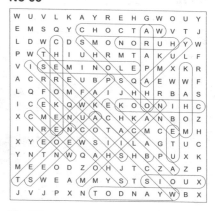

No 64

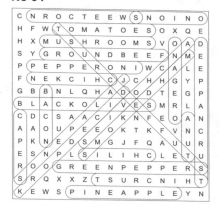

No 65

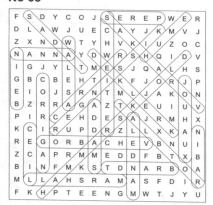

No 66

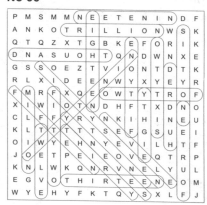

Solutions

No 67

No 68

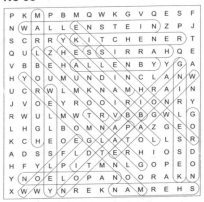

No 69

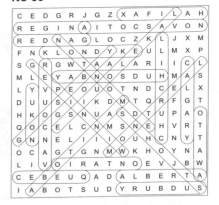

No 70

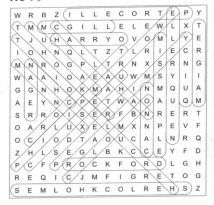

No 71

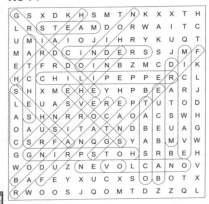

No 72

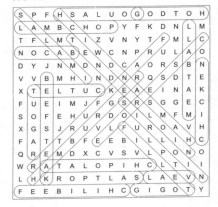

Solutions

No 73

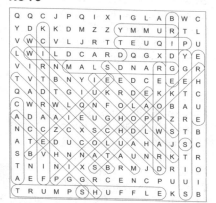

No 74

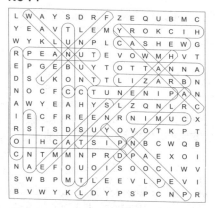

No 75

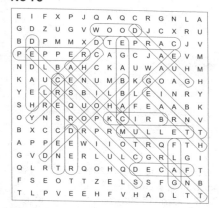

No 76

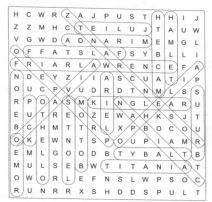

No 77

Solutions

No 1

Across: 1 Circus, 7 Clerical, 8 Run, 9 Secret, 10 Able, 11 Nymph, 13 Deviate, 15 Partial, 17 Recur, 21 Wade, 22 Season, 23 Dot, 24 Regional, 25 Trader.

Down: 1 Carton, 2 Ransom, 3 Scare, 4 Neither, 5 Finalize, 6 Wallet, 12 Pathetic, 14 Passing, 16 Azalea, 18 Candid, 19 Rector, 20 Fault.

No 2

Across: 1 Abated, 5 Utopia, 8 Lawn, 9 Avenge, 10 Sheaf, 11 Cage, 12 Isle, 13 Harass, 15 Soda, 17 Kiss, 19 Recede, 20 Aids, 21 Drab, 22 Salve, 24 Garnet, 25 Loud, 26 Roller, 27 Stamen.

Down: 2 Bravado, 3 Tense, 4 Dice, 5 Unafraid, 6 Obelisk, 7 Ageless, 14 Ancestor, 15 Stagger, 16 Arsenal, 18 Stature, 21 Delta, 23 Lens.

No 3

Across: 1 Shoe, 3 Feminine, 9 Menthol, 10 Rifle, 11 Sierra Nevada, 14 Eat, 16 Udder, 17 Lie, 18 Cash register, 21 Opera, 22 Ailment, 23 Open-eyed, 24 News.

Down: 1 Semester, 2 Ounce, 4 Eel, 5 Irreversible, 6 Infidel, 7 Even, 8 Thoroughfare, 12 Nudge, 13 Detritus, 15 Trapeze, 19 Theme, 20 Coco, 22 Ale.

No 4

Across: 1 Brass, 4 Crowbar, 8 Ego, 9 Salsa, 10 Scale, 11 Battleship, 13 Eleven, 15 Hairdo, 18 Prosperous, 22 Alike, 23 Horde, 24 Née, 25 Sighted, 26 Renal.

Down: 1 Besotted, 2 Ad-lib, 3 Seattle, 4 Cockle, 5 Oasis, 6 Brazier, 7 Reef, 12 Foretell, 14 Earring, 16 Another, 17 Behind, 19 Scent, 20 Siren, 21 Dais.

No 5

Across: 1 Shrimp, 7 Spacious, 8 Axis, 10 Dahlia, 11 Emit, 12 Abbey, 13 Decibel, 17 Stencil, 19 Bogus, 21 Boss, 23 Tragic, 25 Cope, 26 Research, 27 Stress.

Down: 1 Star Wars, 2 Raid, 3 Psalm, 4 Cadaver, 5 Aide, 6 Futile, 9 Sateen, 14 Ironic, 15 Listless, 16 Cistern, 18 Trowel, 20 Paths, 22 Seem, 24 Cote.

No 6

Across: 1 Attaché cases, 9 Grass, 10 Scion, 11 The, 12 Inane, 13 Species, 14 Muster, 16 Assess, 20 Chortle, 22 Socks, 24 Rut, 25 Upper, 26 Abase, 27 Show business.

Down: 2 Tiara, 3 Austere, 4 Honest, 5 Caste, 6 Suicide, 7 Sinus, 8 Egoism, 15 Scorpio, 17 Sustain, 18 Sister, 19 Series, 20 Clubs, 21 Throb, 23 Class.

No 7

Across: 1 Bistro, 4 Picnic, 7 Silver, 9 Eschewed, 11 Stop, 14 America, 15 Bier, 16 Sham, 17 Spinach, 18 Yell, 21 Biennial, 22 Embalm, 24 Recess, 25 Indent.

Down: 1 Basis, 2 Salvo, 3 Roe, 4 Practicable, 5 Camera-shy, 6 Card, 8 Repetitious, 10 Entail, 12 Taipei, 13 Parsonage, 19 Erase, 20 Limit, 21 Beer, 23 Man.

Solutions

No 8
Across: 1 Satsuma, 8 Pro rata,
9 Dismiss, 10 Exiled, 12 Severe,
13 Typographer, 17 Accost,
20 Retina, 23 Earning, 24 Nervous,
25 Surgeon.
Down: 1 Sudden, 2 Testify, 3 Unite,
4 Apse, 5 Force, 6 Badge, 7 Backer,
11 Digit, 12 Stair, 14 Edifice,
15 Banana, 16 Margin, 18 Chart,
19 Salon, 21 Error, 22 Less.

No 9
Across: 4 Assuage, 8 Ennui,
9 Recording, 10 Adieu, 11 Sensitive,
13 Crease, 16 Jet set, 20 Temperate,
23 Links, 24 Apartheid, 25 Eyrie,
26 Putrefy.
Down: 1 Ceramic, 2 Entitle, 3 Virus,
4 Ascent, 5 Servile, 6 Alibi, 7 Eagle,
12 Vie, 14 Rue, 15 Sheathe,
17 Spin-dry, 18 Two step, 19 Bakery,
20 Tramp, 21 Meant, 22 Elder.

No 10
Across: 1 Parapet, 5 Genus, 8 Rot,
9 Shangri-la, 10 Shame, 12 Gave,
13 Ravage, 15 Lees, 17 Dart,
20 Harass, 22 Beau, 23 Piton,
25 South-east, 26 See, 27 Cadet,
28 Lenient.
Down: 1 Parasol, 2 Retrace,
3 Poster, 4 Teat, 6 Enraged, 7 Shave,
11 Bass, 14 Acre, 16 Shuttle,
18 Artiste, 19 Tangent, 21 Spot on,
22 Basic, 24 Bail.

No 11
Across: 1 Ballet, 3 Callus,
7 Nonetheless, 10 Streamer,
11 Acne, 13 Latch, 14 Bagel,
18 Amid, 19 Breeding, 21 Electric
eye, 22 Saucer, 23 Census.

Down: 1 Banish, 2 Entrance,
4 Amen, 5 Sequel, 6 Fever,
8 Narrative, 9 Secretive, 12 Baseline,
15 Harass, 16 Broth, 17 Egress,
20 Were.

No 12
Across: 1 Shift key, 5 Fang,
8 Asteroid, 10 Refusal, 11 Corps,
12 Heartache, 15 Surprises,
18 Hinge, 19 Rhubarb, 22 Earliest,
23 T-bar, 24 Reversal.
Down: 1 Scarce, 2 Interior, 3 Thrash,
4 Emir, 6 Adds, 7 Grille, 9 Decree,
13 Emigre, 14 Countess, 15 Strict,
16 Shelve, 17 Lentil, 20 Urea,
21 Base.

No 13
Across: 1 Classic, 7 Sahara,
9 Squeeze, 10 Crepe, 11 Reek,
12 Taper, 16 Salem, 17 Gala,
21 Jeans, 22 Chariot, 23 Clever,
24 Hearing.
Down: 1 Consort, 2 Albumen,
3 Screw, 4 Fancier, 5 Eager, 6 Babel,
8 Decadence, 13 Parsley, 14 Ravioli,
15 Parting, 18 Eject, 19 Baker,
20 Fauna.

No 14
Across: 1 Screen, 4 Metric,
9 Afghani, 10 Supreme, 11 Ensue,
12 Easel, 14 Squad, 15 Serve,
17 Stave, 18 Examine, 20 Surmise,
21 Sparse, 22 Parent.
Down: 1 Shares, 2 Register,
3 Erase, 5 Elapsed, 6 Race,
7 Cereal, 8 Discourtesy, 13 Set
aside, 14 Serious, 15 Shears,
16 Defect, 17 Syria, 19 Aria.

Solutions

No 15
Across: 1 Aspic, 4 Anguish, 8 Stopper, 9 Leper, 10 Those, 11 Athlete, 12 Punish, 13 Rhesus, 16 Stellar, 18 Pious, 20 Arena, 21 Cuisine, 22 Extreme, 23 Remit.
Down: 1 Asset, 2 Pronouncement, 3 Cypress, 4 Abroad, 5 Gulch, 6 Impressionism, 7 Harness, 12 Passage, 14 Happier, 15 Oracle, 17 Leave, 19 Swept.

No 16
Across: 1 Materialism, 9 Scant, 10 Ace, 11 React, 12 Sieve, 13 Cataract, 16 Kerosene, 18 Traps, 21 Tired, 22 Rye, 23 Bathe, 24 Star-crossed.
Down: 2 Andante, 3 Eastern, 4 Italic, 5 Lotus, 6 Shade, 7 Agriculture, 8 Level-headed, 14 Hostess, 15 Reprove, 17 Editor, 19 Agent, 20 Sober.

No 17
Across: 1 Earnest, 6 Bus, 8 Aroma, 9 Tactics, 10 Bigot, 11 Panpipes, 13 Staple, 15 Corner, 18 Betrayed, 19 Teens, 21 Sternum, 22 Slate, 23 Ere, 24 Linseed.
Down: 2 Adamant, 3 Eligible, 4 Tassel, 5 Bomb, 6 Bargain, 7 Slither, 12 Fourteen, 13 Scuttle, 14 Adverse, 16 Execute, 17 Vessel, 20 Scar.

No 18
Across: 1 Cassette, 5 Babe, 9 Reactor, 10 Enrol, 11 Pallbearer, 14 Leaked, 15 Waffle, 17 Transverse, 20 Prior, 21 Avocado, 22 Saga, 23 Reverent.
Down: 1 Corn, 2 Seat, 3 Extrasensory, 4 Thrill, 6 Aircraft, 7 Enlarges, 8 General store, 12 Platypus, 13 Parading, 16 Berate, 18 Came, 19 Colt.

No 19
Across: 1 Drachma, 5 Snipe, 7 Aries, 8 Scarlet, 9 Ovation, 10 Label, 11 Dressy, 13 Rabies, 18 Aides, 20 Sponsor, 21 Collide, 22 Gelid, 23 Aside, 24 Tetanus.
Down: 1 Diamond, 2 Agitate, 3 Huskies, 4 Absent, 5 Shawl, 6 Precede, 12 Ruinous, 14 Amongst, 15 Insulin, 16 Strides, 17 Aspect, 19 Suite.

No 20
Across: 1 Caress, 4 Biopsy, 7 Nipper, 8 Disclose, 12 Defend, 14 Famine, 15 Basket, 16 Aerate, 18 Vertebra, 22 Coarse, 23 Battle, 24 Sleepy.
Down: 1 Cent, 2 Empire, 3 Sordid, 4 Bass, 5 Oval, 6 Yule, 9 Cease, 10 Sanity, 11 Sedate, 13 Niece, 16 Abacus, 17 Rebate, 18 Verb, 19 Text, 20 Bike, 21 Deny.

No 21
Across: 1 Dross, 4 Spatula, 7 Being, 8 Intranet, 9 Bliss, 11 Icebound, 15 Timeless, 17 Scrap, 19 Pakistan, 20 Caper, 21 Depress, 22 Shrug.
Down: 1 Delicious, 2 Oak tree, 3 Senator, 4 Spleen, 5 Treble, 6 Links, 10 Seasoning, 12 Tedious, 13 Weather, 14 Career, 16 Images, 18 Chase.

Solutions

No 22
Across: 1 Solar system, 7 Liberate, 8 Torn, 9 System, 11 Strife, 13 Manor, 14 Cheek, 17 Assist, 20 Rustle, 22 Diva, 23 Shanghai, 24 Penetrating.
Down: 1 Splash, 2 Avert, 3 Stammer, 4 Stems, 5 Ester, 6 Bunker, 10 Swans, 12 Inert, 14 Corsair, 15 Bandit, 16 Sewing, 18 Inane, 19 Taste, 21 Sight.

No 23
Across: 1 Sigh, 3 Nightcap, 9 Riddles, 10 Lease, 11 Egypt, 12 Embargo, 13 Typist, 15 Hounds, 17 Terrace, 18 Heads, 20 Olive, 21 Israeli, 22 Sheathed, 23 Stag.
Down: 1 Surreptitious, 2 Giddy, 4 Instep, 5 Half-brothers, 6 Chagrin, 7 Prepossessing, 8 Old Testament, 14 Porcine, 16 Devise, 19 Adept.

No 24
Across: 1 Pagans, 8 Charcoal, 9 Morale, 10 Needless, 11 Geisha, 12 Runner-up, 16 Tapeworm, 18 Excess, 21 Protocol, 23 Exotic, 24 Pitiless, 25 Surfer.
Down: 2 Adore, 3 Amass, 4 Scenario, 5 Cake, 6 Scalpel, 7 Nassau, 11 Gait, 13 Nameless, 14 Plus, 15 Certain, 17 Afraid, 19 Choir, 20 Slice, 22 Crew.

No 25
Across: 1 Stallion, 5 Bare, 8 Llama, 9 Salvage, 10 Slavery, 12 Possess, 14 Speckle, 16 Transit, 18 Mariner, 19 Inner, 20 So-so, 21 Megabyte.
Down: 1 Silo, 2 Amazes, 3 Leap years, 4 Obsess, 6 Awaken, 7 Everyone, 11 Argentina, 12 Pastimes, 13 Madras, 14 Starve, 15 Kidney, 17 Erie.

No 26
Across: 7 Maharaja, 8 Away, 9 Kilo, 10 Site, 11 Cat, 13 Cameo, 14 Masonry, 16 Gateway, 18 Pedal, 21 Irk, 22 Wage, 23 Part, 25 Fare, 26 Eyeglass.
Down: 1 Patina, 2 Barometer, 3 False, 4 Factual, 5 Fad, 6 Bazaar, 12 Totem pole, 15 Cabaret, 17 Aerial, 19 Afresh, 20 Jewel, 24 Bed.

No 27
Across: 1 Crass, 7 Ragtime, 8 Rap, 9 Premature, 11 Blade, 12 Republic, 16 Wide-eyed, 20 Abode, 21 Elocution, 23 Ark, 24 Texture, 25 Radar.
Down: 1 Caribou, 2 Appeal, 3 Supper, 4 True, 5 Stately, 6 Never, 10 Mauve, 13 Elect, 14 Educate, 15 Breaker, 17 Danger, 18 Coward, 19 Berth, 22 Idea.

No 28
Across: 1 Signet, 7 Root beer, 8 Versus, 10 Try out, 11 Ravel, 13 Seismic, 16 Applied, 17 Beret, 20 Falter, 22 Sorrow, 24 Reprieve, 25 Needed.
Down: 1 Shiver, 2 Gear, 3 Tress, 4 Bootleg, 5 Obey, 6 Deputize, 9 Steal, 12 Appeared, 14 Spear, 15 Debrief, 18 Toward, 19 Aspen, 21 Turf, 23 Road.

No 29
Across: 1 Duchess, 7 Avarice, 8 Nasal, 10 Inexact, 11 Scene, 12 Diagnosis, 16 Universal, 18 Samoa, 20 Toaster, 23 Annul, 24 Edition, 25 Dynasty.
Down: 1 Dress, 2 Confetti, 3 Saliva, 4 Fame, 5 Lira, 6 Dentist, 9 Sledge, 13 Nelson, 14 Stimulus, 15 Curtsey, 17 Strand, 19 Array, 21 Acid, 22 Toil.

Solutions

No 30

Across: 1 Morass, 5 Bishop, 8 Errand, 9 Starts, 10 Are, 11 Revel, 13 Sterling, 15 Rejoices, 16 Spent, 19 Nut, 21 Office, 22 Weaken, 23 Biceps, 24 Goatee.

Down: 2 Ourselves, 3 Adage, 4 Soda, 5 Baseless, 6 Shackle, 7 Peso, 12 Insincere, 13 Sickness, 14 Combine, 17 Plaza, 18 Tomb, 20 Twig.

No 31

Across: 1 Foretaste, 8 Largo, 9 Surge, 10 Annie, 11 Rhyme, 12 Sadism, 13 Mantis, 17 Repel, 20 Aloha, 22 Await, 23 Chaos, 24 Endurance.

Down: 1 Flora, 2 Refined, 3 Theseus, 4 Source, 5 Elder, 6 Gravy, 7 Confess, 12 Service, 14 Amateur, 15 Trodden, 16 Placid, 18 Petal, 19 Lapse, 21 Andre.

No 32

Across: 1 Charm, 7 Laundry, 8 Acronym, 9 Someone, 12 Identity, 14 Idol, 16 Suds, 18 Clearing, 20 Darling, 23 Astride, 24 Illness, 25 Bleat.

Down: 1 Claudius, 2 Abrade, 3 Mane, 4 Alms, 5 Anterior, 6 Bronco, 10 Oxygen, 11 Tin can, 13 Nestling, 15 Ligament, 17 Unable, 19 Iodine, 21 Gasp, 22 Stab.

No 33

Across: 1 Mature, 4 Litmus, 7 Ninepins, 8 Tops, 9 Arabs, 10 Foresee, 12 Skewer, 13 Elicit, 15 Riposte, 18 Mania, 20 Lean, 21 Aardvark, 22 Sneeze, 23 Fleece.

Down: 1 Manna, 2 Tonnage, 3 Repossess, 4 Lasso, 5 Moons, 6 Suspect, 11 Role model, 12 Surplus, 14 Concave, 16 Place, 17 Tease, 19 Ankle.

No 34

Across: 1 Discus, 4 Sortie, 7 Slur, 8 Scavenge, 10 Corset, 12 Sleuth, 14 Leaves, 17 Simmer, 19 Mahogany, 21 Solo, 22 Nectar, 23 Statue.

Down: 1 Dusk, 2 Carves, 3 Sunset, 4 Smears, 5 Revere, 6 Ill-gotten, 9 Tolerable, 11 Eve, 13 Lei, 15 Violet, 16 Skater, 17 Stylus, 18 Miasma, 20 Cone.

No 35

Across: 1 Steam, 4 Jackpot, 8 Perdition, 9 Drill, 10 Ebullient, 13 Ratify, 14 Caring, 16 Stop press, 19 Eases, 20 Animation, 22 Timbers, 23 Eerie.

Down: 1 Shudder, 2 Exhibitionism, 3 Maple, 4 Jar, 5 Chill, 6 Prime Minister, 7 Tenet, 11 Buyer, 12 Lochs, 15 Gristle, 16 Smart, 17 Peace, 18 Sense, 21 Its.

No 36

Across: 1 Zeal, 3 Warmed up, 9 Coroner, 10 Sisal, 11 Helix, 12 Sunlit, 14 Nickel, 16 Renege, 18 Marine, 19 Prank, 22 Onion, 23 Sterile, 24 Symmetry, 25 Hers.

Down: 1 Zucchini, 2 Aural, 4 Arrest, 5 Misinterpret, 6 Despise, 7 Pale, 8 Inexperience, 13 Feckless, 15 Cranium, 17 Geyser, 20 Abide, 21 Toss.

Solutions

No 37

Across: 1 Tenable, 5 Costa, 8 Nationalism, 9 Oaths, 11 Enhance, 13 Spider, 14 Spoils, 17 Proffer, 18 Inset, 19 Intravenous, 22 Soggy, 23 Hosiery.

Down: 1 Tenuous, 2 Net, 3 Bookshelf, 4 Elated, 5 Chi, 6 Semantics, 7 Afire, 10 Tailoring, 12 Happiness, 15 Satisfy, 16 Broach, 17 Pants, 20 Toy, 21 Ore.

No 38

Across: 1 Jackal, 5 Slake, 9 Right away, 10 Breve, 11 Piecemeal, 13 Solemn, 15 Beggar, 19 Strenuous, 21 Roost, 22 Attention, 24 Style, 25 Carpet.

Down: 2 Angle, 3 Kit, 4 Lawyer, 5 Sky blue, 6 Angel, 7 Enterprising, 8 Preposterous, 12 Cue, 14 Mistake, 16 Gnu, 17 Critic, 18 Dowry, 20 Opine, 23 Nor.

No 39

Across: 4 Selects, 7 One-time, 8 Beach, 9 Brake, 10 Tar, 11 Amend, 12 Santa Cruz, 14 Submarine, 17 Pilau, 18 Lea, 19 Islet, 21 Endue, 22 Colonel, 23 Stylish.

Down: 1 Comb, 2 Regain, 3 Time capsule, 4 Sector, 5 Chapel, 6 Schedule, 8 Brazzaville, 12 Suppress, 13 Gladly, 15 Blanch, 16 Inland, 20 Talc.

No 40

Across: 1 Czech Republic, 7 Safe, 8 Soften, 9 Seeks, 10 Nuts, 12 Impede, 13 Gaunt, 15 Nabob, 18 Cliche, 20 Fete, 21 Liner, 22 Chisel, 23 Ails, 24 Panic-stricken.

Down: 1 Casino, 2 Cress, 3 Ripen, 4 Passion, 5 Lithesome, 6 Cancel, 11 Tradition, 14 Trellis, 16 Ice-cap, 17 Reason, 19 Anger, 20 Franc.

No 41

Across: 1 Blanc, 5 Posy, 7 Eczema, 8 Align, 9 Synthetic, 10 Ear, 11 Rejoinder, 15 Perimeter, 19 Ape, 20 Athletics, 21 Idiot, 22 Crisis, 23 Feat, 24 Tiger.

Down: 1 Beaker, 2 Apiary, 3 Censor, 4 Dextrose, 5 Pageant, 6 Shrivel, 12 Electric, 13 Bedtime, 14 Dialect, 16 Resist, 17 Casing, 18 Debtor.

No 42

Across: 1 Scald, 4 Scallop, 8 Air, 9 Sylvester, 10 Prime, 11 Sapient, 13 Contact lenses, 15 Aimless, 17 Ideal, 19 Grapevine, 21 Pan, 22 Sniffed, 23 Tarry.

Down: 1 Swamp, 2 Arraign, 3 Desperate, 4 Self-satisfied, 5 Are, 6 Lithe, 7 Pirates, 12 President, 13 Charges, 14 Sleeper, 16 Miami, 18 Lanky, 20 Elf.

No 43

Across: 1 Exceeds, 5 Medic, 8 Herbivorous, 9 Coati, 11 Collect, 13 Llamas, 14 Bonsai, 17 Current, 18 Eland, 19 Blood vessel, 22 Uncle, 23 Offence.

Down: 1 Ethical, 2 Car, 3 Eliminate, 4 Scorch, 5 Moo, 6 Dyspepsia, 7 Chest, 10 Anaerobic, 12 Looseleaf, 15 Indulge, 16 Studio, 17 Coypu, 20 Owe, 21 Son.

No 44

Across: 1 Something, 5 Sip, 7 Awning, 8 Canter, 10 Date, 11 Suspend, 13 Asinine, 17 Trample, 19 Chef, 21 Israel, 22 Desire, 23 Sad, 24 Supersede.

Solutions

Down: 1 Seal, 2 Maniac, 3 Tenders, 4 Glass, 5 Setter, 6 Paradise, 9 Asunder, 12 Upstairs, 14 Nuclear, 15 Barred, 16 Beside, 18 Press, 20 Here.

No 45

Across: 1 Osiris, 5 Subway, 8 Bags, 9 Seafarer, 10 Colic, 11 Protest, 14 Tennis, 15 Answer, 17 Hacksaw, 19 Baste, 21 Pleasing, 23 Inch, 24 String, 25 Engulf.

Down: 2 Soap opera, 3 Russian, 4 Sash, 5 Stairway, 6 Boast, 7 Are, 12 Sceptical, 13 Escaping, 16 Sparing, 18 Khaki, 20 Ogre, 22 Lit.

No 46

Across: 1 Secret agent, 7 Ova, 8 Polynesia, 9 Lettuce, 11 Trade, 14 Senile, 15 Bypass, 16 Rowel, 19 Bedside, 21 Restraint, 23 Can, 24 Documentary.

Down: 1 Sepal, 2 Ray, 3 Trencher, 4 Exact, 5 Tonga, 6 Hapless, 10 Tribe, 12 Ropes, 13 Absentee, 14 Surface, 17 Wound, 18 Lyric, 20 Entry, 22 Ant.

No 47

Across: 1 Soup, 3 Christen, 7 Demerara, 8 Lode, 9 Enlist, 10 Tested, 11 Steer, 12 Cross, 15 Landed, 18 Brazil, 19 Lima, 20 Placidly, 21 Unsettle, 22 Avid.

Down: 1 Sadden, 2 Preside, 3 Chapter, 4 Roast, 5 Sells, 6 Endless, 11 Station, 12 Cabbage, 13 Ocarina, 14 Played, 16 Drape, 17 Depot.

No 48

Across: 1 Wick, 3 Bachelor, 9 Trivial, 10 Perdu, 11 Embed, 12 Decline, 13 Salver, 15 Nought, 18 Stamina, 19 Dusky, 21 Lying, 22 Orinoco, 23 Distress, 24 Dead.

Down: 1 Witness, 2 Climb, 4 Allude, 5 Hypochondria, 6 Lurking, 7 Route, 8 Middle finger, 14 Lead-ins, 16 Thyroid, 17 Famous, 18 Salad, 20 Shove.

No 49

Across: 1 Grubby, 7 Monocle, 8 Aboard, 9 Venture, 10 Siesta, 13 China, 15 Buff, 16 Lion, 17 These, 18 Spouse, 21 Appease, 23 Cognac, 24 Caraway, 25 Boiler.

Down: 2 Rabbi, 3 Burst, 4 Code, 5 Contralto, 6 Reverence, 10 Substance, 11 Soft-pedal, 12 Acre, 14 Ides, 19 Photo, 20 Share, 22 Slab.

No 50

Across: 1 Farmland, 5 Crag, 7 Artless, 8 Sneaker, 9 Several, 11 Assign, 14 Castle, 16 Radiant, 18 Enthral, 21 Seminar, 22 Axle, 23 New World.

Down: 1 Fuss, 2 Repels, 3 Luck, 4 Nears, 5 Colleges, 6 Gasoline, 10 Epic, 11 Ambrosia, 12 Incisive, 13 Noon, 15 Terror, 17 Terse, 19 Thaw, 20 Land.

No 51

Across: 1 Should, 7 Rational, 8 Art, 9 Select, 10 Laid, 11 Ditch, 13 Century, 15 Spanner, 17 Myths, 21 Bows, 22 Suitor, 23 Oat, 24 Rehearse, 25 Rugged.

Solutions

Down: 1 Stared, 2 Outset, 3 Drier, 4 Stutter, 5 Toiletry, 6 Caviar, 12 Canister, 14 Berserk, 16 Proper, 18 Throng, 19 Skated, 20 Viper.

No 52

Across: 1 Across, 5 Scruff, 8 Buds, 9 Reamer, 10 Eagle, 11 Diet, 12 Idle, 13 Genius, 15 Crop, 17 Miss, 19 Asleep, 20 Aims, 21 Slay, 22 Pasha, 24 Ethics, 25 Rate, 26 Unless, 27 Pastry.

Down: 2 Courier, 3 Onset, 4 Song, 5 Sure-fire, 6 Realism, 7 Forceps, 14 Ellipsis, 15 Chateau, 16 Pastime, 18 Scatter, 21 Saris, 23 Snip.

No 53

Across: 1 Scab, 3 Inviting, 9 Morning, 10 Sushi, 11 Hydrotherapy, 14 Not, 16 Etude, 17 Due, 18 Indigestible, 21 Alien, 22 Florida, 23 Lingered, 24 Cede.

Down: 1 Symphony, 2 Acrid, 4 Nag, 5 Insurrection, 6 Insipid, 7 Gain, 8 Disobedience, 12 House, 13 Delegate, 15 Tension, 19 Baize, 20 Hail, 22 Fee.

No 54

Across: 1 Cubit, 4 Slander, 8 Act, 9 Rural, 10 Arson, 11 Evil-minded, 13 Eldest, 15 Dredge, 18 Unassuming, 22 Event, 23 Tie in, 24 Eke, 25 Destroy, 26 Range.

Down: 1 Carefree, 2 Barge, 3 Talkies, 4 Stigma, 5 Again, 6 Descend, 7 Rand, 12 Defiance, 14 Donkeys, 16 Roister, 17 Pulley, 19 Satyr, 20 Glean, 21 Bead.

No 55

Across: 1 Sorbet, 7 Approval, 8 Mess, 10 Hasten, 11 Grid, 12 Eclat, 13 Persist, 17 Officer, 19 Board, 21 This, 23 Turner, 25 Role, 26 Key-rings, 27 Pliers.

Down: 1 Sombrero, 2 Rush, 3 Tasty, 4 Spaniel, 5 Gong, 6 Caries, 9 Salami, 14 Shower, 15 Tidiness, 16 Setting, 18 Fuhrer, 20 Crisp, 22 Sort, 24 Rode.

No 56

Across: 1 Tuberculosis, 9 Abash, 10 Grave, 11 Elm, 12 Guess, 13 Sardine, 14 Debase, 16 Lapdog, 20 Soldier, 22 Frill, 24 All, 25 Along, 26 Irate, 27 Dispensation.

Down: 2 Usage, 3 Ephesus, 4 Clumsy, 5 Lager, 6 Seabird, 7 Swede, 8 Jagged, 15 Bilious, 17 Afflict, 18 Galley, 19 Fracas, 20 Stand, 21 Ingle, 23 Imago.

No 57

Across: 1 Cosmic, 4 Saline, 7 Careen, 9 Effusion, 11 Acme, 14 Re-elect, 15 Iris, 16 Unit, 17 Tussled, 18 East, 21 Emphatic, 22 Thrice, 24 Embers, 25 Behead.

Down: 1 Cocoa, 2 Scram, 3 Ice, 4 Self-neglect, 5 Lassitude, 6 Earn, 8 Necessitous, 10 Orbits, 12 Curium, 13 Erstwhile, 19 Arise, 20 Tread, 21 Else, 23 Hoe.

No 58

Across: 1 Pockets, 8 Emanate, 9 Terrier, 10 Stares, 12 Bridle, 13 Femme fatale, 17 Absurd, 20 Drowse, 23 Airlift, 24 Express, 25 Sincere.

Solutions

Down: 1 Potash, 2 Carnage, 3 Exile, 4 Sere, 5 Mayor, 6 Fated, 7 Deafen, 11 Speed, 12 Beard, 14 Low tide, 15 Barber, 16 Beetle, 18 Swipe, 19 Rebel, 21 Rerun, 22 Pass.

No 59

Across: 4 Sampler, 8 Tango, 9 Cartridge, 10 Poilu, 11 Sacrilege, 13 Normal, 16 Fiesta, 20 Dexterous, 23 Circa, 24 San Marino, 25 Peeve, 26 Dungeon.

Down: 1 Utopian, 2 Incisor, 3 Focus, 4 Spruce, 5 Martini, 6 Ladle, 7 Reeve, 12 Got, 14 One, 15 Acetate, 17 Snorkel, 18 Ashamed, 19 Lotion, 20 Dosed, 21 Xenon, 22 Scope.

No 60

Across: 1 Shampoo, 5 Actor, 8 Oar, 9 Paternity, 10 Blaze, 12 Icon, 13 Theirs, 15 Rasp, 17 Tsar, 20 Abrupt, 22 Beds, 23 Avail, 25 Assistant, 26 Era, 27 Shrew, 28 Scruple.

Down: 1 Slobber, 2 Arrears, 3 Puppet, 4 Oath, 6 Consist, 7 Rayon, 11 Limp, 14 Hart, 16 Passive, 18 Shake up, 19 Release, 21 Tatter, 22 Brass, 24 Bans.

No 61

Across: 1 Sandal, 3 Radius, 7 Reservation, 10 Examiner, 11 Ague, 13 Sheet, 14 Laity, 18 Alto, 19 Jubilant, 21 Intelligent, 22 Serene, 23 Haggis.

Down: 1 Street, 2 Airliner, 4 Akin, 5 Sachet, 6 Caret, 8 Spaghetti, 9 Negotiate, 12 Basilica, 15 Canvas, 16 Bugle, 17 Status, 20 Stun.

No 62

Across: 1 Defacing, 5 Boat, 8 Anaconda, 10 Epistle, 11 Fichu, 12 Selection, 15 Washboard, 18 Ahead, 19 Isthmus, 22 Sanguine, 23 Tang, 24 Generous.

Down: 1 Dwarfs, 2 Fiancees, 3 Chorus, 4 Nude, 6 Omit, 7 Tavern, 9 Appear, 13 Exodus, 14 Impetigo, 15 Weight, 16 Dangle, 17 Idlers, 20 Thin, 21 Sate.

No 63

Across: 1 Swollen, 7 Panama, 9 Cortege, 10 Siege, 11 Reed, 12 Coney, 16 Nacre, 17 Calm, 21 Learn, 22 Crouton, 23 Stereo, 24 Wanders.

Down: 1 Sincere, 2 Oversee, 3 Libel, 4 Hamster, 5 Cater, 6 Eaves, 8 Democracy, 13 Pannier, 14 Lattice, 15 Ominous, 18 Clasp, 19 Gavel, 20 Dozen.

No 64

Across: 1 Claret, 4 Halves, 9 Avenues, 10 Stipend, 11 Evade, 12 Tardy, 14 Alias, 15 Seeds, 17 Stage, 18 A priori, 20 Orifice, 21 Shandy, 22 Settee.

Down: 1 Chalet, 2 Amenable, 3 Educe, 5 Anoints, 6 Vote, 7 Sundry, 8 Association, 13 Royalist, 14 Astound, 15 Smarts, 16 Delete, 17 Spice, 19 Rota.

No 65

Across: 1 Skimp, 4 Swanson, 8 Anthill, 9 Dregs, 10 Terra, 11 Restive, 12 Travel, 13 Spring, 16 Prickle, 18 Claws, 20 Lunar, 21 Bullion, 22 Deliver, 23 Dingy.

Solutions

Down: 1 Slant, 2 International, 3 Private, 4 Salary, 5 Andes, 6 Specification, 7 Nest egg, 12 Toppled, 14 Pickled, 15 Member, 17 Kirov, 19 Sunny.

No 66

Across: 1 Acquisitive, 9 Seize, 10 Sir, 11 Input, 12 Spain, 13 Struggle, 16 Hacienda, 18 Elves, 21 Stale, 22 Spa, 23 Minim, 24 Assassinate.

Down: 2 Compare, 3 Upstage, 4 Spinal, 5 Trees, 6 Vista, 7 Swiss cheese, 8 Transparent, 14 Kinsman, 15 Inhabit, 17 Amends, 19 Vials, 20 Samba.

No 67

Across: 1 Osmosis, 6 Rim, 8 Obese, 9 Pillion, 10 Point, 11 Nineteen, 13 Stench, 15 Heresy, 18 Bereaved, 19 Snail, 21 Triumph, 22 Erode, 23 Nod, 24 Retired.

Down: 2 Ski lift, 3 Sciatica, 4 Sonnet, 5 Hemp, 6 Relieve, 7 Mystery, 12 Benedict, 13 Session, 14 Engaged, 16 Steeple, 17 Jester, 20 Look.

No 68

Across: 1 Disowned, 5 Skip, 9 Abalone, 10 Brave, 11 Perpetuate, 14 Cornet, 15 Heroic, 17 Icebreaker, 20 Elide, 21 Leotard, 22 Togs, 23 Crescent.

Down: 1 Draw, 2 Slap, 3 Wholehearted, 4 Exempt, 6 Krakatoa, 7 Pretence, 8 Obstreperous, 12 Accident, 13 Freezing, 16 Sailor, 18 Cane, 19 Edit.

No 69

Across: 1 Cardiac, 5 Smash, 7 Radii, 8 Scanner, 9 Crevice, 10 Petty, 11 Saddle, 13 Cohere, 18 Crumb, 20 Secured, 21 Caprice, 22 Abhor, 23 Atone, 24 Tidings.

Down: 1 Caracas, 2 Redhead, 3 Initial, 4 Casket, 5 Sharp, 6 Shelter, 12 Abreast, 14 Orchard, 15 Earthen, 16 Endures, 17 Assert, 19 Bride.

No 70

Across: 1 Stolid, 4 Porous, 7 Always, 8 Taste bud, 12 Fossil, 14 Hearse, 15 Candle, 16 Rented, 18 Analysis, 22 Scrape, 23 Access, 24 Adagio.

Down: 1 Soak, 2 Loaves, 3 Distil, 4 Paws, 5 Ride, 6 Sold, 9 There, 10 Ulster, 11 Domain, 13 Inlay, 16 Russia, 17 Nutria, 18 Area, 19 Lace, 20 Skis, 21 Zero.

No 71

Across: 1 Scalp, 4 Succeed, 7 Party, 8 Aperture, 9 Recap, 11 Endanger, 15 Wariness, 17 Speak, 19 Gracious, 20 Hoard, 21 Wet suit, 22 Shred.

Down: 1 Secateurs, 2 Already, 3 Posting, 4 Swerve, 5 Craven, 6 Extra, 10 Persisted, 12 Viscous, 13 Recover, 14 Walrus, 16 Adrift, 18 Phone.

No 72

Across: 1 Predecessor, 7 Pine tree, 8 Roll, 9 Sharif, 11 Pestle, 13 Bowel, 14 Shape, 17 Myriad, 20 Borzoi, 22 Alga, 23 Narrates, 24 Ferris wheel.

Solutions

Down: 1 Papist, 2 Drear, 3 Careful, 4 Sweep, 5 Orris, 6 Allied, 10 Amour, 12 Topaz, 14 Suburbs, 15 Embalm, 16 Tinsel, 18 Image, 19 Donor, 21 Roach.

No 73
Across: 1 Boar, 3 Literati, 9 Spoiler, 10 Scowl, 11 No-one, 12 Portico, 13 Septic, 15 Likens, 17 Carrier, 18 Edged, 20 Agora, 21 Grammar, 22 Spacemen, 23 Stud.
Down: 1 Business class, 2 Amoco, 4 Irrupt, 5 Ex-serviceman, 6 Agonize, 7 Ill-considered, 8 Illegitimate, 14 Pergola, 16 Brogue, 19 Gamut.

No 74
Across: 1 Menace, 8 Moonbeam, 9 Zagreb, 10 Obsolete, 11 Essays, 12 Shutting, 16 Charades, 18 Trance, 21 Massacre, 23 Amount, 24 Reverend, 25 Yonder.
Down: 2 Exams, 3 Aorta, 4 Embossed, 5 Loss, 6 Ability, 7 Fasten, 11 Eric, 13 Unsteady, 14 Game, 15 Prosper, 17 Heaven, 19 Acorn, 20 Canoe, 22 Crew.

No 75
Across: 1 Supposed, 5 Trip, 8 Liars, 9 Tuneful, 10 Reagent, 12 Sundown, 14 Chassis, 16 Art deco, 18 Topical, 19 Large, 20 Yarn, 21 Arboreal.
Down: 1 Sole, 2 Platen, 3 Oasthouse, 4 Extern, 6 Rafter, 7 Politics, 11 Armadillo, 12 Stealthy, 13 Stupor, 14 Collar, 15 Soiree, 17 Bell.

No 76
Across: 7 Lonesome, 8 Aunt, 9 Otis, 10 Slip, 11 Fan, 13 Crank, 14 Palaver, 16 Make way, 18 Fatty, 21 Urn, 22 Hi-fi, 23 Auld, 25 Data, 26 Teenager.

Down: 1 Co-star, 2 Personnel, 3 Douse, 4 Seminar, 5 Bad, 6 In case, 12 Catamaran, 15 Variety, 17 Airman, 19 Tiller, 20 Biped, 24 Cap.

No 77
Across: 1 Scamp, 7 Radical, 8 For, 9 Synagogue, 11 Rouse, 12 Resident, 16 Two-timer, 20 Email, 21 Film stars, 23 Hod, 24 Ivanhoe, 25 Testy.
Down: 1 Saffron, 2 Air gun, 3 Purser, 4 Iron, 5 Disobey, 6 Fleet, 10 Alive, 13 Evict, 14 Comment, 15 Holiday, 17 Resent, 18 Washes, 19 Affix, 22 Apex.

No 78
Across: 1 Acacia, 7 Mainstay, 8 Elapse, 10 In situ, 11 Steep, 13 Hassock, 16 Pretzel, 17 Boxer, 20 Labels, 22 Dining, 24 Neurotic, 25 Tinned.
Down: 1 Abbess, 2 Aura, 3 Amber, 4 Minimal, 5 Isis, 6 Particle, 9 Pleat, 12 Threaten, 14 Sworn, 15 Density, 18 Regard, 19 Edict, 21 Euro, 23 Ivan.

No 79
Across: 1 Command, 7 Realize, 8 Umbra, 10 Worn-out, 11 Tests, 12 Horseshoe, 16 Scarlatti, 18 Bogey, 20 Rustler, 23 Guest, 24 Chuckle, 25 Tyranny.
Down: 1 Coast, 2 Moussaka, 3 Drawer, 4 Fair, 5 Biro, 6 Settler, 9 Bushel, 13 Edible, 14 Heighten, 15 Ostrich, 17 Target, 19 Yummy, 21 Scud, 22 Lake.

Solutions

No 1

		V	E	N	U	S		P		P	L	U	T	O	
S				A		E	P	O	C	H				R	
T		M		S		T		I		A	R	C		I	
A	B	E	R	R	A	T	I	O	N			S		O	
R		R		O		T			T			E		N	
F		C		T			M	O	O	N		E			
O		U		A		S			F		M	A	R	S	
R		R	E	T	R	O	G	R	A	D	E		T		
M		Y		I		L			P		T		H		
A			C	O	M	A		C	O	M	E	T		U	
T		E		N		R			A		O			R	
I		U		C			S	U	P	E	R	N	O	V	A
O		R		U					S		I			A	
N		O		R	E	D	S	H	I	F	T			N	
		P		V					S		E			U	
P	L	A	N	E	T				U					S	
									N				I	T	

No 2

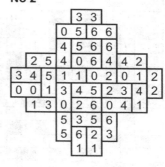

No 3

5	4	3	1	2	6
4	1	6	2	5	3
2	3	4	6	1	5
1	2	5	3	6	4
6	5	1	4	3	2
3	6	2	5	4	1

No 4

Start in the grey-shaded square

2S	1W	2S	2W	2W
1E	2S	1E	1E	2S
1N	2E		1S	2N
1S	1W	2N	1W	1N
2E	2N	2E	2W	1W

No 5

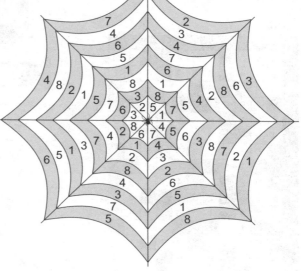

No 6

1 Pisces, 2 Slalom,
3 Mont Blanc,
4 Codicil, 5 Laughing
gas, 6 Seismology,
7 Yard, 8 Daniel
Defoe, 9 Epidermis,
10 Spearmint,
11 Twenty-one.
The gemstone is:
PERIDOT

Solutions

No 7

S	P	L	I	T		S		S	A	N	D
H		A		E	X	T	R	A			O
I	N	N	E	R		U		L	U	L	L
P		O		R	A	N	G	E	R		L
B	A	L	S	A		N			G		A
U		I		C		E	N	D	E	A	R
I	N	N	U	E	N	D	O			L	
L			S		O		I	N	T	E	R
D	I	S	E	A	S	E	S		H		E
E		E		R	E	V	E	L	E	R	S
R	A	T	I	O		E		I		I	
	W			S	T	R	A	P	P	E	D
B	E	A	R	E	R		B		A		E
R		P		I		R	I	P	E	N	
O		S	T	A	P	L	E		R		
W	H	E	Y		L		A	L	I	B	I
S			P	E	E	L	S		K		A
E	L	S	E		T		T	R	A	I	L

No 8

1	8	4	3		2	8	1	1	4	0
	9	0	0	4		7	8	2	3	
	5	0	5	0	0		1	0	3	
6	2	5	0	9				0		3
4	4	3	7	7		8	6		2	9
6			7	5	0	8	3	5		
	6		2		9	0	2	7		4
4	5	6	0		4	8	8	5	0	6
7		8		4	0	0	0	9		5
8	9	3	7	8	0		1	5	7	
6	1	0		9	8	5	4		6	

No 9

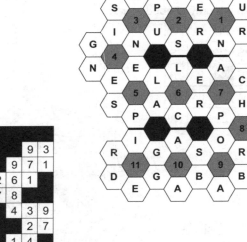

No 10

9	4	8		1	3	4		9	3
2	1	4		3	8	9		9	7	1
8	3		2	5		5	2	6	1
	7	9	6			7	8		
1	2	8		6	3	1		4	3	9
4	9		9	5	2		2	7
	5	7	2	8	6	3		1	4
	3	1			6	9
	9	2		8	9	4	1	5	6
1	7		2	8	1		8	9
9	8	4		1	6	3		8	4	7
	1	5			5	6	2
6	5	9	3		3	7		1	2
4	1	2		9	5	6		5	9	8
9	8		2	3	1		1	5	6

Solutions

No 11

A		G		P	E	R	T	A	I	N	E	D
S	N	I	P	E		U		B		I		U
K		N		T	A	N	G	Y		C	O	S
A	N	G	L	E		N		S	P	E	A	K
N		H	A	R	D	Y		S	O	R	R	Y
C	R	A	B		U		G		S		S	
E		M	O	R	T	A	L	I	T	Y		S
	N		R		Y		U		M	A	T	H
P	O	K	E	S		S	T	R	A	W		E
A	V	E	R	T		W		A	N	N	U	L
N	A	N		A	L	O	N	G		I		V
I		D		L		R		G	E	N	I	E
C	R	O	O	K	E	D	L	Y		G		D

No 12

S	T	I	R	R	U	P		M	A	W	K	I	S	H
T		T			L		A		I					O
E	V	E	R	Y	B	O	D	Y		D	R	A	F	T
R		M		O		Y		O		E		M		E
I	N	S	A	N	E		T	R	A	N	Q	U	I	L
L			D		S		W			S				
I		S	K	E	L	E	T	O	N		W	I	S	P
Z		E		R		W		B		D		N		E
E	A	S	Y		A	N	N	E	X	I	N	G		R
		S		P		Y		Y		N				F
J	U	I	C	I	E	S	T		S	N	E	E	Z	E
E		O		D		T		I		E		L		C
W	I	N	C	E		R	E	S	U	R	R	E	C	T
E			A			A		L				C		L
L	O	Y	A	L	T	Y		E	M	P	A	T	H	Y

No 13

6	+	9	x	3
−		−		+
2	x	4	+	8
x		+		x
7	−	1	x	5

No 14

4	8	1	20	10	13	4
19	11	3	14	6	18	17
19	2	9	16	1	9	12
15	15	16	17	20	5	1
4	8	2	10	20	12	7
14	16	3	5	6	11	19
3	5	2	7	18	17	13

No 15

C	B	D	E	F	A
A	E	C	D	B	F
F	A	E	C	D	B
D	C	B	F	A	E
E	F	A	B	C	D
B	D	F	A	E	C

No 16

3	1	1	4	4	4
4	2	2	3	3	4
4	2	2	3	3	4
4	1	1	1	1	2
4	1	1	1	1	2
1	3	3	4	4	4

No 17

R	U	T	H			B	A	R	A	B	B	A	S	
		A				B		Q		A			S	
		B	O	A	Z		E		U		T		N	O
		I			E		L		I	S	H	M	A	E	L
L	O	T			C			L		S		T		O
E		H		S	H	A	D	R	A	C	H		H	A	M
A	H	A	B		A					E		A		O
H			R				L	A	B	A	N		N	
	J			S	I	S	E	R	A		A		J	
	O				A			Z			I		A	
	B	E	L	S	H	A	Z	Z	A	R		S	H	E	M
S		S			A			R		R		L		
A	D	A	M		R			U	R	I	A	H		E
U		U		T	H	O	M	A	S		E		V	
L					N			P	I	L	A	T	E	

371

Solutions

No 18

1 Rite (c), 2 Epic (c), 3 Deed (c/a),
4 Herd (a), 5 Teem (a), 6 Tart (c),
7 Vote (a), 8 Pope (c/a), 9 Dead (a),
10 Hard (c), 11 Matt (a), 12 Trot (c),
13 Evil (c), 14 Pink (a), 15 Akin (a),
16 Rain (c), 17 Tack (a), 18 Joke (a),
19 Lime (c), 20 Nick (a), 21 Skid (c),
22 Dial (c), 23 Cake (a), 24 Heel (a),
25 Meal (a), 26 Clan (a), 27 Soon (c),
28 Polo (c/a), 29 Coke (c), 30 Melt (c),
31 Away (c/a), 32 Yard (c), 33 Road (c),
34 Pace (a), 35 Cede (c/a),
36 Same (a).

No 19

1 Salsa, 2 Acetic, 3 Ciabatta,
4 Avocado, 5 Ouzo,
6 Omelette, 7 Edam,
8 Macaroni, 9 Ingredient,
10 Triple sec, 11 Chowder,
12 Ragout, 13 Teetotaller.
The cheese is: CAMEMBERT

No 21

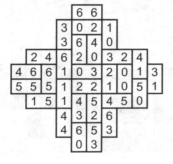

No 20

No 23

No 22

Solutions

No 24

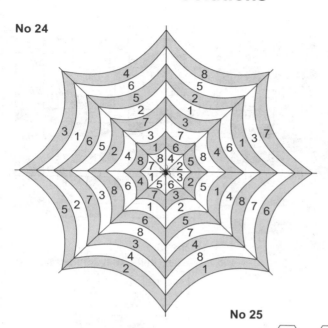

No 25

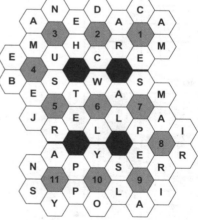

No 26

	1	5		4	3		3	5
8	7	9		9	4		1	2
7	3		6	7	1	5	3	4	8
3	2	8	1		2	4	1		1	2
	9	3	1		7	3	1	8	9
		2	6	9		9	6	
1	3	9	7		8	4	2		1	4
2	1	8		3	7	9		9	6	8
4	8		8	1	6		5	7	2	9
	5	7		4	1	3	
2	1	3	5	4		7	6	8
9	7		9	8	5		1	3	6	2
6	3	5		3	1	6	2		9	1
	2	9		2	7		9	8	3
	1	5		3	9		2	7

No 27

1 Schism, 2 Malta, 3 Ark of the Covenant, 4 Titian, 5 Nassau, 6 Ulna, 7 Archipelago, 8 Orion, 9 Nicaragua, 10 Argentina, 11 Anthropology, 12 Yam.

The fish is: SALMON

373

Solutions

No 28

```
M O B I L E   M   S A M P L E   E
I   I     D W E L T   U   O
M A K I N G   A   A   C   G
I   I   E   N E I G H B O R
C   N   E D I T   N   L   A
  M I N X   N   T   C R O W N
A       E M B A R G O   W   S
V E N O M   O   A   M A N G O
E   O   P A R S N I P     M
R E M I T   N   C   L U S H
S   A   A   D E F Y   Q   J
E N D A N G E R   L   U   A
  O   D A   E   A B O A R D
  R   Z   T H A N K   W   E
I M P E D E   M   E V O K E D
```

No 29

```
W A K E S   F   A D O R N
H   H   P L U M M E T   E
O K A P I   E   E N T E R
L   K   N Y L O N   E   V
E P I C   E   B   P R A Y
  R   H E A R S A Y   B
H I V E   R   C   G O A D
  Z   S U N B E A M   C
F E E T   E   N   Y O K E
U   V   I D L E R   D   V
S C I O N   O   A R I S E
E   C U T L A S S   U   N
D I T T O   F   P U M P S
```

No 30
Start in the grey-shaded square

1E	1E	2E	2S	1W
1N	1S	2W	2W	1W
1S	2S		1S	1N
1E	1E	1N	1S	1N
2N	1W	2E	1W	1N

No 31

5	6	4	3	2	1
3	5	1	6	4	2
4	1	2	5	6	3
1	2	3	4	5	6
2	4	6	1	3	5
6	3	5	2	1	4

No 32

```
S E A T S   S Y R U P
T   M   O B O E   A   R
R E A D Y   L   F   O
U   S   A S B E S T O S
C Y S T   E   C U E   E
K   I   A S T E R N
  S A B L E   D   M
W H I R R   W H E T   A
A   N A U S E A   I C Y
L O G   T U R T L E   B
L   E V E N   E E R I E
S   I   N O D E S   B
  P A P A Y A   C   B
F   T E N   T   H A L O
O U T R I G H T   L   L
C   I   M   O P I N E
U   R   A T O M   G   R
S W E L L   B A N J O
```

No 33

7	+	9	−	2
−		×		+
1	+	4	×	6
+		−		×
5	×	8	+	3

No 34

15	16	8	19	14	12	10
4	3	16	11	13	6	20
9	10	20	7	18	1	13
5	11	16	19	15	6	7
2	17	5	8	17	17	1
14	4	11	12	2	13	15
10	18	9	12	14	3	18

Solutions

No 35

No 36

No 37
The word is:
CONFRONTATIONAL

No 38
PORK, perk, peek, reek, reef, BEEF
GROW, glow, flow, flew, flee, free, TREE
(Alternative solutions are sometimes
possible)

No 39
The words are:
DEBRIS, EMBRYO,
FABRIC, HEBREW,
INBRED, HYBRID

No 40

No 41

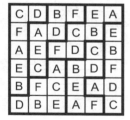

Solutions

No 42
A=102, B=98, C=129, D=142,
E=48, F=200, G=227, H=271,
I=190, J=427, K=498, L=461,
M=925, N=959, O=1884

No 43

F	E	A	T	H	E	R		B	R	A	W	L
L		M		O		E		A		Z		A
E		O		A	C	T	O	R		U	R	N
A	N	N	E	X		A		E	A	R		O
S	I	G	N		T	I	N		T	E	A	L
	C		G	A	R	N	I	S	H			I
O	K	R	A		A		G		L	A	W	N
S			G	U	M	S	H	O	E		E	
M	A	C	E		P	O	T		T	R	I	P
O		A	D	D		V		P	E	A	R	L
S	I	N		O	R	I	E	L		T		E
I		O		M		E	O	I		I		A
S	C	E	N	E		T	H	Y	R	O	I	D

No 44

No 45

D	O	M	E		S	H	O	P	S			B	E	A	M
O					H				B						O
O		H		E		C	E	L	L	A	R	S			R
R	O	T	U	N	D	A			A		T				T
		T			P	L	I	N	T	H					A
E		D		S		A		D		R	I	S	E	R	
S	H	E	L	T	E	R		I		O			X		
T		P		A		T	R	A	N	S	O	M		I	
A		O		I		M		G		M	O	A	T		
T		T	U	R	R	E	T	S		S		N			
E				N				S	T	R	U	T			
	W	A	L	L		T		A		O		M		H	
	O		O		G	R	A	N	G	E		A		A	
R	O	O	F			C		E		N		L		L	
	D		T	R	E	N	C	H	E	S		T	I	L	E

No 46

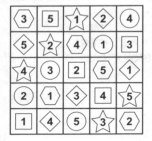

No 47
1 Frog (c), 2 Roof (c), 3 Poor (a), 4 Raft (a),
5 Foam (c), 6 Calm (a), 7 Corn (c),
8 Fret (a), 9 Town (c), 10 Yawn (a),
11 Many (c), 12 Clap (a), 13 Newt (c),
14 Leek (c), 15 Knew (c), 16 Lend (c),
17 Dean (a), 18 Pall (a), 19 Wren (a),
20 Nail (a), 21 Wisp (a), 22 Plow (c),
23 Neon (a), 24 Only (c), 25 Cent (c),
26 Rand (a), 27 Spar (c), 28 Warp (c),
29 Gnaw (a), 30 Goat (c), 31 Talk (a),
32 Deck (c), 33 Each (c), 34 Crab (c),
35 Wall (a), 36 Tall (c).

No 48

```
        1 6
      6 1 6 4
      2 5 5 4
    2 2 3 6 1 3 3 0
  0 2 4 3 4 2 4 1 2 6
  4 5 1 5 0 5 1 3 3 4
    0 6 2 2 3 0 4
        0 0 1 5
        5 6 1 6
          3 5
```

Solutions

No 49

1 Macbeth, 2 Hungary, 3 Yellow, 4 Whitsuntide, 5 Engels, 6 Santiago, 7 Olympus, 8 Sardine, 9 Electron, 10 Northumberland, 11 Darjeeling.
The royal house is: TUDOR

No 50

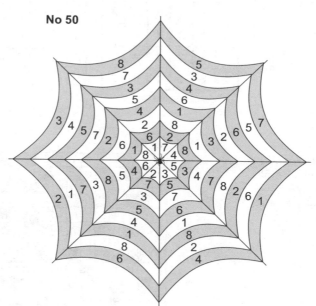

No 51

P	E	N	E	T	R	A	T	I	N	G
	D		T		X			E	A	R
	G		H		S	I	L	V	E	R
D	E	V	I	O	U	S		D	A	Y
E		C		E		P			G	
C	R	A	S	S		F	L	A	R	E	D
O		B		E		A		E		E
M	O	N	O	P	O	L	Y		C	P
P		O		U		M	O	O	S	E
R	U	R	A	L		A		U		N
E		M		C	A	P	T	U	R	E	D
S		A		H		E		S		E
S	P	L	E	E	N		S	H	E	E	N
	I		R		P		O			C
I	T	S		V	I	B	R	A	T	E
	T	O	F	F	E	E		R		U
E	E	L		S		I		I		B
D	O	W	N	T	R	O	D	D	E	N

No 52

2	9		8	9	6		3	2	1		7	3
1	5	4	2	6	3		6	3	5	9	8	7
4	8	9		8	1		2	1		2	4	1
3	7		5	7			4	9		9	2	
		2	3	5	1		7	6	8	9		
9	3	7			6	2	9			8	2	9
5	1	9			2	1	3			5	1	2
4	2	8	1	3	7		6	9	5	7	4	8
		7	9				8	6				
4	3	7	2	1	6		2	7	4	1	3	5
8	7	9			8	9	6		3	9	8	
9	1	6			9	7	1		2	7	9	
	2	7	1	4		9	3	6	8			
9	7		9	4			1	3		4	2	
2	1	6		2	3		3	2		1	9	3
4	2	9	5	3	1		9	4	7	3	8	6
8	9		9	5	8		8	7	9		6	1

Solutions

No 53

6	5	1	3	4	2
3	1	4	2	5	6
5	3	2	4	6	1
4	6	5	1	2	3
2	4	3	6	1	5
1	2	6	5	3	4

No 54

4	1	1	3	3	2
2	1	1	3	3	4
2	1	1	3	3	4
3	3	3	4	4	1
3	3	3	4	4	1
2	2	2	1	1	2

No 55

20	19	7	13	16	6	12
13	1	12	6	12	9	19
11	11	2	18	5	14	17
14	18	15	2	17	5	11
4	19	16	15	10	13	16
8	10	4	7	18	1	9
15	14	3	17	8	3	20

No 56

A=77, B=91, C=142, D=34, E=116, F=168, G=233, H=176, I=150, J=401, K=409, L=326, M=810, N=735, O=1545

No 57

No 58

S	O	C	K	S		F		S	M	A	R	T
P		A		C	L	E	F	T		Z		R
L	U	N	A	R		L		O	V	A	T	E
A		V		A	F	T	E	R		L		N
S	C	A	M	P	I		L	Y	R	E		C
H	O	S	E		S		I		O	A	T	H
	V		R	I	S	O	T	T	O		I	
Y	E	T	I		U		I		S	U	R	F
E		S	T	A	R		S	E	T	T	E	E
L		E		D	E	L	T	A		M		N
L	I	T	H	E		I		G	R	O	W	N
O		S		P	E	N	A	L		S		E
W	H	E	A	T		T		E	X	T	O	L

No 59

1	1	4	6	1		3	8	2	9	4
2		3	8	7	7	2		0		9
5	1	0	5		8	2	9	8		2
5		1		2	7		1	5	8	7
7	8	4	8		2	4	0	0		6
	9		9	2		5	8		5	
5	1	2		5	3	3		6	0	1
6		7	0	0	3	2	4		6	7
1	2	1		5		9	3	4	3	
3		6	0	3	4	4		4		0
7	6	9		6		3	9	0	6	4

Solutions

No 60

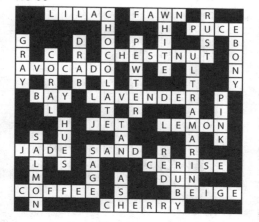

No 61

CORN, core, more, mole, mile, MILL
FORK, work, wore, wire, wise, wish, DISH
(Alternative solutions are sometimes possible)

No 62

The words are:
ABSURD, ASSURE, CASUAL, DISUSE, ISSUES, JESUIT

No 63

1 Sierra Leone, 2 Electra, 3 Alexander, 4 Rialto,
5 Operetta, 6 Antarctica, 7 Ayckbourn, 8 Napalm,
9 Medusa, 10 Agincourt, 11 Tanganyika.
The poultry bird is: TURKEY

No 64

Solutions

No 65

M		E		A		C	O	M	B	A	T
A	M	N	E	S	I	A		I		D	
S		T		P		R	E	N	T	A	L
C	A	R	B	I	N	E		T		G	
A		E		R		S	T	E	R	E	O
R		A		I		S	O	D	A		F
A	T	T	E	N	D		U		D		F
	W		A		A	I	R	L	I	N	E
C	O	S	T	L	Y				A		N
O		O			B	A	L	L	A	D	
P	A	N	C	A	K	E		I		D	
I		N		R		T	R	E	M	O	R
N		E	P	I	C		U		I		O
G	A	T	E	A	U		I		L		U
	W		R		R	A	N	K	I	N	G
L	A	D	I	E	S		O		T		H
	R		O		E	L	U	S	I	V	E
W	E	L	D	E	D			S		A	N

No 66

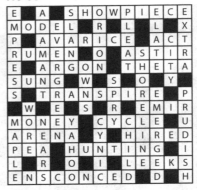

E		A		S	H	O	W	P	I	E	C	E
M	O	D	E	L		R		L		L		X
P		A	V	A	R	I	C	E		A	C	T
R	U	M	E	N		O		A	S	T	I	R
E		A	R	G	O	N		T	H	E	T	A
S	U	N	G		W		S		O		Y	
S		T	R	A	N	S	P	I	R	E		P
	W		E		S		R		E	M	I	R
M	O	N	E	Y		C	Y	C	L	E		U
A	R	E	N	A		Y		H	I	R	E	D
P	E	A		H	U	N	T	I	N	G		I
L		R		O		I		L	E	E	K	S
E	N	S	C	O	N	C	E	D		D		H

No 67

Start in the grey-shaded square

1S	2S	2S	1W	1S
2S	1N	1W	1N	1W
2N	2S		2S	2N
2E	2E	2N	1E	1S
2N	1N	2W	1W	2N

No 68

9	–	3	x	5
–		+		x
7	–	6	x	1
+		x		+
4	x	2	+	8

No 69

No 70

S	I	D	E		M	U	T	U	A	L
W		I		A		N		N		I
I	N	S	T	R	U	C	T	I	O	N
M		T		I		O		O		S
M	A	I	N	T	E	N	A	N	C	E
I		N		H		S				E
N		C	O	M	I	C	A	L		D
G	E	T		E		I				E
L		I	N	T	R	O	D	U	C	E
Y		V		I		U				H
	P	E	R	C	U	S	S	I	O	N

Solutions

No 71

	W	O	R	S	H	I	P	S		B		R		B
K		U		U			C	H	O	L	E	R	A	
N	A	I	L	B	R	U	S	H		U		J		B
A		E		T		E	N	Q	U	I	R	Y		Y
V	A	N	D	A	L	I	S	M		U		G		H
E		O		I		E	K	E				E		O
	J	O	U	R	N	E	Y	S		T	E	M	P	O
F		S		G		O		E			E			D
I	N	E	P	T		O	U	T	S	I	Z	E	D	
X				R	U	B		T		T				G
A		E		E		V	A	R	I	O	U	S	L	Y
T	I	M	P	A	N	I		M		N				P
I		P		S		A	B	R	A	S	I	O	N	S
O	U	T	P	O	S	T		T			T			Y
N		Y		N		E	X	T	E	R	N	A	L	

No 73

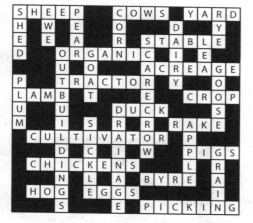

No 72

1 Text (a), 2 Term (c),
3 Real (c), 4 Dart (c),
5 Dent (a), 6 Ease (a),
7 Lynx (c), 8 Mill (c),
9 Link (a), 10 Kind (a),
11 Down (c), 12 Foal (c),
13 Yank (a), 14 Lock (c),
15 Norm (a), 16 Mink (c),
17 Worn (c), 18 Fold (a),
19 Fawn (c), 20 Cuff (c),
21 True (a), 22 Knot (c),
23 Turn (a), 24 Pull (c),
25 Part (a), 26 Flip (c),
27 Fled (c), 28 Food (a),
29 Tool (a), 30 Plod (a),
31 Rant (c), 32 Brim (c),
33 Film (c), 34 Tiff (c),
35 Soft (a), 36 Sofa (c).

No 74

1 Honolulu, 2 Uganda,
3 Aberdeen, 4 North
Sea, 5 Azores,
6 Stansted, 7 Donegal,
8 Leningrad, 9 Death
Valley, 10 Ypres,
11 Snowdon, 12 New
Guinea.
The country is: LIBERIA

No 75

E	D	F	B	C	A
D	B	A	C	E	F
A	C	B	E	F	D
B	F	E	A	D	C
C	A	D	F	B	E
F	E	C	D	A	B

No 76

3	2	2	4	4	2
4	3	3	1	1	1
4	3	3	1	1	1
1	2	2	2	2	3
1	2	2	2	2	3
3	1	1	4	4	4

No 77

5	3	2	1	4
4	2	1	5	3
3	1	5	4	2
1	4	3	2	5
2	5	4	3	1

Solutions

No 78

O		M		P		C		R	
V	I	E	W	E	R		O		E
A		E			E	N	R	O	L
L	I	K	E	L	Y		A		A
			Y			F	L	E	X
W	I	S	E			O			
E		H		J	A	R	G	O	N
A	Z	U	R	E			R		E
R		N		S	Q	U	A	R	E
Y		T		T			B		D

No 79
The word is:
INTERNATIONALLY

No 80
The words are:
BLANCH, CRANKY,
FLANGE, GLANCE,
PEANUT, SCANTY

No 81
A=38, B=103, C=62,
D=125, E=82, F=141,
G=165, H=187, I=207,
J=306, K=352, L=394,
M=658, N=746, O=1404

No 82

S	O	N	I	C		M		P	A	I	L
H		U		O	B	E	S	E			O
A	P	R	O	N		N		S	N	O	W
P		S		C	O	U	N	T			E
E	L	E	V	E	N		U	S	H	E	R
L	A	M		R	E	S	T				C
E	X	A	C	T		A	S	P		Z	
S		I		I	N	N		I	B	E	X
S	E	D	A	N		G	O	T		M	
	M		G	A	S		B	Y	W	A	Y
O	B	O	E		A	L	L		H		E
	R		D	O	G		I	R	O	N	S
	Y		R	O	O	T		L	O	T	
C	O	B	R	A		R	E	V	E	R	E
R		A	L	T	E	R		S		R	
A	M	E	N		I		A	L	O	U	D
W		G	U	E	S	T		M		A	
L	A	Z	E		R		E	L	E	G	Y

No 83

1	4		3	9		9	7		5	4	3
2	6	5	1	4	3	8	9		7	9	8	1
6	8	9		2	1	7		4	9		9	3
	9	6	7	8	4		3	1	6	9	4	2
3	5	2	1		2	6	1		1	5
1	7		2	7		9	6	7	8		9	8
	6	4		2	5		9	5	1
8	7		7	2	1	8		2	7	3	1
6	4	8	9		2	5	1		9	5	2	7
	2	3	5	1		9	7	4	8		3	9
9	3	1		9	2		5	1
2	1		2	7	3	1		2	1		7	1
	7	6		1	2	8		9	8	6	3
4	2	3	5	1	8		5	1	4	2	3
5	1		9	8		7	9	3		9	8	3
9	4	1	7		9	8	7	4	1	3	5	2
	9	6	8		7	1		9	6		9	1

Solutions

No 84

No 85

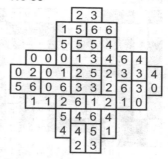

No 86

1 Orchard, 2 Chador, 3 Hoard, 4 Road, 5 Adore, 6 Fedora, 7 Forbade

No 87

7	8	19	2	13	14	2
3	3	12	5	8	8	11
19	18	12	20	9	5	18
7	13	1	15	4	11	6
20	4	1	10	15	6	17
2	9	16	6	1	14	4
10	3	7	16	5	9	17

No 88

S	H	R	U	B		K		R	E	P	E	L
T	E	A		R	A	I	S	E		L		O
A	N	K	L	E		W		L	E	A	S	T
M		E		D	A	I	S	Y		Y	O	U
P	O	D	S		F		C		A	S	P	S
	P		H	A	R	P	O	O	N		R	
B	E	T	A		I		R		G	R	A	Y
	R		R	E	C	I	P	E	S		N	
C	A	S	E		A		I		T	O	O	L
A	T	E		I	N	G	O	T		U		E
R	E	I	G	N		O		H	E	N	N	A
O		Z		C	O	A	T	I		C	A	N
B	E	E	C	H		T		S	W	E	P	T

No 89

1 Gandolfo, 2 *Odyssey*, 3 Yardie, 4 Everglades, 5 Smallpox, 6 Xenophobia, 7 Aficionado, 8 OPEC, 9 Charlemagne, 10 Estonia, 11 Aborigines. The country is: ALGERIA

Solutions

No 90

No 91

No 92

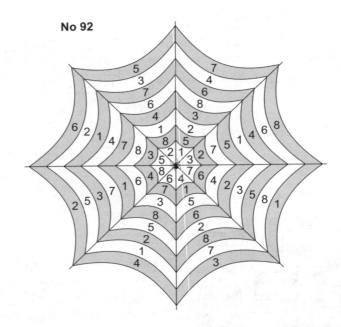

No 93

A=87, B=111, C=96, D=102, E=54, F=198, G=207,
H=198, I=156, J=405, K=405, L=354, M=810,
N=759, O=1569

No 94

The nine-letter
word is:
GUNPOWDER